Praise for *More Effective C++: 35 New Ways to Improve Your Programs and Designs*

"This is an enlightening book on many aspects of C++: both the regions of the language you seldom visit, and the familiar ones you THOUGHT you understood. Only by understanding deeply how the C++ compiler interprets your code can you hope to write robust software using this language. This book is an invaluable resource for gaining that level of understanding. After reading this book, I feel like I've been through a code review with a master C++ programmer, and picked up many of his most valuable insights."
> — Fred Wild, Vice President of Technology,
> Advantage Software Technologies

"This book includes a great collection of important techniques for writing programs that use C++ well. It explains how to design and implement the ideas, and what hidden pitfalls lurk in some obvious alternative designs. It also includes clear explanations of features recently added to C++. Anyone who wants to use these new features will want a copy of this book close at hand for ready reference."
> — Christopher J. Van Wyk, Professor,
> Mathematics and Computer Science, Drew University

"Industrial strength C++ at its best. The perfect companion to those who have read Effective C++.*"*
> — Eric Nagler, C++ Instructor and Author,
> University of California Santa Cruz Extension

"More Effective C++ is a thorough and valuable follow-up to Scott's first book, Effective C++. *I believe that every professional C++ developer should read and commit to memory the tips in both* Effective C++ *and* More Effective C++. *I've found that the tips cover poorly understood, yet important and sometimes arcane facets of the language. I strongly recommend this book, along with his first, to developers, testers, and managers ... everyone can benefit from his expert knowledge and excellent presentation."*
> — Steve Burkett, Software Consultant

More Effective C++

Addison-Wesley Professional Computing Series

Brian W. Kernighan, Consulting Editor

Ken Arnold/John Peyton, *A C User's Guide to ANSI C*

Tom Cargill, *C++ Programming Style*

William R. Cheswick/Steven M. Bellovin, *Firewalls and Internet Security: Repelling the Wily Hacker*

David A. Curry, *UNIX® System Security: A Guide for Users and System Administrators*

Erich Gamma/Richard Helm/Ralph Johnson/John Vlissides, *Design Patterns: Elements of Reusable Object-Oriented Software*

John Lakos, *Large-Scale C++ Software Design*

Scott Meyers, *Effective C++: 50 Specific Ways to Improve Your Programs and Designs*

Scott Meyers, *More Effective C++: 35 New Ways to Improve Your Programs and Designs*

Robert B. Murray, *C++ Strategies and Tactics*

David R. Musser/Atul Saini, *STL Tutorial and Reference Guide: C++ Programming with the Standard Template Library*

John K. Ousterhout, *Tcl and the Tk Toolkit*

Craig Partridge, *Gigabit Networking*

Stephen J. Pendergrast Jr., *Desktop KornShell Graphical Programming*

Radia Perlman, *Interconnections: Bridges and Routers*

David M. Piscitello/A. Lyman Chapin, *Open Systems Networking: TCP/IP and OSI*

Stephen A. Rago, *UNIX® System V Network Programming*

Curt Schimmel, *UNIX® Systems for Modern Architectures: Symmetric Multiprocessing and Caching for Kernel Programmers*

W. Richard Stevens, *Advanced Programming in the UNIX® Environment*

W. Richard Stevens, *TCP/IP Illustrated, Volume 1: The Protocols*

W. Richard Stevens, *TCP/IP Illustrated, Volume 3: TCP for Transactions, HTTP, NNTP, and the UNIX® Domain Protocols*

Gary R. Wright/W. Richard Stevens, *TCP/IP Illustrated, Volume 2: The Implementation*

More Effective C++

35 New Ways to Improve Your Programs and Designs

Scott Meyers

ADDISON-WESLEY PUBLISHING COMPANY

Reading, Massachusetts Menlo Park, California New York
Don Mills, Ontario Wokingham, England Amsterdam Bonn
Sydney Singapore Tokyo Madrid San Juan
Seoul Milan Mexico City Taipei

Many of the designations used by manufacturers and sellers to distinguish their products are claimed as trademarks. Where those designations appear in this book and Addison-Wesley was aware of a trademark claim, the designations have been printed with initial capital letters.

The authors and publishers have taken care in the preparation of this book, but make no expressed or implied warranty of any kind and assume no responsibility for errors or omissions. No liability is assumed for incidental or consequential damages in connection with or arising out of the use of the information of programs contained herein.

The publisher offers discounts on this book when ordered in quantity for special sales. For more information please contact:

Corporate & Professional Publishing Group
Addison-Wesley Publishing Company
One Jacob Way
Reading, Massachusetts 01867

Library of Congress Cataloging-in-Publication Data

Meyers, Scott (Scott Douglas)
    More effective C++ : 35 new ways to improve your programs and
designs / Scott Meyers.
        p.   cm. -- (Addison-Wesley professional computing series)
    Includes bibliographical references and index.
    ISBN 0-201-63371-X (paperback : alk. paper)
    1. C++ (Computer program language)   I. Series.
QA76.73.C153M495   1996
005.13'3--dc20   95-47354
                                                                      CIP

ISBN 0-201-63371-X

Text printed on recycled and acid-free paper
1 2 3 4 5 6 7 8 9 10 CRW 99989796
First Printing, January 1996

For Clancy,
my favorite enemy within.

Contents

Efficiency   81

Techniques   123

Miscellany   252

Recommended Reading   285

An `auto_ptr` Implementation   291

General Index   295

Index of Example Classes, Functions, and Templates   313

Acknowledgments

A great number of people helped bring this book into existence. Some contributed ideas for technical topics, some helped with the process of producing the book, and some just made life more fun while I was working on it.

When the number of contributors to a book is large, it is not uncommon to dispense with individual acknowledgments in favor of a generic "Contributors to this book are too numerous to mention." I prefer to follow the expansive lead of John L. Hennessy and David A. Patterson in *Computer Architecture: A Quantitative Approach* (Morgan Kaufmann, 1990). In addition to motivating the comprehensive acknowledgments that follow, their book provides hard data for the 90-10 rule, which I refer to in Item 16.

The Items

With the exception of direct quotations, all the words in this book are mine. However, many of the ideas I discuss came from others. I have done my best to keep track of who contributed what, but I know I have included information from sources I now fail to recall, foremost among them many posters to the Usenet newsgroups `comp.lang.c++` and `comp.std.c++`.

Many ideas in the C++ community have been developed independently by many people. In what follows, I note only where *I* was exposed to particular ideas, not necessarily where those ideas originated.

Brian Kernighan suggested the use of macros to approximate the syntax of the new C++ casting operators I describe in Item 2.

In Item 3, my warning about deleting an array of derived class objects through a base class pointer is based on material in Dan Saks' "Gotchas" talk, which he's given at several conferences and trade shows.

In Item 5, the proxy class technique for preventing unwanted application of single-argument constructors is based on material in Andrew Koenig's column in the January 1994 *C++ Report*.

James Kanze made a posting to `comp.lang.c++` on implementing postfix increment and decrement operators via the corresponding prefix functions; I use his technique in Item 6.

David Cok, writing me about material I covered in *Effective C++*, brought to my attention the distinction between `operator new` and the `new` operator that is the crux of Item 8. Even after reading his letter, I didn't really understand the distinction, but without his initial prodding, I probably *still* wouldn't.

The notion of using destructors to prevent resource leaks (used in Item 9) comes from section 15.3 of Margaret A. Ellis' and Bjarne Stroustrup's *The Annotated C++ Reference Manual* (see page 285). There the technique is called *resource acquisition is initialization*. Tom Cargill suggested I shift the focus of the approach from resource acquisition to resource release.

Some of my discussion in Item 11 was inspired by material in Chapter 4 of *Taligent's Guide to Designing Programs* (Addison-Wesley, 1994).

My description of over-eager memory allocation for the `DynArray` class in Item 18 is based on Tom Cargill's article, "A Dynamic vector is harder than it looks," in the June 1992 *C++ Report*. A more sophisticated design for a dynamic array class can be found in Cargill's follow-up column in the January 1994 *C++ Report*.

Item 21 was inspired by Brian Kernighan's paper, "An AWK to C++ Translator," at the 1991 USENIX C++ Conference. His use of overloaded operators (sixty-seven of them!) to handle mixed-type arithmetic operations, though designed to solve a problem unrelated to the one I explore in Item 21, led me to consider multiple overloadings as a solution to the problem of temporary creation.

In Item 26, my design of a template class for counting objects is based on a posting to `comp.lang.c++` by Jamshid Afshar.

The idea of a mixin class to keep track of pointers from `operator new` (see Item 27) is based on a suggestion by Don Box. Steve Clamage made the idea practical by explaining how `dynamic_cast` can be used to find the beginning of memory for an object.

The discussion of smart pointers in Item 28 is based in part on Steven Buroff's and Rob Murray's *C++ Oracle* column in the October 1993 *C++ Report*; on Daniel R. Edelson's classic paper, "Smart Pointers: They're Smart, but They're Not Pointers," in the proceedings of the 1992

USENIX C++ Conference; on section 15.9.1 of Bjarne Stroustrup's *The Design and Evolution of C++* (see page 285); on Gregory Colvin's "C++ Memory Management" class notes from C/C++ Solutions '95; and on Cay Horstmann's column in the March-April 1993 issue of the *C++ Report*. I developed some of the material myself, though. Really.

In Item 29, the use of a base class to store reference counts and of smart pointers to manipulate those counts is based on Rob Murray's discussions of the same topics in sections 6.3.2 and 7.4.2, respectively, of his *C++ Strategies and Tactics* (see page 286). The design for adding reference counting to existing classes follows that presented by Cay Horstmann in his March-April 1993 column in the *C++ Report*.

In Item 30, my discussion of lvalue contexts is based on comments in Dan Saks' column in the *C User's Journal* of January 1993. The observation that non-proxy member functions are unavailable when called through proxies comes from an unpublished paper by Cay Horstmann.

The use of runtime type information to build vtbl-like arrays of function pointers (in Item 31) is based on ideas put forward by Bjarne Stroustrup in postings to comp.lang.c++ and in section 13.8.1 of his *The Design and Evolution of C++* (see page 285).

The material in Item 33 is based on several of my *C++ Report* columns in 1994 and 1995. Those columns, in turn, included comments I received from Klaus Kreft about how to use dynamic_cast to implement a virtual operator= that detects arguments of the wrong type.

Much of the material in Item 34 was motivated by Steve Clamage's article, "Linking C++ with other languages," in the May 1992 *C++ Report*. In that same Item, my treatment of the problems caused by functions like strdup was motivated by an anonymous reviewer.

The Book

Reviewing draft copies of a book is hard — and vitally important — work. I am grateful that so many people were willing to invest their time and energy on my behalf. I am especially grateful to Jill Huchital, Tim Johnson, Brian Kernighan, Eric Nagler, and Chris Van Wyk, as they read the book (or large portions of it) more than once. In addition to these gluttons for punishment, complete drafts of the manuscript were read by Katrina Avery, Don Box, Steve Burkett, Tom Cargill, Tony Davis, Carolyn Duby, Bruce Eckel, Read Fleming, Cay Horstmann, James Kanze, Russ Paielli, Steve Rosenthal, Robin Rowe, Dan Saks, Chris Sells, Webb Stacy, Dave Swift, Steve Vinoski, and Fred Wild. Partial drafts were reviewed by Bob Beauchaine, Gerd Hoeren,

Jeff Jackson, and Nancy L. Urbano. Each of these reviewers made comments that greatly improved the accuracy, utility, and presentation of the material you find here.

During preparation of this book, I faced many questions about the emerging ANSI/ISO standard for C++, and I am grateful to Steve Clamage and Dan Saks for taking the time to respond to my incessant email queries.

John Max Skaller and Steve Rumsby conspired to get me the HTML for the draft ANSI C++ standard before it was widely available. Vivian Neou pointed me to the Netscape WWW browser as a stand-alone HTML viewer under (16 bit) Microsoft Windows, and I am deeply grateful to the folks at Netscape Communications for making their fine viewer freely available on such a pathetic excuse for an operating system.

Bryan Hobbs and Hachemi Zenad generously arranged to get me a copy of the internal engineering version of the MetaWare C++ compiler so I could check the code in this book using the latest features of the language. Cay Horstmann helped me get the compiler up and running in the very foreign world of DOS and DOS extenders. Borland provided a beta copy of their most advanced compiler, and Eric Nagler and Chris Sells provided invaluable help in testing code for me on compilers to which I had no access.

Without the staff at the Corporate and Professional Publishing Division of Addison-Wesley, there would be no book, and I am indebted to Kim Dawley, Lana Langlois, Simone Payment, Marty Rabinowitz, Pradeepa Siva, John Wait, and the rest of the staff for their encouragement, patience, and help with the production of this work.

Chris Guzikowski helped draft the back cover copy for this book, and Tim Johnson stole time from his research on low-temperature physics to critique later versions of that text.

Tom Cargill graciously agreed to make his *C++ Report* article on exceptions (see page 287) available at the Addison-Wesley Internet site.

The People

Kathy Reed was responsible for my introduction to programming; surely she didn't deserve to have to put up with a kid like me. Donald French had faith in my ability to develop and present C++ teaching materials when I had no track record. He also introduced me to John Wait, my editor at Addison-Wesley, an act for which I will always be grateful. The triumvirate at Beaver Ridge — Jayni Besaw, Lorri Fields, and Beth McKee — provided untold entertainment on my breaks as I worked on the book.

My wife, Nancy L. Urbano, put up with me and put up with me and put up with me as I worked on the book, continued to work on the book, and kept working on the book. How many times did she hear me say we'd do something after the book was done? Now the book is done, and we will do those things. She amazes me. I love her.

Finally, I must acknowledge our puppy, Persephone, whose existence changed our world forever. Without her, this book would have been finished both sooner and with less sleep deprivation, but also with substantially less comic relief.

Introduction

These are heady days for C++ programmers. Commercially available less than a decade, C++ has nevertheless emerged as the language of choice for systems programming on nearly all major computing platforms. Companies and individuals with challenging programming problems increasingly embrace the language, and the question faced by those who do not use C++ is often *when* they will start, not *if*. Standardization of C++ is essentially complete, and the breadth and scope of the accompanying library — which both dwarfs and subsumes that of C — makes it possible to write rich, complex programs without sacrificing portability or implementing common algorithms and data structures from scratch. C++ compilers continue to proliferate, the features they offer continue to expand, and the quality of the code they generate continues to improve. Tools and environments for C++ development grow ever more abundant, powerful, and robust. Commercial libraries all but obviate the need to write code in many application areas.

As the language has matured and our experience with it has increased, our needs for information about it have changed. In 1990, people wanted to know *what* C++ was. By 1992, they wanted to know *how* to make it work. Now C++ programmers ask higher-level questions: How can I design my software so it will adapt to future demands? How can I improve the efficiency of my code without compromising its correctness or making it harder to use? How can I implement sophisticated functionality not directly supported by the language?

In this book, I answer these questions and many others like them.

This book shows how to design and implement C++ software that is *more effective*: more likely to behave correctly; more robust in the face of exceptions; more efficient; more portable; makes better use of language features; adapts to change more gracefully; works better in a mixed-language environment; is easier to use correctly; is harder to use incorrectly. In short, software that's just *better*.

The material in this book is divided into 35 Items. Each Item summarizes the accumulated wisdom of the C++ programming community on a particular topic. Most Items take the form of guidelines, and the explanation accompanying each guideline describes why the guideline exists, what happens if you fail to follow it, and under what conditions it may make sense to violate the guideline anyway.

Items fall into several categories. Some concern particular language features, especially newer features with which you may have little experience. For example, Items 9 through 15 are devoted to exceptions. Other Items explain how to combine the features of the language to achieve higher-level goals. Items 25 through 31, for instance, describe how to constrain the number or placement of objects, how to create functions that act "virtual" on the type of more than one object, how to create "smart pointers," and more. Still other Items address broader topics; Items 16 through 24 focus on efficiency. No matter what the topic of a particular Item, each takes a no-nonsense approach to the subject. In *More Effective C++*, you learn how to *use* C++ more effectively. The descriptions of language features that make up the bulk of most C++ texts are in this book mere background information.

An implication of this approach is that you should be familiar with C++ before reading this book. I take for granted that you understand classes, protection levels, virtual and nonvirtual functions, etc., and I assume you are acquainted with the concepts behind templates and exceptions. At the same time, I don't expect you to be a language expert, so when poking into lesser-known corners of C++, I always explain what's going on.

The C++ in *More Effective C++*

The C++ I describe in this book is the language specified by the working papers of the ANSI/ISO standardization committee in the fall of 1995. In all likelihood, this means I use a few features your compilers don't yet support. Don't worry. The only "new" feature I assume you have is templates, and templates are now almost universally available. I use exceptions, too, but that use is largely confined to Items 9 through 15, which are specifically devoted to exceptions. If you don't have access to a compiler offering exceptions, that's okay. It won't affect your ability to take advantage of the material in the other parts of the book. Furthermore, you should read Items 9 through 15 even if you don't have support for exceptions, because those items examine issues you need to understand in any case.

I recognize that just because the standardization committee blesses a feature or endorses a practice, there's no guarantee that the feature is present in current compilers or the practice is applicable to existing environments. When faced with a discrepancy between theory (what the committee says) and practice (what actually works), I discuss both, though my bias is toward things that work. Because I discuss both, this book will aid you as your compilers approach conformance with the standard. It will show you how to use existing constructs to approximate language features your compilers don't yet support, and it will guide you when you decide to transform workarounds into newly-supported features.

Notice that I refer to your *compilers* — plural. Different compilers implement varying approximations to the standard, so I encourage you to develop your code under at least two compilers. Doing so will help you avoid inadvertent dependence on one vendor's proprietary language extension or its misinterpretation of the standard. It will also help keep you away from the bleeding edge of compiler technology, i.e., from new features supported by only one vendor. Such features are often poorly implemented (buggy or slow — frequently both), and upon their introduction, the C++ community lacks experience to advise you in their proper use. Blazing trails can be exciting, but when your goal is producing reliable code, it's often best to let others test the waters before jumping in.

There are two constructs you'll see in this book that may not be familiar to you. Both are relatively recent language extensions. Some compilers support them, but if your compilers don't, you can easily approximate them with features you do have.

The first construct is the `bool` type, which has as its values the keywords `true` and `false`. If your compilers haven't implemented `bool`, there are two ways to approximate it. One is to use a global enum:

```
enum bool { false, true };
```

This allows you to overload functions on the basis of whether they take a `bool` or an `int`, but it has the disadvantage that the built-in comparison operators (i.e., `==`, `<`, `>=`, etc.) still return `int`s. As a result, code like the following will not behave the way it's supposed to:

```
void f(int);
void f(bool);

int x, y;
...
f( x < y );                         // calls f(int), but it
                                    // should call f(bool)
```

The enum approximation may thus lead to code whose behavior changes when you submit it to a compiler that truly supports `bool`.

An alternative is to use a typedef for `bool` and constant objects for `true` and `false`:

```
typedef int bool;

const bool false = 0;
const bool true = 1;
```

This is compatible with the traditional semantics of C and C++, and the behavior of programs using this approximation won't change when they're ported to `bool`-supporting compilers. The drawback is that you can't differentiate between `bool` and `int` when overloading functions. Both approximations are reasonable. Choose the one that best fits your circumstances.

The second new construct is really four constructs, the casting forms `static_cast`, `const_cast`, `dynamic_cast`, and `reinterpret_cast`. If you're not familiar with these casts, you'll want to turn to Item 2 and read all about them. Not only do they do more than the C-style casts they replace, they do it better. I use these new casting forms whenever I need to perform a cast in this book.

There is more to C++ than the language itself. There is also the standard library. Where possible, I employ the standard `string` class instead of using raw `char*` pointers, and I encourage you to do the same. `string` objects are no more difficult to manipulate than `char*`-based strings, and they relieve you of most memory-management concerns. Furthermore, `string` objects are less susceptible to memory leaks if an exception is thrown (see Items 9 and 10). A well-implemented `string` class can hold its own in an efficiency contest with its `char*` equivalent, and it may even do better. (For insight into how this could be, see Item 29.) If you don't have access to an implementation of the standard `string` class, you almost certainly have access to *some* string-like class. Use it. Just about anything is preferable to raw `char*`s.

I use data structures from the standard library whenever I can. Such data structures are drawn from the Standard Template Library (the "STL" — see Item 35). The STL includes bitsets, vectors, lists, queues, stacks, maps, sets, and more, and you should prefer these standardized data structures to the ad hoc equivalents you might otherwise be tempted to write. Your compilers may not have the STL bundled in, but don't let that keep you from using it. Several vendors offer STL implementations and, thanks to Hewlett Packard, you can FTP an implementation from the Internet; the FTP site is `butler.hpl.hp.com`. (Look in the `stl` directory.)

If you currently use a library of algorithms and data structures and are happy with it, there's no need to switch to the STL just because it's "standard." However, if you have a choice between using an STL component or writing your own code from scratch, you should lean toward using the STL. Remember code reuse? STL (and the rest of the standard library) has lots of code that is very much worth reusing.

Conventions and Terminology

Any time I mention inheritance in this book, I mean public inheritance. If I don't mean public inheritance, I'll say so explicitly. When drawing inheritance hierarchies, I depict base-derived relationships by drawing arrows from derived classes to base classes. For example, here is a hierarchy from Item 31:

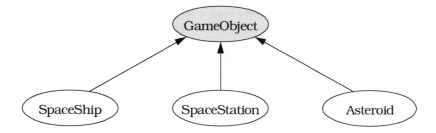

(This notation is the reverse of the convention I employed in *Effective C++*, but I'm now convinced that most C++ practitioners draw inheritance arrows from derived to base classes, and I am happy to follow suit.) Within such diagrams, abstract classes (e.g., GameObject) are shaded and concrete classes (e.g., SpaceShip) are unshaded.

Inheritance gives rise to pointers and references with two different types, a *static type* and a *dynamic type*. The static type of a pointer or reference is its *declared* type. The dynamic type is determined by the type of object it actually *refers* to. Here are some examples based on the classes above:

```
GameObject *pgo =          // static type of pgo is
  new SpaceShip;           // GameObject*, dynamic
                           // type is SpaceShip*

Asteroid *pa = new Asteroid;  // static type of pa is
                              // Asteroid*. So is its
                              // dynamic type

pgo = pa;                  // static type of pgo is
                           // still (and always)
                           // GameObject*. Its
                           // dynamic type is now
                           // Asteroid*
```

```
GameObject& rgo = *pa;              // static type of rgo is
                                    // GameObject, dynamic
                                    // type is Asteroid
```

These examples also demonstrate a naming convention I like. pgo is a pointer-to-GameObject; pa is a pointer-to-Asteroid; rgo is a reference-to-GameObject. I often concoct pointer and reference names in this fashion.

Two of my favorite parameter names are lhs and rhs, abbreviations for "left-hand side" and "right-hand side," respectively. To understand the rationale behind these names, consider a class for representing rational numbers:

```
class Rational { ... };
```

If I wanted a function to compare pairs of Rational objects, I'd declare it like this:

```
bool operator==(const Rational& lhs, const Rational& rhs);
```

That would let me write this kind of code:

```
Rational r1, r2;

...

if (r1 == r2) ...
```

Within the call to operator==, r1 appears on the left-hand side of the "==" and is bound to lhs, while r2 appears on the right-hand side of the "==" and is bound to rhs.

Other abbreviations I employ include *ctor* for "constructor," *dtor* for "destructor," and *RTTI* for C++'s support for runtime type identification (of which dynamic_cast is the most commonly used component).

When you allocate memory and fail to free it, you have a memory leak. Memory leaks arise in both C and C++, but in C++, memory leaks leak more than just memory. That's because C++ automatically calls constructors when objects are created, and constructors may themselves allocate resources. For example, consider this code:

```
class Widget { ... };              // some class — it doesn't
                                   // matter what it is

Widget *pw = new Widget;           // dynamically allocate a
                                   // Widget object

...                                // assume pw is never
                                   // deleted
```

This code leaks memory, because the Widget pointed to by pw is never deleted. However, if the Widget constructor allocates additional resources that are to be released when the Widget is destroyed (such as file descriptors, semaphores, window handles, database locks, etc.), those resources are lost just as surely as the memory is. To emphasize that memory leaks in C++ often leak other resources, too, I usually speak of *resource leaks* in this book rather than memory leaks.

You won't see many inline functions in this book. That's not because I dislike inlining. Far from it, I believe that inline functions are an important feature of C++. However, the criteria for determining whether a function should be inlined can be complex, subtle, and platform-dependent. As a result, I avoid inlining unless there is a point about inlining I wish to make. When you see a non-inline function in *More Effective C++*, that doesn't mean I think it would be a bad idea to declare the function inline, it just means the decision to inline that function is independent of the material I'm examining at that point in the book.

A few C++ features have been *deprecated* by the standardization committee. Such features are slated for eventual removal from the language, because newer features have been added that do what the deprecated features do, but do it better. In this book, I identify deprecated constructs and explain what features replace them. You should try to avoid deprecated features where you can, but there's no reason to be overly concerned about their use. In the interest of preserving backward compatibility for their customers, compiler vendors are likely to support deprecated features for many years.

A *client* is somebody (a programmer) or something (a class or function, typically) that uses the code you write. For example, if you write a Date class (for representing birthdays, deadlines, when the Second Coming occurs, etc.), anybody using that class is your client. Furthermore, any sections of code that use the Date class are your clients as well. Clients are important. In fact, clients are the name of the game! If nobody uses the software you write, why write it? You will find I worry a lot about making things easier for clients, often at the expense of making things more difficult for you, because good software is "clientcentric" — it revolves around clients. If this strikes you as unreasonably philanthropic, view it instead through a lens of self-interest. Do you ever use the classes or functions you write? If so, you're your own client, so making things easier for clients in general also makes them easier for you.

When discussing class or function templates and the classes or functions generated from them, I reserve the right to be sloppy about the difference between the templates and their instantiations. For example, if Array is a class template taking a type parameter T, I may refer to a particular instantiation of the template as an Array, even though

Array<T> is really the name of the class. Similarly, if swap is a function template taking a type parameter T, I may refer to an instantiation as swap instead of swap<T>. In cases where this kind of shorthand might be unclear, I include template parameters when referring to template instantiations.

Reporting Bugs, Making Suggestions, Getting Book Updates

I have tried to make this book as accurate, readable, and useful as possible, but I know there is room for improvement. If you find an error of any kind — technical, grammatical, typographical, *whatever* — please tell me about it. I will try to correct the mistake in future printings of the book, and if you are the first person to report it, I will gladly add your name to the book's acknowledgments. If you have other suggestions for improvement, I welcome those, too.

I continue to collect guidelines for effective programming in C++. If you have ideas for new guidelines, I'd be delighted if you'd share them with me. Send your guidelines, your comments, your criticisms, and your bug reports to:

Scott Meyers
c/o Editor-in-Chief, Corporate and Professional Publishing
Addison-Wesley Publishing Company
1 Jacob Way
Reading, MA 01867
U. S. A.

Alternatively, you may send electronic mail to johnw@aw.com.

I maintain a list of changes to this book since its first printing, including bug-fixes, clarifications, and technical updates. This list, along with other book-related information, is available from Addison-Wesley at World Wide Web URL http://www.aw.com/cp/mec++.html. It is also available via anonymous FTP from ftp.aw.com in the directory cp/mec++. If you would like a copy of the list of changes to this book, but you lack access to the Internet, please send a request to one of the addresses above, and I will see that the list is sent to you.

Enough preliminaries. On with the show!

Basics

Ah, the basics. Pointers, references, casts, arrays, constructors — you can't get much more basic than that. All but the simplest C++ programs use most of these features, and many programs use them all.

In spite of our familiarity with these parts of the language, sometimes they can still surprise us. This is especially true for programmers making the transition from C to C++, because the concepts behind references, dynamic casts, default constructors, and other non-C features are usually a little murky.

This chapter describes the differences between pointers and references and offers guidance on when to use each. It introduces the new C++ syntax for casts and explains why the new casts are superior to the C-style casts they replace. It examines the C notion of arrays and the C++ notion of polymorphism, and it describes why mixing the two is an idea whose time will never come. Finally, it considers the pros and cons of default constructors and suggests ways to work around language restrictions that encourage you to have one when none makes sense.

By heeding the advice in the items that follow, you'll make progress toward a worthy goal: producing software that expresses your design intentions clearly and correctly.

Item 1: Distinguish between pointers and references

Pointers and references *look* different enough (pointers use the "*" and "->" operators, references use " ."), but they seem to do similar things. Both pointers and references let you refer to other objects indirectly. How, then, do you decide when to use one and not the other?

First, recognize that there is no such thing as a null reference. A reference must *always* refer to some object. As a result, if you have a variable whose purpose is to refer to another object, but it is possible that there might not be an object to refer to, you should make the variable a pointer, because then you can set it to null. On the other hand, if the variable must *always* refer to an object, i.e., if your design does not allow for the possibility that the variable is null, you should probably make the variable a reference.

"But wait," you wonder, "what about underhandedness like this?"

```
char *pc = 0;                    // set pointer to null

char& rc = *pc;                  // make reference refer to
                                 // dereferenced null pointer
```

Well, this is evil, pure and simple. The results are undefined (compilers can generate output to do anything they like), and people who write this kind of code should be shunned until they agree to cease and desist. If you have to worry about things like this in your software, you're probably best off avoiding references entirely. Either that or finding a better class of programmers to work with. We'll henceforth ignore the possibility that a reference can be "null."

Because a reference must refer to an object, C++ requires that references be initialized:

```
string& rs;                      // error! References must
                                 // be initialized

string s("xyzzy");

string& rs = s;                  // okay, rs refers to s
```

Pointers are subject to no such restriction:

```
string *ps;                      // uninitialized pointer:
                                 // valid but risky
```

The fact that there is no such thing as a null reference implies that it can be more efficient to use references than to use pointers. That's because there's no need to test the validity of a reference before using it:

```
void printDouble(const double& rd)
{
    cout << rd;                  // no need to test rd; it
}                                // must refer to a double
```

Pointers, on the other hand, should generally be tested against null:

```
void printDouble(const double *pd)
{
  if (pd) {                      // check for null pointer
    cout << *pd;
  }
}
```

Another important difference between pointers and references is that pointers may be reassigned to refer to different objects. A reference, however, *always* refers to the object with which it is initialized:

```
string s1("Nancy");
string s2("Clancy");

string& rs = s1;              // rs refers to s1

string *ps = &s1;            // ps points to s1

rs = s2;                     // rs still refers to s1,
                             // but s1's value is now
                             // "Clancy"

ps = &s2;                    // ps now points to s2;
                             // s1 is unchanged
```

In general, you should use a pointer whenever you need to take into account the possibility that there's nothing to refer to (in which case you can set the pointer to null) or whenever you need to be able to refer to different things at different times (in which case you can change where the pointer points). You should use a reference whenever you know there will always be an object to refer to and you also know that once you're referring to that object, you'll never want to refer to anything else.

There is one other situation in which you should use a reference, and that's when you're implementing certain operators. The most common example is operator[]. This operator typically needs to return something that can be used as the target of an assignment:

```
vector<int> v(10);   // create an int vector of size 10;
                     // vector is a template in the
                     // standard C++ library (see Item 35)
v[5] = 10;           // the target of this assignment is
                     // the return value of operator[]
```

If operator[] returned a pointer, this last statement would have to be written this way:

```
*v[5] = 10;
```

But this makes it look like v is a vector of pointers, which it's not. For this reason, you'll almost always want operator[] to return a reference.

References, then, are the feature of choice when you *know* you have something to refer to, when you'll *never* want to refer to anything else, and when implementing operators whose syntactic requirements make the use of pointers undesirable. In all other cases, stick with pointers.

Item 2:   Prefer C++-style casts

Consider the lowly cast. Nearly as much a programming pariah as the
goto, it nonetheless endures, because when worse comes to worst and
push comes to shove, casts can be necessary. Casts are especially necessary when worse comes to worst and push comes to shove.

Still, C-style casts are not all they might be. For one thing, they're
rather crude beasts, letting you cast pretty much any type to pretty
much any other type. It would be nice to be able to specify more precisely the purpose of each cast. There is a great difference, for example,
between a cast that changes a pointer-to-const-object into a pointer-
to-non-const-object (i.e., a cast that changes only the constness of an
object) and a cast that changes a pointer-to-base-class-object into a
pointer-to-derived-class-object (i.e., a cast that completely changes an
object's type). Traditional C-style casts make no such distinctions.
(This is hardly a surprise. C-style casts were designed for C, not C++.)

A second problem with casts is that they are hard to find. Syntactically, casts consist of little more than a pair of parentheses and an
identifier, and parentheses and identifiers are used everywhere in C++.
This makes it tough to answer even the most basic cast-related questions, questions like, "Are any casts used in this program?" That's because human readers are likely to overlook casts, and tools like grep
cannot distinguish them from non-cast constructs that are syntactically similar.

C++ addresses the shortcomings of C-style casts by introducing four
new cast operators, static_cast, const_cast, dynamic_cast, and
reinterpret_cast. For most purposes, all you need to know about
these operators is that what you are accustomed to writing like this,

```
(type) expression
```

you should now generally write like this:

```
static_cast<type>(expression)
```

For example, suppose you'd like to cast an int to a double to force an
expression involving ints to yield a floating point value. Using C-style
casts, you could do it like this:

```
int firstNumber, secondNumber;

...

double result = ((double)firstNumber)/secondNumber;
```

With the new casts, you'd write it this way:

```
double result = static_cast<double>(firstNumber)/secondNumber;
```

Now *there's* a cast that's easy to see, both for humans and for programs.

static_cast has basically the same power and meaning as the general-purpose C-style cast. It also has the same kind of restrictions. For example, you can't cast a struct into an int or a double into a pointer using static_cast any more than you can with a C-style cast. Furthermore, static_cast can't change the constness of an expression, because another new cast, const_cast, is designed specifically to do that.

The other new C++ casts are used for more restricted purposes. const_cast is used to cast away the constness or volatileness of an expression. By using a const_cast, you emphasize (to both humans and compilers) that the only thing you want to change through the cast is the constness or volatileness of something. This meaning is enforced by compilers. If you try to employ const_cast for anything other than modifying the constness or volatileness of an expression, your cast will be rejected. Here are some examples:

```
class Widget { ... };
class SpecialWidget: public Widget { ... };

void update(SpecialWidget *psw);

const SpecialWidget sw;

update(&sw);                    // error! can't pass a const
                                // SpecialWidget* to a function
                                // taking a SpecialWidget*

update(const_cast<SpecialWidget*>(&sw));
                                // fine, the constness of sw is
                                // explicitly cast away (and sw may
                                // now be changed inside update)

update((SpecialWidget*)&sw);
                                // same as above, but using a
                                // harder-to-recognize C-style cast

Widget *pw = new SpecialWidget;

update(pw);                     // error! pw's type is Widget*, but
                                // update takes a SpecialWidget*

update(const_cast<SpecialWidget*>(pw));
                                // error! const_cast can be used only
                                // to affect constness or volatileness,
                                // never to cast down the inheritance
                                // hierarchy
```

By far the most common use of const_cast is to cast away the constness of an object.

The second specialized type of cast, dynamic_cast, is used to perform *safe casts* down or across an inheritance hierarchy. That is, you use dynamic_cast to cast pointers or references to base class objects into pointers or references to derived or sibling base class objects in such a way that you can determine whether the casts succeeded.[†] Failed casts are indicated by a null pointer (when casting pointers) or an exception (when casting references):

```
Widget *pw;

...

update(dynamic_cast<SpecialWidget*>(pw));
                          // fine, passes to update a pointer
                          // to the SpecialWidget pw points to
                          // if pw really points to one,
                          // otherwise passes the null pointer

void updateViaRef(SpecialWidget &rsw);

updateViaRef(dynamic_cast<SpecialWidget&>(*pw));   ViaRef
                          // fine, passes to update the
                          // SpecialWidget pw points to if pw
                          // really points to one, otherwise
                          // throws an exception
```

dynamic_casts are restricted to helping you navigate inheritance hierarchies. They cannot be applied to types lacking virtual functions (see also Item 24), nor can they cast away constness:

```
int firstNumber, secondNumber;
...
double result = dynamic_cast<double>(firstNumber)/secondNumber;
                          // error! no inheritance is involved

const SpecialWidget sw;
...
update(dynamic_cast<SpecialWidget*>(&sw));
                          // error! dynamic_cast can't cast
                          // away constness
```

If you want to perform a cast on a type where inheritance is not involved, you ~~almost certainly~~ want a static_cast. To cast constness away, you always want a const_cast.

The last of the four new casting forms is reinterpret_cast. This operator is used to perform type conversions whose result is nearly always implementation-defined. As a result, reinterpret_casts are rarely portable.

---

† A second, unrelated use of dynamic_cast is to find the beginning of the memory occupied by an object. We explore that capability in Item 27.

errata ton approximate forms available

The most common use of reinterpret_cast is to cast between function pointer types. For example, suppose you have an array of pointers to functions of a particular type:

```
typedef void (*FuncPtr)();      // a FuncPtr is a pointer
                                // to a function taking no
                                // args and returning void

FuncPtr funcPtrArray[10];       // funcPtrArray is an array
                                // of 10 FuncPtrs
```

Let us suppose you wish (for some unfathomable reason) to place a pointer to the following function into funcPtrArray:

```
int doSomething();
```

You can't do what you want without a cast, because doSomething has the wrong type for funcPtrArray. The functions in funcPtrArray return void, but doSomething returns an int:

```
funcPtrArray[0] = &doSomething;    // error! type mismatch
```

A reinterpret_cast lets you force compilers to see things your way:

```
funcPtrArray[0] =                  // this compiles
   reinterpret_cast<FuncPtr>(&doSomething);
```

Casting function pointers is not portable (C++ offers no guarantee that all function pointers are represented the same way), and in some cases such casts yield incorrect results (see Item 31), so you should avoid casting function pointers unless your back's to the wall and a knife's at your throat. A sharp knife. A *very* sharp knife.

If your compilers lack support for the new casting forms, you can use traditional casts in place of static_cast, const_cast, and reinterpret_cast. Furthermore, you can use macros to approximate the new syntax:

```
#define static_cast(TYPE,EXPR)      ((TYPE)(EXPR))
#define const_cast(TYPE,EXPR)       ((TYPE)(EXPR))
#define reinterpret_cast(TYPE,EXPR) ((TYPE)(EXPR))
```

You'd use the approximations like this:

```
double result = static_cast(double, firstNumber)/secondNumber;

update(const_cast(SpecialWidget*, &sw));

funcPtrArray[0] = reinterpret_cast(FuncPtr, &doSomething);
```

These approximations won't be as safe as the real things, of course, but they will simplify the process of upgrading your code when your compilers support the new casts.

There is no easy way to emulate the behavior of a dynamic_cast, but many libraries provide functions to perform safe inheritance-based casts for you. If you lack such functions and you *must* perform this type of cast, you can fall back on C-style casts for those, too, but then you forego the ability to tell if the casts fail. Needless to say, you can define a macro to look like dynamic_cast, just as you can for the other casts:

```
#define dynamic_cast(TYPE,EXPR)        (TYPE) (EXPR)
```

Remember that this approximation is not performing a true dynamic_cast; there is no way to tell if the cast fails.

I know, I know, the new casts are ugly and hard to type. If you find them too unpleasant to look at, take solace in the knowledge that C-style casts continue to be valid. However, what the new casts lack in beauty they make up for in precision of meaning and easy recognizability. Programs that use the new casts are easier to parse (both for humans and for tools), and they allow compilers to diagnose casting errors that would otherwise go undetected. These are powerful arguments for abandoning C-style casts, and there may also be a third: perhaps making casts ugly and hard to type is a *good* thing.

Item 3:   Never treat arrays polymorphically

One of the most important features of inheritance is that you can manipulate derived class objects through pointers and references to base class objects. Such pointers and references are said to behave *polymorphically* — as if they had multiple types. C++ also allows you to manipulate *arrays* of derived class objects through base class pointers and references. This is no feature at all, because it almost never works the way you want it to.

For example, suppose you have a class BST (for binary search tree objects) and a second class, BalancedBST, that inherits from BST:

```
class BST { ... };
class BalancedBST: public BST { ... };
```

In a real program such classes would be templates, but that's unimportant here, and adding all the template syntax just makes things harder to read. For this discussion, we'll assume BST and BalancedBST objects contain only ints.

Consider a function to print out the contents of each BST in an array of BSTs:

```
void printBSTArray(ostream& s,
                   const BST array[],
                   int numElements)
{
  for (int i = 0; i < numElements; ++i) {
    s << array[i];                  // this assumes an
  }                                 // operator<< is defined
}                                   // for BST objects
```

This will work fine when you pass it an array of BST objects:

```
BST BSTArray[10];

...

printBSTArray(cout, BSTArray, 10);              // works fine
```

Consider, however, what happens when you pass printBSTArray an array of BalancedBST objects:

```
BalancedBST bBSTArray[10];

...

printBSTArray(cout, bBSTArray, 10);             // works fine?
```

Your compilers will accept this function call without complaint, but look again at the loop for which they must generate code:

```
for (int i = 0; i < numElements; ++i) {
  s << array[i];
}
```

Now, array[i] is really just shorthand for an expression involving pointer arithmetic: it stands for *(array+i). We know that array is a pointer to the beginning of the array, but how far away from the memory location pointed to by array is the memory location pointed to by array+i? The distance between them is i*sizeof(*an object in the array*), because there are i objects between array[0] and array[i]. In order for compilers to emit code that walks through the array correctly, they must be able to determine the size of the objects in the array. This is easy for them to do. The parameter array is declared to be of type array-of-BST, so each element of the array must be a BST, and the distance between array and array+i must be i*sizeof(BST).

At least that's how your compilers look at it. But if you've passed an array of BalancedBST objects to printBSTArray, your compilers are probably wrong. In that case, they'd assume each object in the array is the size of a BST, but each object would actually be the size of a BalancedBST. Derived classes usually have more data members than their base classes, so derived class objects are usually larger than base class objects. We thus expect a BalancedBST object to be larger than a

BST object. If it is, the pointer arithmetic generated for `printBSTArray` will be wrong for arrays of `BalancedBST` objects, and there's no telling what will happen when `printBSTArray` is invoked on a `BalancedBST` array. Whatever does happen, it's a good bet it won't be pleasant.

The problem pops up in a different guise if you try to delete an array of derived class objects through a base class pointer. Here's one way you might innocently attempt to do it:

```
// delete an array, but first log a message about its
// deletion
void deleteArray(ostream& logStream, BST array[])
{
  logStream << "Deleting array at address "
            << static_cast<void*>(array) << '\n';

  delete [] array;
}

BalancedBST *balTreeArray =        // create a BalancedBST
  new BalancedBST[50];             // array

...

deleteArray(cout, balTreeArray);   // log its deletion
```

You can't see it, but there's pointer arithmetic going on here, too. When an array is deleted, a destructor for each element of the array must be called (see Item 8). When compilers see the statement

```
delete [] array;
```

they must generate code that does something like this:

```
// destruct the objects in *array in the inverse order
// in which they were constructed
for (int i = the number of elements in the array - 1;
     i >= 0;
     --i)
  {
    array[i].BST::~BST();          // call array[i]'s
  }                                // destructor
```

Just as this kind of loop failed to work when you wrote it, it will fail to work when your compilers write it, too. The language specification says the result of deleting an array of derived class objects through a base class pointer is undefined, but we know what that really means: executing the code is almost certain to lead to grief. Polymorphism and pointer arithmetic simply don't mix. Array operations almost always involve pointer arithmetic, so arrays and polymorphism don't mix.

Note that you're unlikely to make the mistake of treating an array poly-morphically if you avoid having a concrete class (like `BalancedBST`) inherit from another concrete class (such as BST). As Item 33 explains, designing your software so that concrete classes never inherit from one another has many benefits. I encourage you to turn to Item 33 and read all about them.

Item 4: Avoid gratuitous default constructors

A default constructor (i.e., a constructor that can be called with no arguments) is the C++ way of saying you can get something for nothing. Constructors initialize objects, so default constructors initialize objects without any information from the place where the object is being created. Sometimes this makes perfect sense. Objects that act like numbers, for example, may reasonably be initialized to zero or to undefined values. Objects that act like pointers (see Item 28) may reasonably be initialized to null or to undefined values. Data structures like linked lists, hash tables, maps, and the like may reasonably be initialized to empty containers.

Not all objects fall into this category. For many objects, there is no reasonable way to perform a complete initialization in the absence of outside information. For example, every (legal) worker in the United States must have a Social Security number, so it would rarely make sense to model U.S. workers without insisting that a Social Security number be provided. An object representing an entry in an address book makes no sense unless the name of the thing being entered is provided. In some companies, all equipment must be tagged with a corporate ID number, and creating an object to model a piece of equipment in such companies is nonsensical unless the appropriate ID number is provided.

In a perfect world, classes in which objects could reasonably be created from nothing would contain default constructors and classes in which information was required for object construction would not. Alas, ours is not the best of all possible worlds, so we must take additional concerns into account. In particular, if a class lacks a default constructor, there are restrictions on how you can use that class.

Consider a class for company equipment in which the corporate ID number of the equipment is a mandatory constructor argument:

```
class EquipmentPiece {
public:
  EquipmentPiece(int IDNumber);
  ...
};
```

Because EquipmentPiece lacks a default constructor, its use may be problematic in three contexts. The first is the creation of arrays. There is, in general, no way to specify constructor arguments for objects in arrays, so it is not usually possible to create arrays of Equipment-Piece objects:

```
EquipmentPiece bestPieces[10];        // error! No way to call
                                      // EquipmentPiece ctors

EquipmentPiece *bestPieces =
    new EquipmentPiece[10];           // error! same problem
```

There are three ways to get around this restriction. A solution for non-heap arrays is to provide the necessary arguments at the point where the array is defined:

```
int ID1, ID2, ID3, ..., ID10;        // variables to hold
                                      // equipment ID numbers
    ...

EquipmentPiece bestPieces[] = {       // fine, ctor arguments
    ID1, ID2, ID3, ..., ID10          // are provided
};
```

[handwritten margin note: Equipment Piece(ID1) " (ID2) ...]

Unfortunately, there is no way to extend this strategy to heap arrays.

A more general approach is to use an array of *pointers* instead of an array of objects:

```
typedef EquipmentPiece* PEP;         // a PEP is a pointer to
                                     // an EquipmentPiece

PEP bestPieces[10];                  // fine, no ctors called

PEP *bestPieces = new PEP[10];       // also fine
```

Each pointer in the array can then be made to point to a different EquipmentPiece object:

```
for (int i = 0; i < 10; ++i)
    bestPieces[i] = new EquipmentPiece( ID Number );
```

There are two disadvantages to this approach. First, you have to remember to delete all the objects pointed to by the array. If you forget, you have a resource leak. Second, the total amount of memory you need increases, because you need the space for the pointers as well as the space for the EquipmentPiece objects.

You can avoid the space penalty if you allocate the raw memory for the array, then use "placement new" (see Item 8) to construct the EquipmentPiece objects in the memory:

```
// allocate enough raw memory for an array of 10
// EquipmentPiece objects; see Item 8 for details on
// the operator new[] function
void *rawMemory =
  operator new[](10*sizeof(EquipmentPiece));

// make bestPieces point to it so it can be treated as a
// EquipmentPiece array
EquipmentPiece *bestPieces =
  static_cast<EquipmentPiece*>(rawMemory);

// construct the EquipmentPiece objects in the memory
// using "placement new" (see Item 8)
for (int i = 0; i < 10; ++i)
  new (&bestPieces[i]) EquipmentPiece( ID Number );
```

Notice that you still have to provide a constructor argument for each EquipmentPiece object. This technique (as well as the array-of-pointers idea) allows you to create arrays of objects when a class lacks a default constructor; it doesn't show you how to bypass required constructor arguments. There is no way to do that. If there were, it would defeat the purpose of constructors, which is to *guarantee* that objects are initialized.

The downside to using placement new, aside from the fact that most programmers are unfamiliar with it (which will make maintenance more difficult), is that you must manually call destructors on the objects in the array when you want them to go out of existence, then you must manually deallocate the raw memory by calling operator delete[] (again, see Item 8):

```
// destruct the objects in bestPieces in the inverse
// order in which they were constructed
for (int i = 9; i >= 0; --i)
  bestPieces[i].~EquipmentPiece();

// deallocate the raw memory
operator delete[](rawMemory);
```

If you forget this requirement and use the normal array-deletion syntax, your program will behave unpredictably. That's because the result of deleting a pointer that didn't come from the new operator is undefined:

```
delete [] bestPieces;          // undefined! bestPieces
                               // didn't come from the new
                               // operator
```

For more information on the new operator, placement new and how they interact with constructors and destructors, see Item 8.

The second problem with classes lacking default constructors is that they are ineligible for use with many template-based container classes. That's because it's a common requirement for such templates that the type used to instantiate the template provide a default constructor. This requirement almost always grows out of the fact that inside the template, an array of the template parameter type is being created. For example, a template for an `Array` class might look something like this:

```
template<class T>
class Array {
public:
  Array(int size);
  ...

private:
  T *data;
};

template<class T>
Array<T>::Array(int size)
{
  data = new T[size];            // calls T::T() for each
  ...                            // element of the array
}
```

In most cases, careful template design can eliminate the need for a default constructor. For example, the standard `vector` template (which generates classes that act like extensible arrays) has no requirement that its type parameter have a default constructor. Unfortunately, many templates are designed in a manner that is anything but careful. That being the case, classes without default constructors will be incompatible with many templates. As C++ programmers learn more about template design, this problem should recede in significance. How long it will take for that to happen, however, is anyone's guess.

The final consideration in the to-provide-a-default-constructor-or-not-to-provide-a-default-constructor dilemma has to do with virtual base classes. Virtual base classes lacking default constructors are a pain to work with. That's because the arguments for virtual base class constructors must be provided by the most derived class of the object being constructed. As a result, a virtual base class lacking a default constructor requires that *all* classes derived from that class — no matter how far removed — must know about, understand the meaning of, and provide for the virtual base class's constructors' arguments. Authors of derived classes neither expect nor appreciate this requirement.

Because of the restrictions imposed on classes lacking default constructors, some people believe *all* classes should have them, even if a default constructor doesn't have enough information to fully initialize objects of that class. For example, adherents to this philosophy might modify EquipmentPiece as follows:

```
class EquipmentPiece {
public:
  EquipmentPiece(int IDNumber = UNSPECIFIED);
  ...

private:
  static const int UNSPECIFIED;   // magic ID number value
                                  // meaning no ID was
};                                // specified
```

This allows EquipmentPiece objects to be created like this:

```
EquipmentPiece e;                 // now okay
```

Such a transformation almost always complicates the other member functions of the class, because there is no longer any guarantee that the fields of an EquipmentPiece object have been meaningfully initialized. Assuming it makes no sense to have an EquipmentPiece without an ID field, most member functions must check to see if the ID is present. If it's not, they'll have to figure out how to stumble on anyway. Often it's not clear how to do that, and many implementations choose a solution that offers nothing but expediency: they throw an exception or they call a function that terminates the program. When that happens, it's difficult to argue that the overall quality of the software has been improved by including a default constructor in a class where none was warranted.

Inclusion of meaningless default constructors affects the efficiency of classes, too. If member functions have to test to see if fields have truly been initialized, clients of those functions have to pay for the time those tests take. Furthermore, they have to pay for the code that goes into those tests, because that makes executables and libraries bigger. They also have to pay for the code that handles the cases where the tests fail. All those costs are avoided if a class's constructors ensure that all fields of an object are correctly initialized. Often default constructors can't offer that kind of assurance, so it's best to avoid them in classes where they make no sense. That places some limits on how such classes can be used, yes, but it also guarantees that when you *do* use such classes, you can expect that the objects they generate are fully initialized and are efficiently implemented.

Operators

Overloadable operators — you gotta love 'em! They allow you to give your types the same syntax as C++'s built-in types, yet they let you put a measure of power into the functions *behind* the operators that's unheard of for the built-ins. Of course, the fact that you can make symbols like "+" and "==" do anything you want also means you can use overloaded operators to produce programs best described as impenetrable. Adept C++ programmers know how to harness the power of operator overloading without descending into the incomprehensible.

Regrettably, it is easy to make the descent. Single-argument constructors and implicit type conversion operators are particularly troublesome, because they can be invoked without there being any source code showing the calls. This can lead to program behavior that is difficult to understand. A different problem arises when you overload operators like && and ||, because the shift from built-in operator to user-defined function yields a subtle change in semantics that's easy to overlook. Finally, many operators are related to one another in standard ways, but the ability to overload operators makes it possible to violate the accepted relationships.

In the items that follow, I focus on explaining when and how overloaded operators are called, how they behave, how they should relate to one another, and how you can seize control of these aspects of overloaded operators. With the information in this chapter under your belt, you'll be overloading (or *not* overloading) operators like a pro.

Item 5: Be wary of user-defined conversion functions

C++ allows compilers to perform implicit conversions between types. In honor of its C heritage, for example, the language allows silent conversions from char to int and from short to double. This is why you can pass a short to a function that expects a double and still have the call succeed. The more frightening conversions in C — those that may lose information — are also present in C++, including conversion of int to short and double to (of all things) char.

You can't do anything about such conversions, because they're hard-coded into the language. When you add your own types, however, you have more control, because you can choose whether to provide the functions compilers are allowed to use for implicit type conversions.

Two kinds of functions allow compilers to perform such conversions: *single-argument constructors* and *implicit type conversion operators*. A single-argument constructor is a constructor that may be called with only one argument. Such a constructor may declare a single parameter or it may declare multiple parameters, with each parameter after the first having a default value. Here are two examples:

```
class Name {                        // for names of things
public:
  Name(const string& s);           // converts string to
                                    // Name
  ...

};
class Rational {                    // for rational numbers
public:
  Rational(int numerator = 0,      // converts int to
           int denominator = 1);   // Rational
  ...

};
```

An implicit type conversion operator is simply a member function with a strange-looking name: the word operator followed by a type specification. You aren't allowed to specify a type for the function's return value, because the type of the return value is basically just the name of the function. For example, to allow Rational objects to be implicitly converted to doubles (which might be useful for mixed-mode arithmetic involving Rational objects), you might define class Rational like this:

```
class Rational {
public:
  ...
  operator double() const;         // converts Rational to
};                                  // double
```

This function would be automatically invoked in contexts like this:

```
Rational r(1, 2);                   // r has the value 1/2

double d = 0.5 * r;                 // converts r to a double,
                                    // then does multiplication
```

Perhaps all this is review. That's fine, because what I really want to explain is why you usually don't want to provide type conversion functions of *any* ilk.

The fundamental problem is that such functions often end up being called when you neither want nor expect them to be. The result can be incorrect and unintuitive program behavior that is maddeningly difficult to diagnose.

Let us deal first with implicit type conversion operators, as they are the easiest case to handle. Suppose you have a class for rational numbers similar to the one above, and you'd like to print Rational objects as if they were a built-in type. That is, you'd like to be able to do this:

```
Rational r(1, 2);

cout << r;                           // should print "1/2"
```

Further suppose you forgot to write an operator<< for Rational objects. You would probably expect that the attempt to print r would fail, because there is no appropriate operator<< to call. You would be mistaken. Your compilers, faced with a call to a function called operator<< that takes a Rational, would find that no such function existed, but they would then try to find an acceptable sequence of implicit type conversions they could apply to make the call succeed. The rules defining which sequences of conversions are acceptable are complicated, but in this case your compilers would discover they could make the call succeed by implicitly converting r to a double by calling Rational::operator double. The result of the code above would be to print r as a floating point number, not as a rational number. This is hardly a disaster, but it demonstrates the disadvantage of implicit type conversion operators: their presence can lead to the *wrong function* being called (i.e., one other than the one intended).

The solution is to replace the operators with equivalent functions that don't have the syntactically magic names. For example, to allow conversion of a Rational object to a double, replace operator double with a function called something like asDouble:

```
class Rational {
public:
  ...
  double asDouble() const;        // converts Rational
};                                // to double
```

Such a member function must be called explicitly:

```
Rational r(1, 2);

cout << r;                           // error! No operator<<
                                     // for Rationals
```

```
cout << r.asDouble();              // fine, prints r as a
                                   // double
```

In most cases, the inconvenience of having to call conversion functions explicitly is more than compensated for by the fact that unintended functions can no longer be silently invoked. In general, the more experience C++ programmers have, the more likely they are to eschew type conversion operators. The members of the committee working on the standard C++ library (see Item 35), for example, are among the most experienced in the business, and perhaps that's why the string class they added to the library contains no implicit conversion from a string object to a C-style char*. Instead, there's an explicit member function, c_str, that performs that conversion. Coincidence? I think not.

Implicit conversions via single-argument constructors are more difficult to eliminate. Furthermore, the problems these functions cause are in many cases worse than those arising from implicit type conversion operators.

As an example, consider a class template for array objects. These arrays allow clients to specify upper and lower index bounds:

```
template<class T>
class Array {
public:
  Array(int lowBound, int highBound);
  Array(int size);

  T& operator[](int index);

  ...

};
```

The first constructor in the class allows clients to specify a range of array indices, for example, from 10 to 20. As a two-argument constructor, this function is ineligible for use as a type-conversion function. The second constructor, which allows clients to define Array objects by specifying only the number of elements in the array (in a manner similar to that used with built-in arrays), is different. It *can* be used as a type conversion function, and that can lead to endless anguish.

For example, consider a template specialization for comparing Array<int> objects and some code that uses such objects:

```
bool operator==( const Array<int>& lhs,
                 const Array<int>& rhs);
```

```
Array<int> a(10);
Array<int> b(10);

...

for (int i = 0; i < 10; ++i)
  if (a == b[i]) {              // oops! "a" should be "a[i]"
    do something for when
    a[i] and b[i] are equal;
  }
  else {
    do something for when they're not;
  }
```

We intended to compare each element of a to the corresponding element in b, but we accidentally omitted the subscripting syntax when we typed a. Certainly we expect this to elicit all manner of unpleasant commentary from our compilers, but they will complain not at all. That's because they see a call to operator== with arguments of type Array<int> (for a) and int (for b[i]), and though there is no operator== function taking those types, our compilers notice they can convert the int into an Array<int> object by calling the Array<int> constructor that takes a single int as an argument. This they proceed to do, thus generating code for a program we never meant to write, one that looks like this:

```
for (int i = 0; i < 10; ++i)
  if (a == static_cast< Array<int> >(b[i])) ...
```

Each iteration through the loop thus compares the contents of a with the contents of a temporary array of size b[i] (whose contents are presumably undefined). Not only is this unlikely to behave in a satisfactory manner, it is also tremendously inefficient, because each time through the loop we both create and destroy a temporary Array<int> object (see Item 19).

The drawbacks to implicit type conversion operators can be avoided by simply failing to declare the operators, but single-argument constructors cannot be so easily waved away. After all, you may really *want* to offer single-argument constructors to your clients. At the same time, you may wish to prevent compilers from calling such constructors indiscriminately. Fortunately, there is a way to have it all. In fact, there are two ways: the easy way and the way you'll have to use if your compilers don't yet support the easy way.

The easy way is to avail yourself of one of the newest C++ features, the explicit keyword. This feature was introduced specifically to address the problem of implicit type conversion, and its use is about as straightforward as can be. Constructors can be declared explicit, and if they are, compilers are prohibited from invoking them for purposes of implicit type conversion. Explicit conversions are still legal, however:

```
template<class T>
class Array {
public:
  ...
  explicit Array(int size);        // note use of "explicit"
  ...
};

Array<int> a(10);                  // okay, explicit ctors can
                                   // be used as usual for
                                   // object construction

Array<int> b(10);                  // also okay

if (a == b[i]) ...                 // error! no way to
                                   // implicitly convert
                                   // int to Array<int>

if (a == Array<int>(b[i])) ...     // okay, the conversion
                                   // from int to Array<int> is
                                   // explicit (but the logic of
                                   // the code is suspect)

if (a == static_cast< Array<int> >(b[i])) ...
                                   // equally okay, equally
                                   // suspect

if (a == (Array<int>)b[i]) ...     // C-style casts are also
                                   // okay, but the logic of
                                   // the code is still suspect
```

In the example using static_cast (see Item 2), the space separating the two ">" characters is no accident. If the statement were written like this,

```
if (a == static_cast<Array<int>>(b[i])) ...
```

it would have a different meaning. That's because C++ compilers parse ">>" as a single token. Without a space between the ">" characters, the statement would generate a syntax error.

If your compilers don't yet support explicit, you'll have to fall back on home-grown methods for preventing the use of single-argument constructors as implicit type conversion functions. Such methods are obvious only *after* you've seen them.

I mentioned earlier that there are complicated rules governing which sequences of implicit type conversions are legitimate and which are not. One of those rules is that no sequence of conversions is allowed to contain more than one user-defined conversion (i.e., a call to a single-argument constructor or an implicit type conversion operator). By constructing your classes properly, you can take advantage of this rule so that the object constructions you want to allow are legal, but the implicit conversions you don't want to allow are illegal.

Consider the `Array` template again. You need a way to allow an integer specifying the size of the array to be used as a constructor argument, but you must at the same time prevent the implicit conversion of an integer into a temporary `Array` object. You accomplish this by first creating a new class, `ArraySize`. Objects of this type have only one purpose: they represent the size of an array that's about to be created. You then modify `Array`'s single-argument constructor to take an `ArraySize` object instead of an `int`. The code looks like this:

```
template<class T>
class Array {
public:

  class ArraySize {              // this class is new
  public:
    ArraySize(int numElements): theSize(numElements) {}
    int size() const { return theSize; }

  private:
    int theSize;
  };

  Array(int lowBound, int highBound);
  Array(ArraySize size);         // note new declaration

  ...

};
```

Here you've nested `ArraySize` inside `Array` to emphasize the fact that it's always used in conjunction with that class. You've also made `ArraySize` public in `Array` so that anybody can use it. Good.

Consider what happens when an `Array` object is defined via the class's single-argument constructor:

```
Array<int> a(10);
```

Your compilers are asked to call a constructor in the `Array<int>` class that takes an `int`, but there is no such constructor. Compilers realize they can convert the `int` argument into a temporary `ArraySize` object, and that `ArraySize` object is just what the `Array<int>` constructor needs, so compilers perform the conversion with their usual gusto. This allows the function call (and the attendant object construction) to succeed.

The fact that you can still construct `Array` objects with an `int` argument is reassuring, but it does you little good unless the type conversions you want to avoid are prevented. They are. Consider this code again:

```
bool operator==( const Array<int>& lhs,
                 const Array<int>& rhs);

Array<int> a(10);
Array<int> b(10);

...

for (int i = 0; i < 10; ++i)
  if (a == b[i]) ...          // oops! "a" should be "a[i]";
                              // this is now an error
```

Compilers need an object of type Array<int> on the right-hand side of the "==" in order to call operator== for Array<int> objects, but there is no single-argument constructor taking an int argument. Furthermore, compilers cannot consider converting the int into a temporary ArraySize object and then creating the necessary Array<int> object from this temporary, because that would call for two user-defined conversions, one from int to ArraySize and one from ArraySize to Array<int>. Such a conversion sequence is *verboten*, so compilers must issue an error for the code attempting to perform the assignment.

The use of the ArraySize class in this example might look like a special-purpose hack, but it's actually a specific instance of a more general technique. Classes like ArraySize are often called *proxy classes*, because each object of such a class stands for (is a proxy for) some other object. An ArraySize object is really just a stand-in for the integer used to specify the size of the Array being created. Proxy objects can give you control over aspects of your software's behavior — in this case implicit type conversions — that is otherwise beyond your grasp, so it's well worth your while to learn how to use them. How, you might wonder, can you acquire such learning? One way is to turn to Item 30; it's devoted to proxy classes.

Before you turn to proxy classes, however, reflect a bit on the lessons of this Item. Granting compilers license to perform implicit type conversions usually leads to more harm than good, so don't provide conversion functions unless you're *sure* you want them.

Item 6: Distinguish between prefix and postfix forms of increment and decrement operators

Long, long ago (the late '80s) in a language far, far away (C++ at that time), there was no way to distinguish between prefix and postfix invocations of the ++ and -- operators. Programmers being programmers, they kvetched about this omission, and C++ was extended to allow overloading both forms of increment and decrement operators.

There was a syntactic problem, however, and that was that overloaded functions are differentiated on the basis of the parameter types they take, but neither prefix nor postfix increment or decrement takes an argument. To surmount this linguistic pothole, it was decreed that postfix forms take an int argument, and compilers silently pass 0 as that int when those functions are called:

```
class UPInt {                    // "unlimited precision int"
public:
  UPInt& operator++();           // prefix ++
  const UPInt operator++(int);   // postfix ++

  UPInt& operator--();           // prefix --
  const UPInt operator--(int);   // postfix --

  UPInt& operator+=(int);        // a += operator for UPInts
                                 // and ints

  ...

};

UPInt i;

++i;                             // calls i.operator++();
i++;                             // calls i.operator++(0);

--i;                             // calls i.operator--();
i--;                             // calls i.operator--(0);
```

This convention is a little on the odd side, but you'll get used to it. More important to get used to, however, is this: the prefix and postfix forms of these operators return *different types*. In particular, prefix forms return a reference, postfix forms return a const object. We'll focus here on the prefix and postfix ++ operators, but the story for the -- operators is analogous.

From your days as a C programmer, you may recall that the prefix form of the increment operator is sometimes called "increment and fetch," while the postfix form is often known as "fetch and increment." These two phrases are important to remember, because they all but act as formal specifications for how prefix and postfix increment should be implemented:

```
// prefix form: increment and fetch
UPInt& UPInt::operator++()
{
  *this += 1;                    // increment
  return *this;                  // fetch
}
```

```
// postfix form: fetch and increment
const UPInt UPInt::operator++(int)
{
  UPInt oldValue = *this;              // fetch
  ++(*this);                           // increment

  return oldValue;                     // return what was
}                                      // fetched
```

Note how the postfix operator makes no use of its parameter. This is typical. The only purpose of the parameter is to distinguish prefix from postfix function invocation. Many compilers issue warnings if you fail to use named parameters in the body of the function to which they apply, and this can be annoying. To avoid such warnings, a common strategy is to omit names for parameters you don't plan to use; that's what's been done above.

It's clear why postfix increment must return an object (it's returning an old value), but why a const object? Imagine that it did not. Then the following would be legal:

```
UPInt i;

i++++;                               // apply postfix increment
                                     // twice
```

This is the same as

```
i.operator++(0).operator++(0);
```

and it should be clear that the second invocation of operator++ is being applied to the object returned from the first invocation.

There are two reasons to abhor this. First, it's inconsistent with the behavior of the built-in types. A good rule to follow when designing classes is *when in doubt, do as the ints do*, and the ints most certainly do not allow double application of postfix increment:

```
int i;

i++++;                               // error!
```

The second reason is that double application of postfix increment almost never does what clients expect it to. As noted above, the second application of operator++ in a double increment changes the value of the object returned from the first invocation, *not* the value of the original object. Hence, if

```
i++++;
```

were legal, i would be incremented only once. This is counterintuitive and confusing (for both ints and UPInts), so it's best prohibited.

C++ prohibits it for ints, but you must prohibit it yourself for classes you write. The easiest way to do this is to make the return type of postfix increment a const object. Then when compilers see

```
i++++;              // same as i.operator++(0).operator++(0);
```

they recognize that the const object returned from the first call to operator++ is being used to call operator++ again. operator++, however, is a non-const member function, so const objects — such as those returned from postfix operator++ — can't call it. If you've ever wondered if it makes sense to have functions return const objects, now you know: sometimes it does, and postfix increment and decrement are examples.

If you're the kind who worries about efficiency, you probably broke into a sweat when you first saw the postfix increment function. That function has to create a temporary object for its return value (see Item 19), and the implementation above also creates an explicit temporary object (oldValue) that has to be constructed and destructed. The prefix increment function has no such temporaries. This leads to the possibly startling conclusion that, for efficiency reasons alone, clients of UPInt should prefer prefix increment to postfix increment unless they really need the behavior of postfix increment. Let us be explicit about this. When dealing with user-defined types, prefix increment should be used whenever possible, because it's inherently more efficient.

Let us make one more observation about the prefix and postfix increment operators. Except for their return values, they do the same thing: they increment a value. That is, they're *supposed* to do the same thing. How can you be sure the behavior of postfix increment is consistent with that of prefix increment? What guarantee do you have that their implementations won't diverge over time, possibly as a result of different programmers maintaining and enhancing them? Unless you've followed the design principle embodied by the code above, you have no such guarantee. That principle is that postfix increment and decrement should be implemented *in terms of* their prefix counterparts. You then need only maintain the prefix versions, because the postfix versions will automatically behave in a consistent fashion.

As you can see, mastering prefix and postfix increment and decrement is easy. Once you know their proper return types and that the postfix operators should be implemented in terms of the prefix operators, there's very little more to learn.

Item 7: Never overload &&, ||, or ,

Like C, C++ employs short-circuit evaluation of boolean expressions. This means that once the truth or falsehood of an expression has been determined, evaluation of the expression ceases, even if some parts of the expression haven't yet been examined. For example, in this case,

```
char *p;

...

if ((p != 0) && (strlen(p) > 10)) ...
```

there is no need to worry about invoking `strlen` on p if it's a null pointer, because if the test of p against 0 fails, `strlen` will never be called. Similarly, given

```
int rangeCheck(int index)
{
  if ((index < lowerBound) || (index > upperBound)) ...

  ...

}
```

index will never be compared to upperBound if it's less than lower-Bound.

This is the behavior that has been drummed into C and C++ programmers since time immemorial, so this is what they expect. Furthermore, they write programs whose correct behavior *depends* on short-circuit evaluation. In the first code fragment above, for example, it is important that `strlen` not be invoked if p is a null pointer, because the standard for C++ states (as does the standard for C) that the result of invoking `strlen` on a null pointer is undefined.

C++ allows you to customize the behavior of the && and || operators for user-defined types. You do it by overloading the functions opera-tor&& and operator||, and you can do this at the global scope or on a per-class basis. If you decide to take advantage of this opportunity, however, you must be aware that you are changing the rules of the game quite radically, because you are replacing short-circuit semantics with *function call* semantics. That is, if you overload operator&&, what looks to you like this,

```
if (expression1 && expression2) ...
```

looks to compilers like one of these:

```
if (expression1.operator&&(expression2)) ...
                                // when operator&& is a
                                // member function
```

```
if (operator&&(expression1, expression2)) ...
                                    // when operator&& is a
                                    // global function
```

This may not seem like that big a deal, but function call semantics differ from short-circuit semantics in two crucial ways. First, when a function call is made, *all* parameters must be evaluated, so when calling the functions operator&& and operator||, *both* parameters are evaluated. There is, in other words, no short circuit. Second, the language specification leaves undefined the order of evaluation of parameters to a function call, so there is no way of knowing whether expression1 or expression2 will be evaluated first. This stands in stark contrast to short-circuit evaluation, which *always* evaluates its arguments in left-to-right order.

As a result, if you overload && or ||, there is no way to offer programmers the behavior they both expect and have come to depend on. So don't overload && or ||.

The situation with the comma operator is similar, but before we delve into that, I'll pause and let you catch the breath you lost when you gasped, "The comma operator? There's a *comma* operator?" There is indeed.

The comma operator is used to form *expressions*, and about the only time you're likely to see it in the wild is in the update part of a for loop. The following function, for example, is based on one in the second edition of Kernighan's and Ritchie's classic *The C Programming Language* (Prentice-Hall, 1988):

```
// reverse string s in place
void reverse(char s[])
{
  for (int i = 0, j = strlen(s)-1;
       i < j;
       ++i, --j)                    // aha! the comma operator!
  {
    int c = s[i];
    s[i] = s[j];
    s[j] = c;
  }
}
```

Here, i is incremented and j is decremented in the final part of the for loop. It is convenient to use the comma operator here, because only an expression is valid in the final part of a for loop; separate statements to change the values of i and j would be illegal.

Just as there are rules in C++ defining how && and || behave for built-in types, there are rules defining how the comma operator behaves for such types. An expression containing a comma is evaluated by first evaluating the part of the expression to the left of the comma, then evaluating the expression to the right of the comma; the result of the overall comma expression is the value of the expression on the right. So in the final part of the loop above, compilers first evaluate ++i, then --j, and the result of the comma expression is the value returned from --j.

Perhaps you're wondering why you need to know this. You need to know because you need to mimic this behavior if you're going to take it upon yourself to write your own comma operator. Unfortunately, you can't perform the requisite mimicry.

If you write operator, as a non-member function, you'll never be able to guarantee that the left-hand expression is evaluated before the right-hand expression, because both expressions will be passed as arguments in a function call (to operator,). But you have no control over the order in which a function's arguments are evaluated. So the non-member approach is definitely out.

That leaves only the possibility of writing operator, as a member function. Even here you can't rely on the left-hand operand to the comma operator being evaluated first, because compilers are not constrained to do things that way. Hence, you can't overload the comma operator and also guarantee it will behave the way it's supposed to. It therefore seems imprudent to overload it at all.

You may be wondering if there's an end to this overloading madness. After all, if you can overload the comma operator, what *can't* you overload? As it turns out, there are limits. You can't overload the following operators:

.	.*	::	?:
new	delete	sizeof	typeid
static_cast	dynamic_cast	const_cast	reinterpret_cast

You can overload these:

operator new			operator delete					
operator new[]			operator delete[]					
+	−	*	/	%	^	&	|	~
!	=	<	>	+=	−=	*=	/=	%=
^=	&=	|=	<<	>>	>>=	<<=	==	!=
<=	>=	&&	||	++	−−	,	->*	->
()	[]							

(For information on the new and delete operators, as well as operator new, operator delete, operator new[], and operator delete[], see Item 8.)

Of course, just because you can overload these operators is no reason to run off and do it. The purpose of operator overloading is to make programs easier to read, write, and understand, not to dazzle others with your knowledge that comma is an operator. If you don't have a good reason for overloading an operator, don't overload it. In the case of &&, ||, and ,, it's difficult to have a good reason, because no matter how hard you try, you can't make them behave the way they're supposed to.

Item 8: Understand the different meanings of new and delete

It occasionally seems as if people went out of their way to make C++ terminology difficult to understand. Case in point: the difference between the *new operator* and *operator new*.

When you write code like this,

```
string *ps = new string("Memory Management");
```

the new you are using is the new operator. This operator is built into the language and, like sizeof, you can't change its meaning: it always does the same thing. What it does is twofold. First, it allocates enough memory to hold an object of the type requested. In the example above, it allocates enough memory to hold a string object. Second, it calls a constructor to initialize an object in the memory that was allocated. The new operator always does those two things; you can't change its behavior in any way.

What you can change is *how* the memory for an object is allocated. The new operator calls a function to perform the requisite memory allocation, and you can rewrite or overload that function to change its behavior. The name of the function the new operator calls to allocate memory is operator new. Honest.

The operator new function is usually declared like this:

```
void * operator new(size_t size);
```

The return type is void*, because this function returns a pointer to raw, uninitialized memory. (If you like, you can write a version of operator new that initializes the memory to some value before returning a pointer to it, but this is not commonly done.) The size_t parameter specifies how much memory to allocate. You can overload operator new by adding additional parameters, but the first parameter must always be of type `size_t`.

You'll probably never want to call `operator new` directly, but on the off chance you do, you'll call it just like any other function:

```
void *rawMemory = operator new(sizeof(string));
```

Here `operator new` will return a pointer to a chunk of memory large enough to hold a `string` object.

Like `malloc`, `operator new`'s only responsibility is to allocate memory. It knows nothing about constructors. All `operator new` understands is memory allocation. It is the job of the `new` operator to take the raw memory that `operator new` returns and transform it into an object. When your compilers see a statement like

```
string *ps = new string("Memory Management");
```

they must generate code that more or less corresponds to this:

```
void *memory =                              // get raw memory
  operator new(sizeof(string));             // for a string
                                            // object

call string::string("Memory Management")    // initialize the
on *memory;                                 // object in the
                                            // memory

string *ps =                                // make ps point to
  static_cast<string*>(memory);             // the new object
```

Notice that the second step above involves calling a constructor, something you, a mere programmer, are prohibited from doing. Your compilers are unconstrained by mortal limits, however, and they can do whatever they like. That's why you must use the `new` operator if you want to conjure up a heap-based object: you can't directly call the constructor necessary to initialize the object (including such crucial components as its vtbl — see Item 24).

Placement new

There are times when you really *want* to call a constructor directly. Invoking a constructor on an existing object makes no sense, because constructors initialize objects, and an object can only be initialized — given its first value — once. But occasionally you have some raw memory that's already been allocated, and you need to construct an object in the memory you have. A special version of `operator new` called *placement new* allows you to do it.

As an example of how placement new might be used, consider this:

```
class Widget {
public:
  Widget(int widgetSize);
  ...
};

Widget * constructWidgetInBuffer(void *buffer,
                                 int widgetSize)
{
  return new (buffer) Widget(widgetSize);
}
```

This function returns a pointer to a Widget object that's constructed *within* the buffer passed to the function. Such a function might be useful for applications using shared memory or memory-mapped I/O, because objects in such applications must be placed at specific addresses or in memory allocated by special routines. (For a different example of how placement new can be used, see Item 3.)

Inside constructWidgetInBuffer, the expression being returned is

```
new (buffer) Widget(widgetSize)
```

This looks a little strange at first, but it's just a use of the new operator in which an additional argument (buffer) is being specified for the implicit call that the new operator makes to operator new. The operator new thus called must, in addition to the mandatory size_t argument, accept a void* parameter that points to the memory the object being constructed is to occupy. That operator new *is* placement new, and it looks like this:

```
void * operator new(size_t, void *location)
{
  return location;
}
```

This is probably simpler than you expected, but this is all placement new needs to do. After all, the purpose of operator new is to find memory for an object and return a pointer to that memory. In the case of placement new, the caller already knows what the pointer to the memory should be, because the caller knows where the object is supposed to be placed. All placement new has to do, then, is return the pointer that's passed into it. (The unused (but mandatory) size_t parameter has no name to keep compilers from complaining about its not being used; see Item 6.) Placement new is part of the standard C++ library. To use placement new, all you have to do is #include <new.h>.

If we step back from placement new for a moment, we'll see that the relationship between the new operator and operator new, though perhaps terminologically confusing, is conceptually straightforward. If you want to create an object on the heap, use the new operator. It both allocates memory and calls a constructor for the object. If you only want to allocate memory, call operator new; no constructor will be called. If you want to customize the memory allocation that takes place when heap objects are created, write your own version of operator new and use the new operator; it will automatically invoke your custom version of operator new. If you want to construct an object in memory you've already got a pointer to, use placement new.

Deletion and Memory Deallocation

To avoid resource leaks, every dynamic allocation must be matched by an equal and opposite deallocation. The function operator delete is to the built-in delete operator as operator new is to the new operator. When you say something like this,

```
string *ps;
...
delete ps;                        // use the delete operator
```

your compilers must generate code both to destruct the object ps points to and to deallocate the memory occupied by that object.

The memory deallocation is performed by the operator delete function, which is usually declared like this:

```
void operator delete(void *memoryToBeDeallocated);
```

Hence,

```
delete ps;
```

causes compilers to generate code that approximately corresponds to this:

```
ps->~string();              // call the object's dtor

operator delete(ps);        // deallocate the memory
                            // the object occupied
```

One implication of this is that if you want to deal only with raw, uninitialized memory, you should bypass the new and delete operators entirely. Instead, you should call operator new to get the memory and operator delete to return it to the system:

```
void *buffer =                   // allocate enough
  operator new(50*sizeof(char)); // memory to hold 50
                                 // chars; call no ctors

...

operator delete(buffer);         // deallocate the memory;
                                 // call no dtors
```

This is the C++ equivalent of calling `malloc` and `free`.

If you use placement `new` to create an object in some memory, you should avoid using the `delete` operator on that memory. That's because the `delete` operator calls `operator delete` to deallocate the memory, but the memory containing the object wasn't allocated by `operator new` in the first place; placement `new` just returned the pointer that was passed to it. Who knows where that pointer came from? Instead, you should undo the effect of the constructor by explicitly calling the object's destructor:

```
// functions for allocating and deallocating memory in
// shared memory
void * mallocShared(size_t size);
void freeShared(void *memory);

void *sharedMemory = mallocShared(sizeof(Widget));

Widget *pw =                                  // as above,
  constructWidgetInBuffer( sharedMemory, 10); // placement
                                              // new is used

...

delete pw;           // undefined! sharedMemory came from
                     // mallocShared, not operator new

pw->~Widget();       // fine, destructs the Widget pointed to
                     // by pw, but doesn't deallocate the
                     // memory containing the Widget

freeShared(pw);      // fine, deallocates the memory pointed
                     // to by pw, but calls no destructor
```

As this example demonstrates, if the raw memory passed to placement `new` was itself dynamically allocated (through some unconventional means), you must still deallocate that memory if you wish to avoid a memory leak.

Arrays

So far so good, but there's farther to go. Everything we've examined so far concerns itself with only one object at a time. What about array allocation? What happens here?

```
string *ps = new string[10];    // allocate an array of
                                // objects
```

The `new` being used is still the `new` operator, but because an array is being created, the `new` operator behaves slightly differently than in the case of single-object creation. For one thing, memory is no longer allocated by `operator new`. Instead, it's allocated by the array-allocation equivalent, a function called `operator new[]` (often referred to as "array new.") Like operator new, operator new[] can be overloaded. This allows you to seize control of memory allocation for arrays in the same way you can control memory allocation for single objects.

(operator new[] is a relatively recent addition to C++, so your compilers may not support it yet. If they don't, the global version of operator new will be used to allocate memory for every array, regardless of the type of objects in the array. Customizing array-memory allocation under such compilers is daunting, because it requires that you rewrite the global operator new. This is not a task to be undertaken lightly. By default, the global operator new handles *all* dynamic memory allocation in a program, so any change in its behavior has a dramatic and pervasive effect. Furthermore, there is only one global operator new, so if you decide to claim it as your own, you instantly render your software incompatible with any library that makes the same decision. (See also Item 27.) As a result of these considerations, custom memory management for arrays is not usually a reasonable design decision for compilers lacking support for operator new[].)

The second way in which the new operator behaves differently for arrays than for objects is in the number of constructor calls it makes. For arrays, a constructor must be called for *each object* in the array:

```
string *ps =              // call operator new[] to allocate
  new string[10];         // memory for 10 string objects,
                          // then call the default string
                          // ctor for each array element
```

Similarly, when the delete operator is used on an array, it calls a destructor for each array element and then calls operator delete[] to deallocate the memory:

```
delete [] ps;             // call the string dtor for each
                          // array element, then call
                          // operator delete[] to
                          // deallocate the array's memory
```

Just as you can replace or overload operator delete, you can replace or overload operator delete[]. There are some restrictions on how they can be overloaded, however; consult a good C++ text for details. (For ideas on good C++ texts, see the recommendations beginning on page 285.)

So there you have it. The new and delete operators are built-in and beyond your control, but the memory allocation and deallocation functions they call are not. When you think about customizing the behavior of the new and delete operators, remember that you can't really do it. You can modify *how* they do what they do, but *what* they do is fixed by the language.

Exceptions

The addition of exceptions to C++ changes things. Profoundly. Radically. Possibly uncomfortably. The use of raw, unadorned pointers, for example, becomes risky. Opportunities for resource leaks increase in number. It becomes more difficult to write constructors and destructors that behave the way we want them to. Special care must be taken to prevent program execution from abruptly halting. Executables and libraries typically increase in size and decrease in speed.

And these are just the things we know. There is much the C++ community does not know about writing programs using exceptions, including, for the most part, how to do it correctly. There is as yet no agreement on a body of techniques that, when applied routinely, leads to software that behaves predictably and reliability when exceptions are thrown. (For insight into some of the issues involved, see the article by Tom Cargill I refer to on page 287.)

We do know this much: programs that behave well in the presence of exceptions do so because they were *designed* to, not because they happen to. Exception-safe programs are not created by accident. The chances of a program behaving well in the presence of exceptions when it was not designed for exceptions are about the same as the chances of a program behaving well in the presence of multiple threads of control when it was not designed for multi-threaded execution: about zero.

That being the case, why use exceptions? Error codes have sufficed for C programmers ever since C was invented, so why mess with exceptions, especially if they're as problematic as I say? The answer is simple: exceptions cannot be ignored. If a function signals an exceptional condition by setting a status variable or returning an error code, there is no way to guarantee the function's caller will check the variable or examine the code. As a result, execution may continue long past the point where the condition was encountered. If the function signals the condition by throwing an exception, however, and that exception is not caught, program execution immediately ceases.

This is behavior that C programmers can approach only by using `set-jmp` and `longjmp`. But `longjmp` exhibits a serious deficiency when used with C++: it fails to call destructors for local objects when it adjusts the stack. Most C++ programs depend on such destructors being called, so `setjmp` and `longjmp` make a poor substitute for true exceptions. If you need a way of signaling exceptional conditions that cannot be ignored, and if you must ensure that local destructors are called when searching the stack for code that can handle exceptional conditions, you need C++ exceptions. It's as simple as that.

Because we have much to learn about programming with exceptions, the Items that follow comprise an incomplete guide to writing exception-safe software. Nevertheless, they introduce important considerations for anyone using exceptions in C++. By heeding the guidance in the material below, you'll improve the correctness, robustness, and efficiency of the software you write, and you'll sidestep many problems that commonly arise when working with exceptions.

Item 9: Use destructors to prevent resource leaks

Say good-bye to pointers. Admit it: you never really liked them that much anyway.

Okay, you don't have to say good-bye to *all* pointers, but you do need to say *sayonara* to pointers that are used to manipulate local resources. Suppose, for example, you're writing software at the Shelter for Adorable Little Animals, an organization that finds homes for puppies and kittens. Each day the shelter creates a file containing information on the adoptions it arranged that day, and your job is to write a program to read these files and do the appropriate processing for each adoption.

A reasonable approach to this task is to define an abstract base class, ALA ("Adorable Little Animal"), plus concrete derived classes for puppies and kittens. A virtual function, `processAdoption`, handles the necessary species-specific processing:

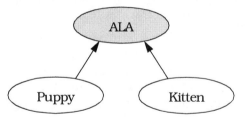

```
class ALA {
public:
  virtual void processAdoption() = 0;
  ...
};

class Puppy: public ALA {
public:
  virtual void processAdoption();
  ...
};

class Kitten: public ALA {
public:
  virtual void processAdoption();
  ...
};
```

You'll need a function that can read information from a file and produce either a Puppy object or a Kitten object, depending on the information in the file. This is a perfect job for a *virtual constructor*, a kind of function described in Item 25. For our purposes here, the function's declaration is all we need:

```
// read animal information from s, then return a pointer
// to a newly allocated object of the appropriate type
ALA * readALA(istream& s);
```

The heart of your program is likely to be a function that looks something like this:

```
void processAdoptions(istream& dataSource)
{
  while (dataSource) {              // while there's data
    ALA *pa = readALA(dataSource);  // get next animal
    pa->processAdoption();          // process adoption
    delete pa;                      // delete object that
  }                                 // readALA returned
}
```

This function loops through the information in dataSource, processing each entry as it goes. The only mildly tricky thing is the need to remember to delete pa at the end of each iteration. This is necessary because readALA creates a new heap object each time it's called. Without the call to delete, the loop would contain a resource leak.

Now consider what would happen if pa->processAdoption threw an exception. processAdoptions fails to catch exceptions, so the exception would propagate to processAdoptions's caller. In doing so, all statements in processAdoptions after the call to pa->processAdoption would be skipped, and that means pa would never be deleted. As a result, anytime pa->processAdoption throws an exception, processAdoptions contains a resource leak.

Plugging the leak is easy enough,

```
void processAdoptions(istream& dataSource)
{
  while (dataSource) {
    ALA *pa = readALA(dataSource);

    try {
      pa->processAdoption();
    }
    catch (...) {            // catch all exceptions

      delete pa;             // avoid resource leak when an
                             // exception is thrown

      throw;                 // propagate exception to caller
    }
    delete pa;               // avoid resource leak when no
  }                          // exception is thrown
}
```

but then you have to litter your code with try and catch blocks. More importantly, you are forced to duplicate cleanup code that is common to both normal and exceptional paths of control. In this case, the call to delete must be duplicated. Like all replicated code, this is annoying to write and difficult to maintain, but it also *feels wrong*. Regardless of whether we leave processAdoptions by a normal return or by throwing an exception, we need to delete pa, so why should we have to say that in more than one place?

We don't have to if we can somehow move the cleanup code that must always be executed into the destructor for an object local to processAdoptions. That's because local objects are always destroyed when leaving a function, regardless of how that function is exited. (The only exception to this rule is when you call longjmp, and this shortcoming of longjmp is the primary reason why C++ has support for exceptions in the first place.) Our real concern, then, is moving the delete from processAdoptions into a destructor for an object local to processAdoptions.

The solution is to replace the pointer pa with an object that *acts like* a pointer. That way, when the pointer-like object is (automatically) destroyed, we can have its destructor call delete. Objects that act like pointers, but do more, are called *smart pointers*, and, as Item 28 explains, you can make pointer-like objects very smart indeed. In this case, we don't need a particularly brainy pointer, we just need a pointer-like object that knows enough to delete what it points to when the pointer-like object goes out of scope.

It's not difficult to write a class for such objects, but we don't need to. The standard C++ library contains a class template called `auto_ptr` that does just what we want. Each `auto_ptr` class takes a pointer to a heap object in its constructor and deletes that object in its destructor. Boiled down to these essential functions, `auto_ptr` looks like this:

```
template<class T>
class auto_ptr {
public:
  auto_ptr(T *p = 0): ptr(p) {}     // save ptr to object
  ~auto_ptr() { delete ptr; }       // delete ptr to object

private:
  T *ptr;                            // raw ptr to object
};
```

The standard version of `auto_ptr` is much fancier, and this stripped-down implementation isn't suitable for real use[†] (we must add at least the copy constructor, assignment operator, and pointer-emulating functions discussed in Item 28), but the concept behind it should be clear: use `auto_ptr` objects instead of raw pointers, and you won't have to worry about heap objects not being deleted, not even when exceptions are thrown. (Because the `auto_ptr` destructor uses the single-object form of `delete`, `auto_ptr` is not suitable for use with pointers to *arrays* of objects. If you'd like an `auto_ptr`-like template for arrays, you'll have to write your own.)

Using an `auto_ptr` object instead of a raw pointer, `process-Adoptions` looks like this:

```
void processAdoptions(istream& dataSource)
{
  while (dataSource) {
    auto_ptr<ALA> pa(readALA(dataSource));
    pa->processAdoption();
  }
}
```

This version of `processAdoptions` differs from the original in only two ways. First, pa is declared to be an `auto_ptr<ALA>` object, not a raw ALA* pointer. Second, there is no `delete` statement at the end of the loop. That's it. Everything else is identical, because, except for destruction, `auto_ptr` objects act just like normal pointers. Easy, huh?

---

†. A complete implementation of `auto_ptr` appears on pages 291-294.

The idea behind auto_ptr — using an object to store a resource that needs to be automatically released and relying on that object's destructor to release it — applies to more than just pointer-based resources. Consider a function in a GUI application that needs to create a window to display some information:

```
// this function may leak resources if an exception
// is thrown
void displayInfo(const Information& info)
{
  WINDOW_HANDLE w(createWindow());

  display info in window corresponding to w;

  destroyWindow(w);
}
```

Many window systems have C-like interfaces that use functions like createWindow and destroyWindow to acquire and release window resources. If an exception is thrown during the process of displaying info in w, the window for which w is a handle will be lost just as surely as any other dynamically allocated resource.

The solution is the same as it was before. Create a class whose constructor and destructor acquire and release the resource:

```
// class for acquiring and releasing a window handle
class WindowHandle {
public:
  WindowHandle(WINDOW_HANDLE handle): w(handle) {}
  ~WindowHandle() { destroyWindow(w); }

  operator WINDOW_HANDLE() { return w; }     // see below
private:
  WINDOW_HANDLE w;

  // The following functions are declared private to prevent
  // multiple copies of a WINDOW_HANDLE from being created.
  // See Item 28 for a discussion of a more flexible approach.
  WindowHandle(const WindowHandle&);
  WindowHandle& operator=(const WindowHandle&);
};
```

This looks just like the auto_ptr template, except that assignment and copying are explicitly prohibited, and there is an implicit conversion operator that can be used to turn a WindowHandle into a WINDOW_HANDLE. This capability is essential to the practical application of a WindowHandle object, because it means you can use a WindowHandle just about anywhere you would normally use a raw WINDOW_HANDLE. (See Item 5, however, for why you should generally be leery of implicit type conversion operators.)

Given the `WindowHandle` class, we can rewrite `displayInfo` as follows:

```
// this function avoids leaking resources if an
// exception is thrown
void displayInfo(const Information& info)
{
  WindowHandle w(createWindow());

  display info in window corresponding to w;

}
```

Even if an exception is thrown within `displayInfo`, the window created by `createWindow` will always be destroyed.

By adhering to the rule that resources should be encapsulated inside objects, you can usually avoid resource leaks in the presence of exceptions. But what happens if an exception is thrown while you're in the process of acquiring a resource, e.g., while you're in the constructor of a resource-acquiring class? What happens if an exception is thrown during the automatic destruction of such resources? Don't constructors and destructors call for special techniques? They do, and you can read about them in Items 10 and 11.

Item 10: **Prevent resource leaks in constructors**

Imagine you're developing software for a multimedia address book. Such an address book might hold, in addition to the usual textual information of a person's name, address, and phone numbers, a picture of the person and the sound of their voice (possibly giving the proper pronunciation of their name).

To implement the book, you might come up with a design like this:

```
class Image {                    // for image data
public:
  Image(const string& imageDataFileName);
  ...
};

class AudioClip {                // for audio data
public:
  AudioClip(const string& audioDataFileName);
  ...
};

class PhoneNumber { ... };        // for holding phone numbers
```

```
class BookEntry {                       // for each entry in the
public:                                 // address book

  BookEntry(const string& name,
            const string& address = "",
            const string& imageFileName = "",
            const string& audioClipFileName = "");
  ~BookEntry();

  // phone numbers are added via this function
  void addPhoneNumber(const PhoneNumber& number);
  ...

private:
  string theName;                    // person's name
  string theAddress;                 // their address
  list<PhoneNumber> thePhones;       // their phone numbers
  Image *theImage;                   // their image
  AudioClip *theAudioClip;           // an audio clip from them
};
```

Each BookEntry must have name data, so you require that as a constructor argument (see Item 3), but the other fields — the person's address and the names of files containing image and audio data — are optional. Note the use of the list class to hold the person's phone numbers. This is one of several container classes that are part of the standard C++ library (see Item 35).

A straightforward way to write the BookEntry constructor and destructor is as follows:

```
BookEntry::BookEntry(const string& name,
                     const string& address,
                     const string& imageFileName,
                     const string& audioClipFileName)
: theName(name), theAddress(address),
  theImage(0), theAudioClip(0)
{
  if (imageFileName != "") {
    theImage = new Image(imageFileName);
  }

  if (audioClipFileName != "") {
    theAudioClip = new AudioClip(audioClipFileName);
  }
}

BookEntry::~BookEntry()
{
  delete theImage;
  delete theAudioClip;
}
```

The constructor initializes the pointers theImage and theAudioClip to null, then makes them point to real objects if the corresponding arguments are non-null. The destructor deletes both pointers, thus ensuring that a BookEntry object doesn't give rise to a resource leak. Because C++ guarantees it's safe to delete null pointers, BookEntry's destructor need not check to see if the pointers actually point to something before deleting them.

Everything looks fine here, and under normal conditions everything is fine, but under abnormal conditions — under *exceptional* conditions — things are not fine at all.

Consider what will happen if an exception is thrown during execution of this part of the BookEntry constructor:

```
if (audioClipFileName != "") {
  theAudioClip = new AudioClip(audioClipFileName);
}
```

An exception might arise because operator new (see Item 8) is unable to allocate enough memory for an AudioClip object. One might also arise because the AudioClip constructor itself throws an exception. Regardless of the cause of the exception, if one is thrown within the BookEntry constructor, it will be propagated to the site where the BookEntry object is being created.

Now, if an exception is thrown during creation of the object theAudio-Clip is supposed to point to (thus transferring control out of the BookEntry constructor), who deletes the object that theImage already points to? The obvious answer is that BookEntry's destructor does, but the obvious answer is wrong. BookEntry's destructor will never be called. Never.

C++ destroys only *fully constructed* objects, and an object isn't fully constructed until its constructor has run to completion. So if a BookEntry object b is created as a local object,

```
void testBookEntryClass()
{
  BookEntry b("Addison-Wesley Publishing Company",
              "One Jacob Way, Reading, MA 01867");

  . . .

}
```

and an exception is thrown during construction of b, b's destructor will not be called. Furthermore, if you try to take matters into your own hands by allocating b on the heap and then calling delete if an exception is thrown,

```
void testBookEntryClass()
{
  BookEntry *pb = 0;

  try {
    pb = new BookEntry( "Addison-Wesley Publishing Company",
                        "One Jacob Way, Reading, MA 01867");
    ...
  }
  catch (...) {                   // catch all exceptions

    delete pb;                    // delete pb when an
                                  // exception is thrown

    throw;                        // propagate exception to
  }                               // caller

  delete pb;                      // delete pb normally
}
```

you'll find that the Image object allocated inside BookEntry's constructor is still lost, because no assignment is made to pb unless the new operation succeeds. If BookEntry's constructor throws an exception, pb will be the null pointer, so deleting it in the catch block does nothing except make you feel better about yourself. Using the smart pointer class auto_ptr<BookEntry> (see Item 9) instead of a raw BookEntry* won't do you any good either, because the assignment to pb still won't be made unless the new operation succeeds.

There is a reason why C++ refuses to call destructors for objects that haven't been fully constructed, and it's not simply to make your life more difficult. It's because it would, in many cases, be a nonsensical thing — possibly a harmful thing — to do. If a destructor were invoked on an object that wasn't fully constructed, how would the destructor know what to do? The only way it could know would be if bits had been added to each object indicating how much of the constructor had been executed. Then the destructor could check the bits and (maybe) figure out what actions to take. Such bookkeeping would slow down constructors, and it would make each object larger, too. C++ avoids this overhead, but the price you pay is that partially constructed objects aren't automatically destroyed.

Because C++ won't clean up after objects that throw exceptions during construction, you must design your constructors so that they clean up after themselves. Often, this involves simply catching all possible exceptions, executing some cleanup code, then rethrowing the exception so it continues to propagate. This strategy can be incorporated into the BookEntry constructor like this:

```
BookEntry::BookEntry( const string& name,
                      const string& address,
                      const string& imageFileName,
                      const string& audioClipFileName)
: theName(name), theAddress(address),
  theImage(0), theAudioClip(0)
{
  try {                              // this try block is new
    if (imageFileName != "") {
      theImage = new Image(imageFileName);
    }

    if (audioClipFileName != "") {
      theAudioClip = new AudioClip(audioClipFileName);
    }
  }
  catch (...) {                      // catch any exception

    delete theImage;                 // perform necessary
    delete theAudioClip;             // cleanup actions

    throw;                           // propagate the exception

  }
}
```

There is no need to worry about BookEntry's non-pointer data members. Data members are automatically initialized before a class's constructor is called, so if a BookEntry constructor body begins executing, the object's theName, theAddress, and thePhones data members have already been fully constructed. As fully constructed objects, these data members will be automatically destroyed when the BookEntry object containing them is, and there is no need for you to intervene. Of course, if these objects' constructors call functions that might throw exceptions, *those* constructors have to worry about catching the exceptions and performing any necessary cleanup before allowing them to propagate.

You may have noticed that the statements in BookEntry's catch block are almost the same as those in BookEntry's destructor. Code duplication here is no more tolerable than it is anywhere else, so the best way to structure things is to move the common code into a private helper function and have both the constructor and the destructor call it:

```
class BookEntry {
public:
  ...                              // as before

private:
  ...
  void cleanup();                  // common cleanup statements
};
```

```
void BookEntry::cleanup()
{
  delete theImage;
  delete theAudioClip;
}

BookEntry::BookEntry( const string& name,
                      const string& address,
                      const string& imageFileName,
                      const string& audioClipFileName)
: theName(name), theAddress(address),
  theImage(0), theAudioClip(0)
{
  try {
    ...                          // as before
  }
  catch (...) {
    cleanup();                   // release resources
    throw;                       // propagate exception
  }
}

BookEntry::~BookEntry()
{
  cleanup();
}
```

This is nice, but it doesn't put the topic to rest. Let us suppose we design our BookEntry class slightly differently so that theImage and theAudioClip are *constant* pointers:

```
class BookEntry {
public:
  ...                            // as above

private:
  ...
  Image * const theImage;        // pointers are now
  AudioClip * const theAudioClip; // const
};
```

Such pointers must be initialized via the member initialization lists of BookEntry's constructors, because there is no other way to give const pointers a value. A common temptation is to initialize theImage and theAudioClip like this,

```
// an implementation that may leak resources if an
// exception is thrown
BookEntry::BookEntry(const string& name,
                     const string& address,
                     const string& imageFileName,
                     const string& audioClipFileName)
: theName(name), theAddress(address),
  theImage(imageFileName != ""
           ? new Image(imageFileName)
           : 0),
  theAudioClip(audioClipFileName != ""
               ? new AudioClip(audioClipFileName)
               : 0)
{}
```

but this leads to the problem we originally wanted to eliminate: if an exception is thrown during initialization of theAudioClip, the object pointed to by theImage is never destroyed. Furthermore, we can't solve the problem by adding try and catch blocks to the constructor, because try and catch are statements, and member initialization lists allow only expressions. (That's why we had to use the ?: syntax instead of the if-then-else syntax in the initialization of theImage and theAudioClip.)

Nevertheless, the only way to perform cleanup chores before exceptions propagate out of a constructor is to catch those exceptions, so if we can't put try and catch in a member initialization list, we'll have to put them somewhere else. One possibility is inside private member functions that return pointers with which theImage and theAudio-Clip should be initialized:

```
class BookEntry {
public:
  ...                                    // as above

private:
  ...                                    // data members as above

  Image * initImage(const string& imageFileName);
  AudioClip * initAudioClip(const string&
                            audioClipFileName);
};

BookEntry::BookEntry(const string& name,
                     const string& address,
                     const string& imageFileName,
                     const string& audioClipFileName)
: theName(name), theAddress(address),
  theImage(initImage(imageFileName)),
  theAudioClip(initAudioClip(audioClipFileName))
{}
```

```
// theImage is initialized first, so there is no need to
// worry about a resource leak if this initialization
// fails. This function therefore handles no exceptions
Image * BookEntry::initImage(const string& imageFileName)
{
  if (imageFileName != "") return new Image(imageFileName);
  else return 0;
}

// theAudioClip is initialized second, so it must make
// sure theImage's resources are released if an exception
// is thrown during initialization of theAudioClip. That's
// why this function uses try...catch.
AudioClip * BookEntry::initAudioClip(const string&
                                     audioClipFileName)
{
  try {
    if (audioClipFileName != "") {
      return new AudioClip(audioClipFileName);
    }
    else return 0;
  }
  catch (...) {
    cleanup();
    throw;
  }
}
```

This is perfectly kosher, and it even solves the problem we've been laboring to overcome. The drawback is that code that conceptually belongs in a constructor is now dispersed across several functions, and that's a maintenance headache.

A better solution is to adopt the advice of Item 9 and treat the objects pointed to by theImage and theAudioClip as resources to be managed by local objects. This solution takes advantage of the facts that both theImage and theAudioClip are pointers to dynamically allocated objects and that those objects should be deleted when the pointers themselves go away. This is precisely the set of conditions for which the auto_ptr classes (see Item 9) were designed. We can therefore change the raw pointer types of theImage and theAudioClip to their auto_ptr equivalents:

```
class BookEntry {
public:
  ...                                       // as above

private:
  ...
  const auto_ptr<Image> theImage;        // these are now
  const auto_ptr<AudioClip> theAudioClip; // auto_ptr objects
};
```

Doing this makes BookEntry's constructor leak-safe in the presence of exceptions, and it lets us initialize theImage and theAudioClip using the member initialization list:

```
BookEntry::BookEntry(const string& name,
                     const string& address,
                     const string& imageFileName,
                     const string& audioClipFileName)
: theName(name), theAddress(address),
  theImage(imageFileName != ""
           ? new Image(imageFileName)
           : 0),
  theAudioClip(audioClipFileName != ""
               ? new AudioClip(audioClipFileName)
               : 0)
{}
```

In this design, if an exception is thrown during initialization of the-AudioClip, theImage is already a fully constructed object, so it will automatically be destroyed, just like theName, theAddress, and the-Phones. Furthermore, because theImage and theAudioClip are now objects, they'll be destroyed automatically when the BookEntry object containing them is. Hence there's no need to manually delete what they point to. That simplifies BookEntry's destructor considerably:

```
BookEntry::~BookEntry()
{}                                     // nothing to do!
```

This means you could eliminate BookEntry's destructor entirely.

It all adds up to this: if you replace pointer class members with their corresponding auto_ptr objects, you fortify your constructors against resource leaks in the presence of exceptions, you eliminate the need to manually deallocate resources in destructors, and you allow const member pointers to be handled in the same graceful fashion as non-const pointers.

Dealing with the possibility of exceptions during construction can be tricky, but auto_ptr (and auto_ptr-like classes) can eliminate most of the drudgery. Their use leaves behind code that's not only easy to understand, it's robust in the face of exceptions, too.

Item 11: Prevent exceptions from leaving destructors

There are two situations in which a destructor is called. The first is when an object is destroyed under "normal" conditions, e.g., when it goes out of scope or is explicitly deleted. The second is when an object is destroyed by the exception-handling mechanism during the stack-unwinding part of exception propagation.

That being the case, an exception may or may not be active when a destructor is invoked. Regrettably, there is no way to distinguish between these conditions from inside a destructor.[†] As a result, you must write your destructors under the conservative assumption that an exception *is* active, because if an exception is thrown while another is active, C++ calls the terminate function. That function does just what its name suggests: it terminates execution of your program. Furthermore, it terminates it *immediately*; not even local objects are destroyed.

As an example, consider a Session class for monitoring on-line computer sessions, i.e., things that happen from the time you log in through the time you log out. Each Session object notes the date and time of its creation and destruction:

```
class Session {
public:
  Session();
  ~Session();
  ...

private:
  static void logCreation(Session *objAddr);
  static void logDestruction(Session *objAddr);
};
```

The functions logCreation and logDestruction are used to record object creations and destructions, respectively. We might therefore expect that we could code Session's destructor like this:

```
Session::~Session()
{
  logDestruction(this);
}
```

This looks fine, but consider what would happen if logDestruction throws an exception. The exception would not be caught in Session's destructor, so it would be propagated to the caller of that destructor. But if the destructor was itself being called because some other exception had been thrown, the terminate function would automatically be invoked, and that would stop your program dead in its tracks.

In many cases, this is not what you'll want to have happen. It may be unfortunate that the Session object's destruction can't be logged, it might even be a major inconvenience, but is it really so horrific a pros-

---

†. Now there is. In July 1995, the ANSI/ISO standardization committee for C++ added a function, uncaught_exception, that returns true if an exception is active and has not yet been caught. As I write this in November 1995, the precise semantics of uncaught_exception have yet to be worked out, and I am unaware of any compilers that support it.

pect that the program can't continue running? If not, you'll have to prevent the exception thrown by `logDestruction` from propagating out of `Session`'s destructor. The only way to do that is by using `try` and `catch` blocks. A naive attempt might look like this,

```
Session::~Session()
{
  try {
    logDestruction(this);
  }
  catch (...) {
    cerr << "Unable to log destruction of Session object "
         << "at address "
         << this
         << ".\n";
  }
}
```

but this is probably no safer than our original code. If one of the calls to `operator<<` in the `catch` block results in an exception being thrown, we're back where we started, with an exception leaving the `Session` destructor.

We could always put a `try` block inside the `catch` block, but that seems a bit extreme. Instead, we'll just forget about logging `Session` destructions if `logDestruction` throws an exception:

```
Session::~Session()
{
  try {
    logDestruction(this);
  }
  catch (...) {}
}
```

The `catch` block appears to do nothing, but appearances can be deceiving. That block prevents exceptions thrown from `logDestruction` from propagating beyond `Session`'s destructor. That's all it needs to do. We can now rest easy knowing that if a `Session` object is destroyed as part of stack unwinding, `terminate` will not be called.

There is a second reason why it's bad practice to allow exceptions to propagate out of destructors. If an exception is thrown from a destructor and is not caught there, that destructor won't run to completion. (It will stop at the point where the exception is thrown.) If the destructor doesn't run to completion, it won't do everything it's supposed to do. For example, consider a modified version of the `Session` class where the creation of a session starts a database transaction and the termination of a session ends that transaction:

```
Session::Session()               // to keep things simple,
{                                // this ctor handles no
                                 // exceptions
  logCreation(this);
  startTransaction();            // start DB transaction
}

Session::~Session()
{
  logDestruction(this);
  endTransaction();              // end DB transaction
}
```

Here, if logDestruction throws an exception, the transaction started in the Session constructor will never be ended. In this case, we might be able to reorder the function calls in Session's destructor to eliminate the problem, but if endTransaction might throw an exception, we've no choice but to revert to try and catch blocks.

We thus find ourselves with two good reasons for keeping exceptions from propagating out of destructors. First, it prevents terminate from being called during the stack-unwinding part of exception propagation. Second, it helps ensure that destructors always accomplish everything they are supposed to accomplish. Each argument is convincing in its own right, but together, the case is ironclad.

Item 12: Understand how throwing an exception differs from passing a parameter or calling a virtual function

The syntax for declaring function parameters is almost the same as that for catch clauses:

```
class Widget { ... };            // some class; it makes no
                                 // difference what it is

void f1(Widget w);               // all these functions
void f2(Widget& w);              // take parameters of
void f3(const Widget& w);        // type Widget, Widget&, or
void f4(Widget *pw);             // Widget*
void f5(const Widget *pw);

catch (Widget w) ...             // all these catch clauses
catch (Widget& w) ...            // catch exceptions of
catch (const Widget& w) ...      // type Widget, Widget&, or
catch (Widget *pw) ...           // Widget*
catch (const Widget *pw) ...
```

You might therefore assume that passing an exception from a throw site to a catch clause is basically the same as passing an argument from a function call site to the function's parameter. There are some similarities, to be sure, but there are significant differences, too.

Let us begin with a similarity. You can pass both function parameters and exceptions by value, by reference, or by pointer. What *happens* when you pass parameters and exceptions, however, is quite different. This difference grows out of the fact that when you call a function, control eventually returns to the call site (unless the function fails to return), but when you throw an exception, control does *not* return to the throw site.

Consider a function that both passes a Widget as a parameter and throws a Widget as an exception:

```
// function to read the value of a Widget from a stream
istream operator>>(istream& s, Widget& w);

void passAndThrowWidget()
{
  Widget localWidget;

  cin >> localWidget;     // pass localWidget to operator>>

  throw localWidget;      // throw localWidget as an exception
}
```

When localWidget is passed to operator>>, no copying is performed. Instead, the reference w inside operator>> is bound to localWidget, and anything done to w is really done to localWidget. It's a different story when localWidget is thrown as an exception. Regardless of whether the exception is caught by value or by reference (it can't be caught by pointer — that would be a type mismatch), a copy of localWidget will be made, and it is the *copy* that is passed to the catch clause. This must be the case, because localWidget will go out of scope once control leaves passAndThrowWidget, and when localWidget goes out of scope, its destructor will be called. If localWidget itself were passed to a catch clause, the clause would receive a destructed Widget, an ex-Widget, a former Widget, the carcass of what once was but is no longer a Widget. That would not be useful, and that's why C++ specifies that an object thrown as an exception is *always* copied.

This copying occurs even if the object being thrown is not in danger of being destroyed. For example, if passAndThrowWidget declares localWidget to be static,

```
void passAndThrowWidget()
{
  static Widget localWidget;     // this is now static; it
                                 // will exist until the
                                 // end of the program
```

```
    cin >> localWidget;           // this works as before

    throw localWidget;            // a copy of localWidget is
  }                               // still made and thrown
```

a copy of `localWidget` would still be made when the exception was thrown. This means that even if the exception is caught by reference, it is not possible for the `catch` block to modify `localWidget`; it can only modify a *copy* of `localWidget`. This mandatory copying of exception objects helps explain another difference between parameter passing and throwing an exception: the latter is typically much slower than the former (see Item 15).

When an object is copied for use as an exception, the copying is performed by the object's copy constructor. This copy constructor is the one in the class corresponding to the object's *static* type, not its dynamic type. For example, consider this slightly modified version of `passAndThrowWidget`:

```
    class Widget { ... };
    class SpecialWidget: public Widget { ... };

    void passAndThrowWidget()
    {
      SpecialWidget localSpecialWidget;

      ...

      Widget& rw = localSpecialWidget;   // rw refers to a
                                         // SpecialWidget

      throw rw;                          // this throws an
                                         // exception of type
    }                                    // Widget!
```

Here a `Widget` exception is thrown, even though `rw` refers to a `SpecialWidget`. That's because `rw`'s static type is `Widget`, not `SpecialWidget`. That `rw` actually refers to a `SpecialWidget` is of no concern to your compilers; all they care about is `rw`'s static type. This behavior may not be what you want, but it's consistent with all other cases in which C++ copies objects. Copying is always based on an object's static type (but see Item 25 for a technique that lets you make copies on the basis of an object's dynamic type).

The fact that exceptions are copies of other objects has an impact on how you propagate exceptions from a `catch` block. Consider these two `catch` blocks, which at first glance appear to do the same thing:

```
catch (Widget& w)              // catch Widget exceptions
{
  ...                          // handle the exception

  throw;                       // rethrow the exception so it
}                              // continues to propagate

catch (Widget& w)              // catch Widget exceptions
{
  ...                          // handle the exception

  throw w;                     // propagate a copy of the
}                              // caught exception
```

The only difference between these blocks is that the first one rethrows the current exception, while the second one throws a new copy of the current exception. Setting aside the performance cost of the additional copy operation, is there a difference between these approaches?

There is. The first block rethrows the *current* exception, regardless of its type. In particular, if the exception originally thrown was of type `SpecialWidget`, the first block would propagate a `SpecialWidget` exception, even though w's static type is `Widget`. This is because no copy is made when the exception is rethrown. The second `catch` block throws a *new* exception, which will always be of type `Widget`, because that's w's static type. In general, you'll want to use the

```
throw;
```

syntax to rethrow the current exception, because there's no chance that will change the type of the exception being propagated. Furthermore, it's more efficient, because there's no need to generate a new exception object.

(Incidentally, the copy made for an exception is a *temporary* object. As Item 19 explains, this gives compilers the right to optimize it out of existence. I wouldn't expect your compilers to work that hard, however. Exceptions are supposed to be rare, so it makes little sense for compiler vendors to pour a lot of energy into their optimization.)

Let us examine the three kinds of `catch` clauses that could catch the `Widget` exception thrown by `passAndThrowWidget`. They are:

```
catch (Widget w) ...           // catch exception by value

catch (Widget& w) ...          // catch exception by
                               // reference

catch (const Widget& w) ...    // catch exception by
                               // reference-to-const
```

Right away we notice another difference between parameter passing and exception propagation. A thrown object (which, as explained above, is always a temporary) may be caught by simple reference; it need not be caught by reference-to-const. Passing a temporary object to a non-const reference parameter is not allowed for function calls (see Item 19), but it is for exceptions.

Let us overlook this difference, however, and return to our examination of copying exception objects. We know that when we pass a function argument by value, we make a copy of the passed object, and we store that copy in a function parameter. The same thing happens when we pass an exception by value. Thus, when we declare a catch clause like this,

```
catch (Widget w) ...              // catch by value
```

we expect to pay for the creation of *two* copies of the thrown object, one to create the temporary that all exceptions generate, the second to copy that temporary into w. Similarly, when we catch an exception by reference,

```
catch (Widget& w) ...             // catch by reference

catch (const Widget& w) ...       // also catch by reference
```

we still expect to pay for the creation of a copy of the exception: the copy that is the temporary. In contrast, when we pass function parameters by reference, no copying takes place. When throwing an exception, then, we expect to construct (and later destruct) one more copy of the thrown object than if we passed the same object to a function.

We have not yet discussed throwing exceptions by pointer, but throw by pointer is equivalent to pass by pointer. Either way, a copy of the *pointer* is passed. About all you need to remember is not to throw a pointer to a local object, because that local object will be destroyed when the exception leaves the local object's scope. The catch clause would then be initialized with a pointer to an object that had already been destroyed. This is the behavior the mandatory copying rule is designed to avoid.

The way in which objects are moved from call or throw sites to parameters or catch clauses is one way in which argument passing differs from exception propagation. A second difference lies in what constitutes a type match between caller or thrower and callee or catcher. Consider the sqrt function from the standard math library:

```
double sqrt(double);              // from <math.h>
```

We can determine the square root of an integer like this:

```
int i;

double sqrtOfi = sqrt(i);
```

There is nothing surprising here. The language allows implicit conversion from int to double, so in the call to sqrt, i is silently converted to a double, and the result of sqrt corresponds to that double. (See Item 5 for a fuller discussion of implicit type conversions.) In general, such conversions are not applied when matching exceptions to catch clauses. In this code,

```cpp
void f(int value)
{
  try {
    if (someFunction()) {       // if someFunction() returns
      throw value;              // true, throw an int
      ...
    }
  }
  catch (double d) {            // handle exceptions of
    ...                         // type double here
  }

  ...

}
```

the int exception thrown inside the try block will never be caught by the catch clause that takes a double. That clause catches only exceptions that are exactly of type double; no type conversions are applied. As a result, if the int exception is to be caught, it will have to be by some other (dynamically enclosing) catch clause taking an int or an int& (possibly modified by const or volatile).

Two kinds of conversions *are* applied when matching exceptions to catch clauses. The first is inheritance-based conversions. A catch clause for base class exceptions is allowed to handle exceptions of derived class types, too. For example, consider the diagnostics portion of the hierarchy of exceptions defined by the standard C++ library:

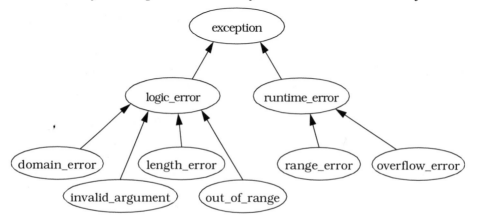

A catch clause for runtime_errors can catch exceptions of type range_error and overflow_error, too, and a catch clause accepting an object of the root class exception can catch any kind of exception derived from this hierarchy.

This inheritance-based exception-conversion rule applies to values, references, and pointers in the usual fashion:

```
catch (runtime_error) ...         // can catch errors of type
catch (runtime_error&) ...        // runtime_error,
catch (const runtime_error&) ...  // range_error, or
                                  // overflow_error

catch (runtime_error*) ...        // can catch errors of type
catch (const runtime_error*) ...  // runtime_error*,
                                  // range_error*, or
                                  // overflow_error*
```

Furthermore, conversions from typed to untyped pointers are allowed, so a catch clause taking a void* pointer will catch an exception of any pointer type:

```
catch (void*) ...                 // catches any exception
                                  // that's a pointer
```

Even here, however, not everything is as it seems. catch clauses are always tried *in the order of their appearance*, so it is possible for an exception of a derived class type to be handled by a catch clause for one of its base class types — even when a catch clause for the derived class is associated with the same try block! For example,

```
try {
  ...
}
catch (logic_error& ex) {         // this block will catch
  ...                             // all logic_error
}                                 // exceptions, even those
                                  // of derived types

catch (invalid_argument& ex) {    // this block can never be
  ...                             // executed, because all
}                                 // invalid_argument
                                  // exceptions will be caught
                                  // by the clause above
```

Contrast this behavior with what happens when you call a virtual function. When you call a virtual function, the function invoked is the one in the class *closest* to the dynamic type of the object invoking the function. You might say that virtual functions employ a "best fit" algorithm, while exception handling follows a "first fit" strategy. Compilers may warn you if a catch clause for a derived class comes after one for a base class (some issue an error, because such code used to be illegal in C++), but your best course of action is preemptive: never put a catch clause for a base class before a catch clause for a derived class. The code above, for example, should be reordered like this:

```
try {
  ...
}
catch (invalid_argument& ex) { // handle invalid_argument
  ...                          // exceptions here
}
catch (logic_error& ex) {      // handle all other
  ...                          // logic_errors here
}
```

There are thus three primary ways in which passing an object to a function or using that object to invoke a virtual function differs from throwing the object as an exception. First, exception objects are always copied; when caught by value, they are copied twice. Objects passed to function parameters need not be copied at all. Second, objects thrown as exceptions are subject to fewer forms of type conversion than are objects passed to functions. Finally, catch clauses are examined in the order in which they appear in the source code, and the first one that can succeed is selected for execution. When an object is used to invoke a virtual function, the function selected is the one that provides the *best* match for the type of the object, even if it's not the first one listed in the source code.

Item 13: Catch exceptions by reference

When you write a catch clause, you must specify how exception objects are to be passed to that clause. You have three choices, just as when specifying how parameters should be passed to functions: by pointer, by value, or by reference.

Let us consider first catch by pointer. In theory, this should be the least inefficient way to implement the invariably slow process of moving an exception from throw site to catch clause (see Item 15). That's because throw by pointer is the only way of moving exception information without copying an object (see Item 12). For example:

```
class exception { ... };        // from the standard C++
                                // library exception
                                // hierarchy (see Item 12)

void someFunction()
{
  static exception ex;          // exception object

  ...
```

```
      throw &ex;                        // throw a pointer to ex

      ...

    }
    void doSomething()
    {
      try {
        someFunction();                 // may throw an exception*
      }
      catch (exception *ex) {           // catches the exception*;
        ...                             // no object is copied
      }
    }
```

This looks neat and tidy, but it's not quite as well-kept as it appears. For this to work, programmers must define exception objects in a way that guarantees the objects exist after control leaves the functions throwing pointers to them. Global and static objects work fine, but it's easy for programmers to forget the constraint. If they do, they typically end up writing code like this:

```
    void someFunction()
    {
      exception ex;                     // local exception object;
                                        // will be destroyed when
                                        // this function's scope is
      ...                               // exited

      throw &ex;                        // throw a pointer to an
      ...                               // object that's about to
    }                                   // be destroyed
```

This is worse than useless, because the catch clause handling this exception receives a pointer to an object that no longer exists.

An alternative is to throw a pointer to a new heap object:

```
    void someFunction()
    {
      ...
      throw new exception;    // throw a pointer to a new heap-
      ...                     // based object (and hope that
    }                         // operator new — see Item 8 —
                              // doesn't itself throw an
                              // exception!)
```

This avoids the I-just-caught-a-pointer-to-a-destroyed-object problem, but now authors of catch clauses confront a nasty question: should they delete the pointer they receive? If the exception object was allocated on the heap, they must, otherwise they suffer a resource leak. If the exception object wasn't allocated on the heap, they mustn't, otherwise they suffer undefined program behavior. What to do?

It's impossible to know. Some clients might pass the address of a global or static object, others might pass the address of an exception on the heap. Catch by pointer thus gives rise to the Hamlet conundrum: to delete or not to delete? It's a question with no good answer. You're best off ducking it.

Furthermore, catch-by-pointer runs contrary to the convention established by the language itself. The four standard exceptions — bad_alloc (thrown when operator new (see Item 8) can't satisfy a memory request), bad_cast (thrown when a dynamic_cast to a reference fails; see Item 2), bad_typeid (thrown when dynamic_cast is applied to a null pointer), and bad_exception (available for unexpected exceptions; see Item 14) — are all objects, not pointers to objects, so you have to catch them by value or by reference, anyway.

Catch-by-value eliminates questions about exception deletion and works with the standard exception types. However, it requires that exception objects be copied *twice* each time they're thrown (see Item 12). It also gives rise to the specter of the *slicing problem*, whereby derived class exception objects caught as base class exceptions have their derivedness "sliced off." Such "sliced" objects *are* base class objects: they lack derived class data members, and when virtual functions are called on them, they resolve to virtual functions of the base class. (Exactly the same thing happens when an object is passed to a function by value.) For example, consider an application employing an exception class hierarchy that extends the standard one:

```
class exception {              // as above, this is a
public:                        // standard exception class

  virtual const char * what() throw();
                               // returns a brief descrip.
  ...                          // of the exception
};

class runtime_error:           // also from the standard
  public exception { ... };    // C++ exception hierarchy

class Validation_error:        // this is a class added by
  public runtime_error {       // a client
public:
  virtual const char *what() throw();
                               // this is a redefinition
  ...                          // of the function declared
};                             // in class exception above
```

```
void someFunction()                 // may throw a validation
{                                   // exception
  ...

  if (a validation test fails) {
    throw Validation_error();
  }

  ...

}
void doSomething()
{
  try {
    someFunction();                 // may throw a validation
  }                                 // exception

  catch (exception ex) {            // catches all exceptions
                                    // in or derived from
                                    // the standard hierarchy

    cerr << ex.what();              // calls exception::what(),
    ...                             // never
  }                                 // Validation_error::what()
}
```

The version of what that is called is that of the base class, even though the thrown exception is of type Validation_error and Validation_error redefines that virtual function. This kind of slicing behavior is almost never what you want.

That leaves only catch-by-reference. Catch-by-reference suffers from none of the problems we have discussed. Unlike catch-by-pointer, the question of object deletion fails to arise, and there is no difficulty in catching the standard exception types. Unlike catch-by-value, there is no slicing problem, and exception objects are copied only once.

If we rewrite the last example using catch-by-reference, it looks like this:

```
void someFunction()                 // nothing changes in this
{                                   // function
  ...

  if (a validation test fails) {
    throw Validation_error();
  }

  ...

}
```

```
void doSomething()
{
  try {
    someFunction();             // no change here
  }
  catch (exception& ex) {       // here we catch by reference
                                // instead of by value

    cerr << ex.what();          // now calls
                                // Validation_error::what(),
    ...                         // not exception::what()
  }
}
```

There is no change at the throw site, and the only change in the catch clause is the addition of an ampersand. This tiny modification makes a big difference, however, because virtual functions in the catch block now work as we expect: functions in Validation_error are invoked if they redefine those in exception.

What a happy confluence of events! If you catch by reference, you side-step questions about object deletion that leave you damned if you do and damned if you don't; you avoid slicing exception objects; you retain the ability to catch standard exceptions; and you limit the number of times exception objects need to be copied. So what are you waiting for? Catch exceptions by reference!

Item 14: Use exception specifications judiciously

There's no denying it: exception specifications have appeal. They make code easier to understand, because they explicitly state what exceptions a function may throw. But they're more than just fancy comments. Compilers are sometimes able to detect inconsistent exception specifications during compilation. Furthermore, if a function throws an exception not listed in its exception specification, that fault is detected at runtime, and the special function unexpected is automatically invoked. Both as a documentation aid and as an enforcement mechanism for constraints on exception usage, then, exception specifications seem attractive.

As is often the case, however, beauty is only skin deep. The default behavior for unexpected is to call terminate, and the default behavior for terminate is to call abort, so the default behavior for a program with a violated exception specification is to halt. Local variables in active stack frames are not destroyed, because abort shuts down program execution without performing such cleanup. A violated exception specification is therefore a cataclysmic thing, something that should almost never happen.

Unfortunately, it's easy to write functions that make this terrible thing occur. Compilers only *partially* check exception usage for consistency with exception specifications. What they do not check for — what the language standard *prohibits* them from rejecting (though they may issue a warning) — is a call to a function that *might* violate the exception specification of the function making the call.

Consider a declaration for a function f1 that has no exception specification. Such a function may throw any kind of exception:

```
extern void f1();                    // might throw anything
```

Now consider a function f2 that claims, through its exception specification, it will throw only exceptions of type int:

```
void f2() throw(int);
```

It is perfectly legal C++ for f2 to call f1, even though f1 might throw an exception that would violate f2's exception specification:

```
void f2() throw(int)
{
  ...
  f1();                    // legal even though f1 might throw
                           // something besides an int
  ...
}
```

This kind of flexibility is essential if new code with exception specifications is to be integrated with older code lacking such specifications.

Because your compilers are content to let you call functions whose exception specifications are inconsistent with those of the routine containing the calls, and because such calls might result in your program's execution being terminated, it's important to write your software in such a way that these kinds of inconsistencies are minimized. A good way to start is to avoid putting exception specifications on templates that take type arguments. Consider this template, which certainly looks as if it couldn't throw any exceptions:

```
// a poorly designed template wrt exception specifications
template<class T>
bool operator==(const T& lhs, const T& rhs) throw()
{
  return &lhs == &rhs;
}
```

This template defines an operator== function for all types. For any pair of objects of the same type, it returns true if the objects have the same address, otherwise it returns false.

This template contains an exception specification stating that the functions generated from the template will throw no exceptions. But that's not necessarily true, because it's possible that operator& (the address-of operator) has been overloaded for some types. If it has, operator& may throw an exception when called from inside operator==. If it does, our exception specification is violated, and off to unexpected we go.

This is a specific example of a more general problem, namely, that there is no way to know *anything* about the exceptions thrown by a template's type parameters. We can almost never provide a meaningful exception specification for a template, because templates almost invariably use their type parameter in some way. The conclusion? Templates and exception specifications don't mix.

A second technique you can use to avoid calls to unexpected is to omit exception specifications on functions making calls to functions that themselves lack exception specifications. This is simple common sense, but there are two cases that are easy to forget. The first is when allowing users to register callback functions:

```cpp
// Function pointer type for a window system callback
// when a window system event occurs
typedef void (*CallBackPtr)(int eventXLocation,
                            int eventYLocation,
                            void *dataToPassBack);

// Window system class for holding onto callback
// functions registered by window system clients
class CallBack {
public:
  CallBack(CallBackPtr fPtr, void *dataToPassBack)
  : func(fPtr), data(dataToPassBack) {}

  void makeCallBack(int eventXLocation,
                    int eventYLocation) const throw();

private:
  CallBackPtr func;             // function to call when
                                // callback is made

  void *data;                   // data to pass to callback
};                              // function

// To implement the callback, we call the registered func-
// tion with event's coordinates and the registered data
void CallBack::makeCallBack(int eventXLocation,
                            int eventYLocation) const throw()
{
  func(eventXLocation, eventYLocation, data);
}
```

Here the call to func in makeCallBack runs the risk of a violated exception specification, because there is no way of knowing what exceptions func might throw.

This problem can be eliminated by tightening the exception specification in the CallBackPtr typedef:

```
typedef void (*CallBackPtr)(int eventXLocation,
                            int eventYLocation,
                            void *dataToPassBack) throw();
```

Given this typedef, it is now an error to register a callback function that fails to guarantee it throws nothing:

```
// a callback function without an exception specification
void callBackFcn1(int eventXLocation,
                  int eventYLocation,
                  void *dataToPassBack);

void *callBackData;

...

CallBack c1(callBackFcn1, callBackData);
                        // error! callBackFcn1
                        // might throw an exception

// a callback function with an exception specification
void callBackFcn2(int eventXLocation,
                  int eventYLocation,
                  void *dataToPassBack) throw();

CallBack c2(callBackFcn2, callBackData);
                        // okay, callBackFcn2 has a
                        // conforming ex. spec.
```

This checking of exception specifications when passing function pointers is a relatively recent addition to the language, so don't be surprised if your compilers don't yet support it. If they don't, it's up to you to ensure you don't make this kind of mistake.

A third technique you can use to avoid calls to unexpected is to handle exceptions "the system" may throw. Of these exceptions, the most common is bad_alloc, which is thrown by operator new and operator new[] when a memory allocation fails (see Item 8). If you use the new operator (again, see Item 8) in any function, you must be prepared for the possibility that the function will encounter a bad_alloc exception.

Now, an ounce of prevention may be better than a pound of cure, but sometimes prevention is hard and cure is easy. That is, sometimes it's easier to cope with unexpected exceptions directly than to prevent them from arising in the first place. If, for example, you're writing software that uses exception specifications rigorously, but you're forced to call functions in libraries that don't use exception specifications, it's impractical to prevent unexpected exceptions from arising, because that would require changing the code in the libraries.

If preventing unexpected exceptions isn't practical, you can exploit the fact that C++ allows you to replace unexpected exceptions with exceptions of a different type. For example, suppose you'd like all unexpected exceptions to be replaced by UnexpectedException objects. You can set it up it like this,

```
class UnexpectedException {};    // all unexpected exception
                                 // objects will be replaced
                                 // by objects of this type

void convertUnexpected()         // function to call if
{                                // an unexpected exception
  throw UnexpectedException();    // is thrown
}
```

and make it happen by replacing the default unexpected function with convertUnexpected:

```
set_unexpected(convertUnexpected);
```

Once you've done this, any unexpected exception results in convert-Unexpected being called. The unexpected exception is then replaced by a new exception of type UnexpectedException. Provided the exception specification that was violated includes UnexpectedException, exception propagation will then continue as if the exception specification had always been satisfied. (If the exception specification does not include UnexpectedException, terminate will be called, just as if you had never replaced unexpected.)

Another way to translate unexpected exceptions into a well known type is to rely on the fact that if the unexpected function's replacement rethrows the current exception, that exception will be replaced by a new exception of the standard type bad_exception. Here's how you'd arrange for that to happen:

```
void convertUnexpected()         // function to call if
{                                // an unexpected exception
  throw;                         // is thrown; just rethrow
}                                // the current exception

set_unexpected(convertUnexpected);
                                 // install convertUnexpected
                                 // as the unexpected
                                 // replacement
```

If you do this and you include bad_exception (or its base class, the standard class exception) in all your exception specifications, you'll never have to worry about your program halting if an unexpected exception is encountered. Instead, any wayward exception will be replaced by a bad_exception, and that exception will be propagated in the stead of the original one.

By now you understand that exception specifications can be a lot of trouble. Compilers perform only partial checks for their consistent usage, they're problematic in templates, they're easy to violate inadvertently, and, by default, they lead to abrupt program termination when they're violated. Exception specifications have another drawback, too, and that's that they result in unexpected being invoked even when a higher-level caller is prepared to cope with the exception that's arisen. For example, consider this code, which is taken almost verbatim from Item 11:

```
class Session {                    // for modeling online
public:                            // sessions
  ~Session();
  ...

private:
  static void logDestruction(Session *objAddr) throw();
};

Session::~Session()
{
  try {
    logDestruction(this);
  }
  catch (...) {}
}
```

The Session destructor calls logDestruction to record the fact that a Session object is being destroyed, but it explicitly catches any exceptions that might be thrown by logDestruction. However, logDestruction comes with an exception specification asserting that it throws no exceptions. Now, suppose some function called by logDestruction throws an exception that logDestruction fails to catch. This isn't supposed to happen, but as we've seen, it isn't difficult to write code that leads to the violation of exception specifications. When this unanticipated exception propagates through logDestruction, unexpected will be called, and, by default, that will result in termination of the program. This is correct behavior, to be sure, but is it the behavior the author of Session's destructor wanted? That author took pains to handle *all possible* exceptions, so it seems almost unfair to halt the program without giving Session's destructor's catch block a chance to work. If logDestruction had no exception specification, this I'm-willing-to-catch-it-if-you'll-just-give-me-a-chance scenario would never arise. (One way to prevent it is to replace unexpected as described above.)

It's important to keep a balanced view of exception specifications. They provide excellent documentation on the kinds of exceptions a function is expected to throw, and for situations in which violating an exception specification is so dire as to justify immediate program termination, they offer that behavior by default. At the same time, they are only partly checked by compilers and they are easy to violate inadvertently. Furthermore, they can prevent high-level exception handlers from dealing with unexpected exceptions, even when they know how to. That being the case, exception specifications are a tool to be applied judiciously. Before adding them to your functions, consider whether the behavior they impart to your software is really the behavior you want.

Item 15: Understand the costs of exception handling

To handle exceptions at runtime, programs must do a fair amount of bookkeeping. At each point during execution, they must be able to identify the objects that require destruction if an exception is thrown; they must make note of each entry to and exit from a try block; and for each try block, they must keep track of the associated catch clauses and the types of exceptions those clauses can handle. This bookkeeping is not free. Nor are the runtime comparisons necessary to ensure that exception specifications are satisfied. Nor is the work expended to destroy the appropriate objects and find the correct catch clause when an exception is thrown. No, exception handling has costs, and you pay at least some of them even if you never use the keywords try, throw, or catch.

Let us begin with the things you pay for even if you never use any exception-handling features. You pay for the space used by the data structures needed to keep track of which objects are fully constructed (see Item 10), and you pay for the time needed to keep these data structures up to date. These costs are typically quite modest. Nevertheless, programs compiled without support for exceptions are typically both faster and smaller than their counterparts compiled with support for exceptions.

In theory, you don't have a choice about these costs: exceptions are part of C++, compilers have to support them, and that's that. You can't even expect compiler vendors to eliminate the costs if you use no exception-handling features, because programs are typically composed of multiple independently generated object files, and just because one object file doesn't do anything with exceptions doesn't mean others don't. Furthermore, even if none of the object files linked to form an executable use exceptions, what about the libraries they're linked with? If *any part* of a program uses exceptions, the rest of the program must support them, too. Otherwise it may not be possible to provide correct exception-handling behavior at runtime.

That's the theory. In practice, most vendors who support exception handling allow you to control whether support for exceptions is included in the code they generate. If you know that no part of your program uses try, throw, or catch, and you also know that no library with which you'll link uses try, throw, or catch, you might as well compile without exception-handling support and save yourself the size and speed penalty you'd otherwise probably be assessed for a feature you're not using. As time goes on and libraries employing exceptions become more common, this strategy will become less tenable, but given the current state of C++ software development, compiling without support for exceptions is a reasonable performance optimization if you have already decided not to use exceptions. It may also be an attractive optimization for libraries that eschew exceptions, provided they can guarantee that exceptions thrown from client code never propagate into the library. This is a difficult guarantee to make, as it precludes client redefinitions of library-declared virtual functions; it also rules out client-defined callback functions.

A second cost of exception-handling arises from try blocks, and you pay it whenever you use one, i.e., whenever you decide you want to be able to catch exceptions. Different compilers implement try blocks in different ways, so the cost varies from compiler to compiler. As a rough estimate, expect your overall code size to increase by 5-10% and your runtime to go up by a similar amount if you use try blocks. This assumes no exceptions are thrown; what we're discussing here is just the cost of *having* try blocks in your programs. To minimize this cost, you should avoid unnecessary try blocks.

Compilers tend to generate code for exception specifications much as they do for try blocks, so an exception specification generally incurs about the same cost as a try block. Excuse me? You say you thought exception specifications were just specifications, you didn't think they generated code? Well, now you have something new to think about.

Which brings us to the heart of the matter, the cost of throwing an exception. In truth, this shouldn't be much of a concern, because exceptions should be rare. After all, they indicate the occurrence of events that are *exceptional*. The 80-20 rule (see Item 16) tells us that such events should almost never have much impact on a program's overall performance. Nevertheless, I know you're curious about just how big a hit you'll take if you throw an exception, and the answer is it's probably a big one. Compared to a normal function return, returning from a function by throwing an exception may be as much as *three orders of magnitude* slower. That's quite a hit. But you'll take it only if you throw an exception, and that should be almost never. If, however, you've been thinking of using exceptions to indicate relatively common conditions like the completion of a data structure traversal or the termination of a loop, now would be an excellent time to think again.

But wait. How can I know this stuff? If support for exceptions is a relatively recent addition to most compilers (it is), and if different compilers implement their support in different ways (they do), how can I say that a program's size will generally grow by about 5-10%, its speed will decrease by a similar amount, and it may run orders of magnitude slower if lots of exceptions are thrown? The answer is frightening: a little rumor and a handful of benchmarks (see Item 23). The fact is that most people — including most compiler vendors — have little experience with exceptions, so though we know there are costs associated with them, it is difficult to predict those costs accurately.

The prudent course of action is to be aware of the costs described in this item, but not to take the numbers very seriously. Whatever the cost of exception handling, you don't want to pay any more than you have to. To minimize your exception-related costs, compile without support for exceptions when that is feasible; limit your use of `try` blocks and exception specifications to those locations where you honestly need them; and throw exceptions only under conditions that are truly exceptional. If you still have performance problems, profile your software (see Item 16) to determine if exception support is a contributing factor. If it is, consider switching to different compilers, ones that provide more efficient implementations of C++'s exception-handling features.

Efficiency

I harbor a suspicion that someone has performed secret Pavlovian experiments on C++ software developers. How else can one explain the fact that when the word "efficiency" is mentioned, scores of programmers start to drool?

In fact, efficiency is no laughing matter. Programs that are too big or too slow fail to find acceptance, no matter how compelling their merits. This is perhaps as it should be. Software is supposed to help us do things better, and it's difficult to argue that slower is better, that demanding 32 megabytes of memory is better than requiring a mere 16, that chewing up 100 megabytes of disk space is better than swallowing only 50. Furthermore, though some programs take longer and use more memory because they perform more ambitious computations, too many programs can blame their sorry pace and bloated footprint on nothing more than bad design and slipshod programming.

Writing efficient programs in C++ starts with the recognition that C++ may well have nothing to do with any performance problems you've been having. If you want to write an efficient C++ program, you must first be able to write an efficient *program*. Too many developers overlook this simple truth. Yes, loops may be unrolled by hand and multiplications may be replaced by shift operations, but such micro-tuning leads nowhere if the higher-level algorithms you employ are inherently inefficient. Do you use quadratic algorithms when linear ones are available? Do you compute the same value over and over? Do you squander opportunities to reduce the average cost of expensive operations? If so, you can hardly be surprised if your programs are described like second-rate tourist attractions: worth a look, but only if you've got some extra time.

The material in this chapter attacks the topic of efficiency from two angles. The first is language-independent, focusing on things you can do in any programming language. C++ provides a particularly appealing implementation medium for these ideas, because its strong support for encapsulation makes it possible to replace inefficient class implementations with better algorithms and data structures that support the same interface.

The second focus is on C++ itself. High-performance algorithms and data structures are great, but sloppy implementation practices can reduce their effectiveness considerably. The most insidious mistake is both simple to make and hard to recognize: creating and destroying too many objects. Superfluous object constructions and destructions act like a hemorrhage on your program's performance, with precious clock-ticks bleeding away each time an unnecessary object is created and destroyed. This problem is so pervasive in C++ programs, I devote four separate items to describing where these objects come from and how you can eliminate them without compromising the correctness of your code.

Programs don't get big and slow only by creating too many objects. Other potholes on the road to high performance include library selection and implementations of language features. In the items that follow, I address these issues, too.

After reading the material in this chapter, you'll be familiar with several principles that can improve the performance of virtually any program you write, you'll know exactly how to prevent unnecessary objects from creeping into your software, and you'll have a keener awareness of how your compilers behave when generating executables.

It's been said that forewarned is forearmed. If so, think of the information that follows as preparation for battle.

Item 16: Remember the 80-20 rule

The 80-20 rule states that 80 percent of a program's resources are used by about 20 percent of the code: 80 percent of the runtime is spent in approximately 20 percent of the code; 80 percent of the memory is used by some 20 percent of the code; 80 percent of the disk accesses are performed for about 20 percent of the code; 80 percent of the maintenance effort is devoted to around 20 percent of the code. The rule has been repeatedly verified through examinations of countless machines, operating systems, and applications. The 80-20 rule is more than just a catchy phrase; it's a guideline about system performance that has both wide applicability and a solid empirical basis.

When considering the 80-20 rule, it's important not to get too hung up on numbers. Some people favor the more stringent 90-10 rule, and there's experimental evidence to back that, too. Whatever the precise numbers, the fundamental point is this: the overall performance of your software is almost always determined by a small part of its constituent code.

As a programmer striving to maximize your software's performance, the 80-20 rule both simplifies and complicates your life. On one hand, the 80-20 rule implies that most of the time you can produce code whose performance is, frankly, rather mediocre, because 80 percent of the time its efficiency doesn't affect the overall performance of the system you're working on. That may not do much for your ego, but it should reduce your stress level a little. On the other hand, the rule implies that if your software has a performance problem, you've got a tough job ahead of you, because you not only have to locate the small pockets of code that are causing the problem, you have to find ways to increase their performance dramatically. Of these tasks, the more troublesome is generally locating the bottlenecks. There are two fundamentally different ways to approach the matter: the way most people do it and the right way.

The way most people locate bottlenecks is to guess. Using experience, intuition, tarot cards and Ouija boards, rumors or worse, developer after developer solemnly proclaims that a program's efficiency problems can be traced to network delays, improperly tuned memory allocators, compilers that don't optimize aggressively enough, or some bonehead manager's refusal to permit assembly language for crucial inner loops. Such assessments are generally delivered with a condescending sneer, and usually both the sneerers and their prognostications are flat-out wrong.

Most programmers have lousy intuition about the performance characteristics of their programs, because program performance characteristics tend to be highly unintuitive. As a result, untold effort is poured into improving the efficiency of parts of programs that will never have a noticeable effect on their overall behavior. For example, fancy algorithms and data structures that minimize computation may be added to a program, but it's all for naught if the program is I/O-bound. Souped-up I/O libraries (see Item 23) may be substituted for the ones shipped with compilers, but there's not much point if the programs using them are CPU-bound.

That being the case, what do you do if you're faced with a slow program or one that uses too much memory? The 80-20 rule means that improving random parts of the program is unlikely to help very much. The fact that programs tend to have unintuitive performance characteristics means that trying to guess the causes of performance bottlenecks is unlikely to be much better than just improving random parts of your program. What, then, *will* work?

What will work is to empirically identify the 20 percent of your program that is causing you heartache, and the way to identify that horrid 20 percent is to use a program profiler. Not just any profiler will do, however. You want one that *directly* measures the resources you are interested in. For example, if your program is too slow, you want a profiler that tells you how much *time* is being spent in different parts of the program. That way you can focus on those places where a significant improvement in local efficiency will also yield a significant improvement in overall efficiency.

Profilers that tell you how many times each statement is executed or how many times each function is called are of limited utility. From a performance point of view, you do not care how many times a statement is executed or a function is called. It is, after all, rather rare to encounter a user of a program or a client of a library who complains that too many statements are being executed or too many functions are being called. If your software is fast enough, nobody cares how many statements are executed, and if it's too slow, nobody cares how few. All they care about is that they hate to wait, and if your program is making them do it, they hate you, too.

Still, knowing how often statements are executed or functions are called can sometimes yield insight into what your software is doing. If, for example, you think you're creating about a hundred objects of a particular type, it would certainly be worthwhile to discover that you're calling constructors in that class thousands of times. Furthermore, statement and function call counts can indirectly help you understand facets of your software's behavior you can't directly measure. If you have no direct way of measuring dynamic memory usage, for example, it may be helpful to know at least how often memory allocation and deallocation functions (e.g., operators `new`, `new[]`, `delete`, and `delete[]` — see Item 8) are called.

Of course, even the best of profilers is hostage to the data it's given to process. If you profile your program while it's processing unrepresentative input data, you're in no position to complain if the profiler leads you to fine-tune parts of your software — the parts making up some 80 percent of it — that have no bearing on its usual performance. Remember that a profiler can only tell you how a program behaved on a particular run (or set of runs), so if you profile a program using input data that is unrepresentative, you're going to get back a profile that is equally unrepresentative. That, in turn, is likely to lead to you to optimize your software's behavior for uncommon uses, and the overall impact on common uses may even be negative.

The best way to guard against these kinds of pathological results is to profile your software using as many data sets as possible. Moreover, you must ensure that each data set is representative of how the software is used by its clients (or at least its most important clients). It is usually easy to acquire representative data sets, because many clients are happy to let you use their data when profiling. After all, you'll then be tuning your software to meet their needs, and that can only be good for both of you.

Item 17: Consider using lazy evaluation

From the perspective of efficiency, the best computations are those you never perform at all. That's fine, but if you don't need to do something, why would you put code in your program to do it in the first place? And if you do need to do something, how can you possibly avoid executing the code that does it?

The key is to be lazy.

Remember when you were a child and your parents told you to clean your room? If you were anything like me, you'd say "Okay," then promptly go back to what you were doing. You would *not* clean your room. In fact, cleaning your room would be the last thing on your mind — *until* you heard your parents coming down the hall to confirm that your room had, in fact, been cleaned. Then you'd sprint to your room and get to work as fast as you possibly could. If you were lucky, your parents would never check, and you'd avoid all the work cleaning your room normally entails.

It turns out that the same delay tactics that work for a five year old work for a C++ programmer. In Computer Science, however, we dignify such procrastination with the name *lazy evaluation*. When you employ lazy evaluation, you write your classes in such a way that they defer computations until the *results* of those computations are required. If the results are never required, the computations are never performed, and neither your software's clients nor your parents are any the wiser.

Perhaps you're wondering exactly what I'm talking about. Perhaps an example would help. Well, lazy evaluation is applicable in an enormous variety of application areas, so I'll describe four.

Reference Counting

Consider this code:

```
class String { ... };    // a string class (the standard
                         // string class may be implemented
                         // as described below, but it
                         // doesn't have to be)
```

```
String s1 = "Hello";

String s2 = s1;                    // call String copy ctor
```

A common implementation for the `String` copy constructor would result in s1 and s2 each having its own copy of "Hello" after s2 is initialized with s1. Such a copy constructor would incur a relatively large expense, because it would have to make a copy of s1's value to give to s2, and that would typically entail allocating heap memory via the `new` operator (see Item 8) and calling `strcpy` to copy the data in s1 into the memory allocated by s2. This is *eager evaluation*: making a copy of s1 and putting it into s2 just because the `String` copy constructor was *called*. At this point, however, there has been no real *need* for s2 to have a copy of the value, because s2 hasn't been used yet.

The lazy approach is a lot less work. Instead of giving s2 a copy of s1's value, we have s2 *share* s1's value. All we have to do is a little book-keeping so we know who's sharing what, and in return we save the cost of a call to `new` and the expense of copying anything. The fact that s1 and s2 are sharing a data structure is transparent to clients, and it certainly makes no difference in statements like the following, because they only read values, they don't write them:

```
cout << s1;                    // read s1's value

cout << s1 + s2;               // read s1's and s2's values
```

In fact, the only time the sharing of values makes a difference is when one or the other string is *modified*; then it's important that only one string be changed, not both. In this statement,

```
s2.convertToUpperCase();
```

it's crucial that only s2's value be changed, not s1's also.

To handle statements like this, we have to implement `String`'s convertToUpperCase function so that it makes a copy of s2's value and makes that value private to s2 before modifying it. Inside convertToUpperCase, we can be lazy no longer: we have to make a copy of s2's (shared) value for s2's private use. On the other hand, if s2 is never modified, we never have to make a private copy of its value. It can continue to share a value as long as it exists. If we're lucky, s2 will never be modified, in which case we'll never have to expend the effort to give it its own value.

The details on making this kind of value sharing work (including all the code) are provided in Item 29, but the idea is lazy evaluation: don't bother to make a copy of something until you really need one. Instead, be lazy — use someone else's copy as long as you can get away with it. In some application areas, you can often get away with it forever.

Distinguishing Reads from Writes

Pursuing the example of reference-counting strings a bit further, we come upon a second way in which lazy evaluation can help us. Consider this code:

```
String s = "Homer's Iliad";      // Assume s is a
                                 // reference-counted string
...

cout << s[3];                    // call operator[] to read s[3]
s[3] = 'x';                      // call operator[] to write s[3]
```

The first call to operator[] is to read part of a string, but the second call is to perform a write. We'd like to be able to distinguish the read call from the write, because reading a reference-counted string is cheap, but writing to such a string may require splitting off a new copy of the string's value prior to the write.

This puts us in a difficult implementation position. To achieve what we want, we need to do different things inside operator[] (depending on whether it's being called to perform a read or a write). How can we determine whether operator[] has been called in a read or a write context? The brutal truth is that we can't. By using lazy evaluation and proxy classes as described in Item 30, however, we can defer the decision on whether to take read actions or write actions until we can determine which is correct.

Lazy Fetching

As a third example of lazy evaluation, imagine you've got a program that uses large objects containing many constituent fields. Such objects must persist across program runs, so they're stored in a database. Each object has a unique object identifier that can be used to retrieve the object from the database:

```
class LargeObject {                 // large persistent objects
public:
  LargeObject(ObjectID id);         // restore object from disk

  const string& field1() const;     // value of field 1
  int field2() const;               // value of field 2
  double field3() const;            // ...
  const string& field4() const;
  const string& field5() const;
  ...

};
```

Now consider the cost of restoring a LargeObject from disk:

```
void restoreAndProcessObject(ObjectID id)
{
  LargeObject object(id);        // restore object

  ...

}
```

Because LargeObject instances are big, getting all the data for such an object might be a costly database operation, especially if the data must be retrieved from a remote database and pushed across a network. In some cases, the cost of reading all that data would be unnecessary. For example, consider this kind of application:

```
void restoreAndProcessObject(ObjectID id)
{
  LargeObject object(id);

  if (object.field2() == 0) {
    cout << "Object " << id << ": null field2.\n";
  }
}
```

Here only the value of field2 is required, so any effort spent setting up the other fields is wasted.

The lazy approach to this problem is to read no data from disk when a LargeObject object is created. Instead, only the "shell" of an object is created, and data is retrieved from the database only when that particular data is needed inside the object. Here's one way to implement this kind of "demand-paged" object initialization:

```
class LargeObject {
public:
  LargeObject(ObjectID id);

  const string& field1() const;
  int field2() const;
  double field3() const;
  const string& field4() const;
  ...

private:
  ObjectID oid;

  mutable string *field1Value;    // see below for a
  mutable int *field2Value;       // discussion of "mutable"
  mutable double *field3Value;
  mutable string *field4Value;
  ...

};
```

```
LargeObject::LargeObject(ObjectID id)
: oid(id), field1Value(0), field2Value(0), field3Value(0), ...
{}

const string& LargeObject::field1() const
{
  if (field1Value == 0) {
    read the data for field 1 from the database and make
    field1Value point to it;
  }

  return *field1Value;
}
```

Each field in the object is represented as a pointer to the necessary data, and the LargeObject constructor initializes each pointer to null. Such null pointers signify fields that have not yet been read from the database. Each LargeObject member function must check the state of a field's pointer before accessing the data it points to. If the pointer is null, the corresponding data must be read from the database before performing any operations on that data.

When implementing lazy fetching, you must confront the problem that null pointers may need to be initialized to point to real data from inside any member function, including const member functions like field1. However, compilers get cranky when you try to modify data members inside const member functions, so you've got to find a way to say, "It's okay, I know what I'm doing." The best way to say that is to declare the pointer fields mutable, which means they can be modified inside any member function, even inside const member functions. That's why the fields inside LargeObject above are declared mutable.

The mutable keyword is a relatively recent addition to C++, so it's possible your vendors don't yet support it. If not, you'll need to find another way to convince your compilers to let you modify data members inside const member functions. One workable strategy is the "fake this" approach, whereby you create a pointer-to-non-const that points to the same object as this does. When you want to modify a data member, you access it through the "fake this" pointer:

```
class LargeObject {
public:
  const string& field1() const;   // unchanged
  ...

private:
  string *field1Value;             // not declared mutable
  ...                              // so that older
};                                 // compilers will accept it
```

```
const string& LargeObject::field1() const
{
  // declare a pointer, fakeThis, that points where this
  // does, but where the constness of the object has been
  // cast away
  LargeObject * const fakeThis =
    const_cast<LargeObject* const>(this);

  if (field1Value == 0) {
    fakeThis->field1Value =        // this assignment is OK,
      the appropriate data         // because what fakeThis
      from the database;           // points to isn't const
  }

  return *field1Value;
}
```

This function employs a const_cast (see Item 2) to cast away the constness of *this. If your compilers don't support const_cast, you can use an old C-style cast:

```
// Use of old-style cast to help emulate mutable
const string& LargeObject::field1() const
{
  LargeObject * const fakeThis = (LargeObject* const)this;

  ...                              // as above

}
```

Look again at the pointers inside LargeObject. Let's face it, it's tedious and error-prone to have to initialize all those pointers to null, then test each one before use. Fortunately, such drudgery can be automated through the use of *smart pointers*, which you can read about in Item 28. If you use smart pointers inside LargeObject, you'll also find you no longer need to declare the pointers mutable. Alas, it's only a temporary respite, because you'll wind up needing mutable once you sit down to implement the smart pointer classes. Think of it as conservation of inconvenience.

Lazy Expression Evaluation

A final example of lazy evaluation comes from numerical applications. Consider this code:

```
template<class T>
class Matrix { ... };            // for homogeneous matrices

Matrix<int> m1(1000, 1000);      // a 1000 by 1000 matrix
Matrix<int> m2(1000, 1000);      // ditto

...

Matrix<int> m3 = m1 + m2;        // add m1 and m2
```

The usual implementation of operator+ would use eager evaluation; in this case it would compute and return the sum of m1 and m2. That's a fair amount of computation (1,000,000 additions), and of course there's the cost of allocating the memory to hold all those values, too.

The lazy evaluation strategy says that's *way* too much work, so it doesn't do it. Instead, it sets up a data structure inside m3 that indicates that m3's value is the sum of m1 and m2. Such a data structure might consist of nothing more than a pointer to each of m1 and m2, plus an enum indicating that the operation on them is addition. Clearly, it's going to be faster to set up this data structure than to add m1 and m2, and it's going to use a lot less memory, too.

Suppose that later in the program, before m3 has been used, this code is executed:

```
Matrix<int> m4(1000, 1000);

...                             // give m4 some values

m3 = m4 * m1;
```

Now we can forget all about m3 being the sum of m1 and m2 (and thereby save the cost of the computation), and in its place we can start remembering that m3 is the product of m4 and m1. Needless to say, we don't perform the multiplication. Why bother? We're lazy, remember?

This example looks contrived, because no good programmer would write a program that computed the sum of two matrices and failed to use it, but it's not as contrived as it seems. No good programmer would deliberately compute a value that's not needed, but during maintenance, it's not uncommon for a programmer to modify the paths through a program in such a way that a formerly useful computation becomes unnecessary. The likelihood of that happening is reduced by defining objects immediately prior to use, but it's still a problem that occurs from time to time.

Nevertheless, if that were the only time lazy evaluation paid off, it would hardly be worth the trouble. A more common scenario is that we need only *part* of a computation. For example, suppose we use m3 as follows after initializing it to the sum of m1 and m2:

```
cout << m3[4];                  // print the 4th row of m3
```

Clearly we can be completely lazy no longer — we've got to compute the values in the fourth row of m3. But let's not be overly ambitious, either. There's no reason we have to compute any *more* than the fourth row of m3; the remainder of m3 can remain uncomputed until it's actually needed. With luck, it never will be.

How likely are we to be lucky? Experience in the domain of matrix computations suggests the odds are in our favor. In fact, lazy evaluation lies behind the wonder that is APL. APL was developed in the 1960s for interactive use by people who needed to perform matrix-based calculations. Running on computers that had less computational horsepower than the chips now found in high-end microwave ovens, APL was seemingly able to add, multiply, and even divide large matrices instantly! Its trick was lazy evaluation. The trick was usually effective, because APL users typically added, multiplied, or divided matrices not because they needed the entire resulting matrix, but only because they needed a small part of it. APL employed lazy evaluation to defer its computations until it knew exactly what part of a result matrix was needed, then it computed only that part. In practice, this allowed users to perform computationally intensive tasks *interactively* in an environment where the underlying machine was hopelessly inadequate for an implementation employing eager evaluation. Machines are faster today, but data sets are bigger and users less patient, so many contemporary matrix libraries continue to take advantage of lazy evaluation.

To be fair, laziness sometimes fails to pay off. If m3 is used in this way,

```
cout << m3;                      // print out all of m3
```

the jig is up and we've got to compute a complete value for m3. Similarly, if one of the matrices on which m3 is dependent is about to be modified, we have to take immediate action:

```
m3 = m1 + m2;                    // remember that m3 is the
                                 // sum of m1 and m2

m1 = m4;                         // now m3 is the sum of m2
                                 // and the OLD value of m1!
```

Here we've got to do something to ensure that the assignment to m1 doesn't change m3. Inside the Matrix<int> assignment operator, we might compute m3's value prior to changing m1 or we might make a copy of the old value of m1 and make m3 dependent on that, but we have to do *something* to guarantee that m3 has the value it's supposed to have after m1 has been the target of an assignment. Other functions that might modify a matrix must be handled in a similar fashion.

Because of the need to store dependencies between values; to maintain data structures that can store values, dependencies, or a combination of the two; and to overload operators like assignment, copying, and addition, lazy evaluation in a numerical domain is a lot of work. On the other hand, it often ends up saving significant amounts of time and space during program runs, and in many applications, that's a payoff that easily justifies the significant effort lazy evaluation requires.

Summary

These four examples show that lazy evaluation can be useful in a variety of domains: to avoid unnecessary copying of objects, to distinguish reads from writes using operator[], to avoid unnecessary reads from databases, and to avoid unnecessary numerical computations. Nevertheless, it's not always a good idea. Just as procrastinating on your clean-up chores won't save you any work if your parents always check up on you, lazy evaluation won't save your program any work if all your computations are necessary. Indeed, if all your computations are essential, lazy evaluation may slow you down and increase your use of memory, because, in addition to having to do all the computations you were hoping to avoid, you'll also have to manipulate the fancy data structures needed to make lazy evaluation possible in the first place. Lazy evaluation is only useful when there's a reasonable chance your software will be asked to perform computations that can be avoided.

There's nothing about lazy evaluation that's specific to C++. The technique can be applied in any programming language, and several languages — notably APL, some dialects of Lisp, and virtually all dataflow languages — embrace the idea as a fundamental part of the language. Mainstream programming languages employ eager evaluation, however, and C++ is mainstream. Yet C++ is particularly suitable as a vehicle for user-implemented lazy evaluation, because its support for encapsulation makes it possible to add lazy evaluation to a class without clients of that class knowing it's been done.

Look again at the code fragments used in the above examples, and you can verify that the class interfaces offer no hints about whether eager or lazy evaluation is used by the classes. That means it's possible to implement a class using a straightforward eager evaluation strategy, but then, if your profiling investigations (see Item 16) show that class's implementation is a performance bottleneck, you can replace its implementation with one based on lazy evaluation. The only change your clients will see (after recompilation or relinking) is improved performance. That's the kind of software enhancement clients love, one that can make you downright proud to be lazy.

Item 18: Amortize the cost of expected computations

In Item 17, I extolled the virtues of laziness, of putting things off as long as possible, and I explained how laziness can improve the efficiency of your programs. In this item, I adopt a different stance. Here, laziness has no place. I now encourage you to improve the performance of your software by having it do *more* than it's asked to do. The philosophy of this item might be called *over-eager evaluation*: doing things *before* you're asked to do them.

Consider, for example, a template for classes representing large collections of numeric data:

```
template<class NumericalType>
class DataCollection {
public:
  NumericalType min() const;
  NumericalType max() const;
  NumericalType avg() const;
  ...
};
```

Assuming the min, max, and avg functions return the current minimum, maximum, and average values of the collection, there are three ways in which these functions can be implemented. Using eager evaluation, we'd examine all the data in the collection when min, max, or avg was called, and we'd return the appropriate value. Using lazy evaluation, we'd have the functions return data structures that could be used to determine the appropriate value whenever the functions' return values were actually used. Using over-eager evaluation, we'd keep track of the running minimum, maximum, and average values of the collection, so when min, max, or avg was called, we'd be able to return the correct value immediately — no computation would be required. If min, max, and avg were called frequently, we'd be able to amortize the cost of keeping track of the collection's minimum, maximum, and average values over all the calls to those functions, and the amortized cost per call would be lower than with eager or lazy evaluation.

The idea behind over-eager evaluation is that if you expect a computation to be requested frequently, you can lower the average cost per request by designing your data structures to handle the requests especially efficiently.

One of the simplest ways to do this is by caching values that have already been computed and are likely to be needed again. For example, suppose you're writing a program to provide information about employees, and one of the pieces of information you expect to be requested frequently is an employee's cubicle number. Further suppose that employee information is stored in a database, but, for most applications, an employee's cubicle number is irrelevant, so the database is not optimized to find it. To avoid having your specialized application unduly stress the database with repeated lookups of employee cubicle numbers, you could write a findCubicleNumber function that caches the cubicle numbers it looks up. Subsequent requests for cubicle numbers that have already been retrieved can then be satisfied by consulting the cache instead of querying the database.

Here's one way to implement findCubicleNumber; it uses a map object from the Standard Template Library (the "STL" — see Item 35) as a local cache:

```
int findCubicleNumber(const string& employeeName)
{
  // define a static map to hold (employee name, cubicle number)
  // pairs. This map is the local cache.
  typedef map<string, int> CubicleMap;
  static CubicleMap cubes;

  // try to find an entry for employeeName in the cache;
  // the STL iterator "it" will then point to the found
  // entry, if there is one (see Item 35 for details)
  CubicleMap::iterator it = cubes.find(employeeName);

  // "it"'s value will be cubes.end() if no entry was
  // found (this is standard STL behavior). If this is
  // the case, consult the database for the cubicle
  // number, then add it to the cache
  if (it == cubes.end()) {
    int cubicle =
      the result of looking up employeeName's cubicle
      number in the database;

    cubes[employeeName] = cubicle;   // add the pair
                                     // (employeeName, cubicle)
                                     // to the cache
    return cubicle;
  }
  else {
    // "it" points to the correct cache entry, which is a
    // (employee name, cubicle number) pair. We want only
    // the second component of this pair, and the member
    // "second" will give it to us
    return (*it).second;
  }
}
```

Try not to get bogged down in the details of the STL code (which will be clearer after you've read Item 35). Instead, focus on the general strategy embodied by this function. That strategy is to use a local cache to replace comparatively expensive database queries with comparatively inexpensive lookups in an in-memory data structure. Provided we're correct in assuming that cubicle numbers will frequently be requested more than once, the use of a cache in findCubicleNumber should reduce the average cost of returning an employee's cubicle number.

(One detail of the code requires explanation. The final statement returns `(*it).second` instead of the more conventional `it->second`. Why? The answer has to do with the conventions followed by the STL. In brief, the iterator `it` is an object, not a pointer, so there is no guarantee that "`->`" can be applied to `it`.[†] The STL does require that "`.`" and "`*`" be valid for iterators, however, so `(*it).second`, though syntactically clumsy, is guaranteed to work.)

Caching is one way to amortize the cost of anticipated computations. Prefetching is another. You can think of prefetching as the computational equivalent of a discount for buying in bulk. Disk controllers, for example, read entire blocks or sectors of data when they read from disk, even if a program asks for only a small amount of data. That's because it's faster to read a big chunk once than to read two or three small chunks at different times. Furthermore, experience has shown that if data in one place is requested, it's quite common to want nearby data, too. This is the infamous *locality of reference* phenomenon, and systems designers rely on it to justify disk caches, memory caches for both instructions and data, and instruction prefetches.

Excuse me? You say you don't worry about such low-level things as disk controllers or CPU caches? No problem. Prefetching can yield dividends for even one as high-level as you. Imagine, for example, you'd like to implement a template for dynamic arrays, i.e., arrays that start with a size of one and automatically extend themselves so that all nonnegative indices are valid:

```
template<class T>          // template for dynamic
class DynArray { ... };     // array-of-T classes

DynArray<double> a;         // at this point, only a[0]
                            // is a legitimate array
                            // element

a[22] = 3.5;                // a is automatically
                            // extended: valid indices
                            // are now 0-22

a[32] = 0;                  // a extends itself again;
                            // now a[0]-a[32] are valid
```

How does a `DynArray` object go about extending itself when it needs to? A straightforward strategy would be to allocate only as much additional memory as needed, something like this:

---

† In July 1995, the ANSI/ISO committee standardizing C++ added a requirement that STL iterators support the "`->`" operator, so `it->second` should now work. Most current STL implementations fail to satisfy this requirement, however, so `(*it).second` is still the more portable construct.

```
template<class T>
T& DynArray<T>::operator[](int index)
{
  if (index < 0) {
    throw an exception;              // negative indices are
  }                                  // still invalid

  if (index > the current maximum index value) {
    call new to allocate enough additional memory so that
    index is valid;
  }

  return the indexth element of the array;
}
```

This approach simply calls new each time it needs to increase the size of the array, but calls to new invoke operator new (see Item 8), and calls to operator new (and operator delete) are usually expensive. That's because they typically result in calls to the underlying operating system, and system calls are generally slower than are in-process function calls. As a result, we'd like to make as few system calls as possible.

An over-eager evaluation strategy employs this reasoning: if we have to increase the size of the array now to accommodate index *i*, the locality of reference principle suggests we'll probably have to increase it in the future to accommodate some other index a bit larger than *i*. To avoid the cost of the memory allocation for the second (anticipated) expansion, we'll increase the size of the DynArray now by *more* than is required to make *i* valid, and we'll hope that future expansions occur within the range we have thereby provided for. For example, we could write DynArray::operator[] like this:

```
template<class T>
T& DynArray<T>::operator[](int index)
{
  if (index < 0) throw an exception;

  if (index > the current maximum index value) {
    int diff = index - the current maximum index value;

    call new to allocate enough additional memory so that
    index+diff is valid;
  }

  return the indexth element of the array;
}
```

This function allocates twice as much memory as needed each time the array must be extended. If we look again at the usage scenario we saw earlier, we note that the DynArray must allocate additional memory only once, even though its logical size is extended twice:

```
DynArray<double> a;              // only a[0] is valid

a[22] = 3.5;                     // new is called to expand
                                 // a's storage through
                                 // index 44; a's logical
                                 // size becomes 23

a[32] = 0;                       // a's logical size is
                                 // changed to allow a[32],
                                 // but new isn't called
```

If a needs to be extended again, that extension, too, will be inexpensive, provided the new maximum index is no greater than 44.

There is a common theme running through this Item, and that's that greater speed can often be purchased at a cost of increased memory usage. Keeping track of running minima, maxima, and averages requires extra space, but it saves time. Caching results necessitates greater memory usage but reduces the time needed to regenerate the results once they've been cached. Prefetching demands a place to put the things that are prefetched, but it reduces the time needed to access those things. The story is as old as Computer Science: you can often trade space for time. (Not always, however. Using larger objects means fewer fit on a virtual memory or cache page. In rare cases, making objects bigger *reduces* the performance of your software, because your paging activity increases, your cache hit rate decreases, or both. How do you find out if you're suffering from such problems? You profile, profile, profile (see Item 16).)

The advice I proffer in this Item — that you amortize the cost of anticipated computations through over-eager strategies like caching and prefetching — is not contradictory to the advice on lazy evaluation I put forth in Item 17. Lazy evaluation is a technique for improving the efficiency of programs when you must support operations whose results are *not always* needed. Over-eager evaluation is a technique for improving the efficiency of programs when you must support operations whose results are *almost always* needed or whose results are often needed more than once. Both are more difficult to implement than run-of-the-mill eager evaluation, but both can yield significant performance improvements in programs whose behavioral characteristics justify the extra programming effort.

Item 19: Understand the origin of temporary objects

When programmers speak amongst themselves, they often refer to variables that are needed for only a short while as "temporaries." For example, in this swap routine,

```
template<class T>
void swap(T& object1, T& object2)
{
  T temp = object1;
  object1 = object2;
  object2 = temp;
}
```

it's common to call `temp` a "temporary." As far as C++ is concerned, however, `temp` is not a temporary at all. It's simply an object local to a function.

True temporary objects in C++ are invisible — they don't appear in your source code. They arise whenever a non-heap object is created but not named. Such *unnamed* objects usually arise in one of two situations: when implicit type conversions are applied to make function calls succeed and when functions return objects. It's important to understand how and why these temporary objects are created and destroyed, because the attendant costs of their construction and destruction can have a noticeable impact on the performance of your programs.

Consider first the case in which temporary objects are created to make function calls succeed. This happens when the type of object passed to a function is not the same as the type of the parameter to which it is being bound. For example, consider a function that counts the number of occurrences of a character in a string:

```
// returns the number of occurrences of ch in str
unsigned int countChar(const string& str, char ch);

char buffer[MAX_STRING_LEN];
char c;

// read in a char and a string; use setw to avoid
// overflowing buffer when reading the string
cin >> c >> setw(MAX_STRING_LEN) >> buffer;

cout << "There are " << countChar(buffer, c)
     << " occurrences of the character " << c
     << " in " << buffer << endl;
```

Look at the call to countChar. The first argument passed is a char array, but the corresponding function parameter is of type const string&. This call can succeed only if the type mismatch can be eliminated, and your compilers will be happy to eliminate it by creating a temporary object of type string. That temporary object is initialized by calling the string constructor with buffer as its argument. The str parameter of countChar is then bound to this temporary string object. When countChar returns, the temporary object is automatically destroyed.

Conversions such as these are convenient (though dangerous — see Item 5), but from an efficiency point of view, the construction and destruction of a temporary string object is an unnecessary expense. There are two general ways to eliminate it. One is to redesign your code so conversions like these can't take place. That strategy is examined in Item 5. An alternative tack is to modify your software so that the conversions are unnecessary. Item 21 describes how you can do that.

These conversions occur only when passing objects by value or when passing to a reference-to-const parameter. They do not occur when passing an object to a reference-to-non-const parameter. Consider this function:

```
void uppercasify(string& str);      // changes all chars in
                                     // str to upper case
```

In the character-counting example, a char array could be successfully passed to countChar, but here, trying to call uppercasify with a char array fails:

```
char subtleBookPlug[] = "Effective C++";

uppercasify(subtleBookPlug);        // error!
```

No temporary is created to make the call succeed. Why not?

Suppose a temporary were created. Then the temporary would be passed to uppercasify, which would modify the temporary so its characters were in upper case. But the actual argument to the function call — subtleBookPlug — would *not be affected*; only the temporary string object generated from subtleBookPlug would be changed. Surely this is not what the programmer intended. That programmer passed subtleBookPlug to uppercasify, and that programmer expected subtleBookPlug to be modified. Implicit type conversion for references-to-non-const objects, then, would allow temporary objects to be changed when programmers expected non-temporary objects to be modified. That's why the language prohibits the generation of temporaries for non-const reference parameters. Reference-to-const parameters don't suffer from this problem, because such parameters, by virtue of being const, can't be changed.

The second set of circumstances under which temporary objects are created is when a function returns an object. For instance, operator+ must return an object that represents the sum of its operands. Given a type Number, for example, operator+ for that type would be declared like this:

```
const Number operator+(const Number& lhs,
                       const Number& rhs);
```

The return value of this function is a temporary, because it has no name: it's just the function's return value. You must pay to construct and destruct this object each time you call operator+. (For an explanation of why the return value is const, see Item 6.)

As usual, you don't want to incur this cost. For this particular function, you can avoid paying by switching to a similar function, operator+=; Item 22 tells you about this transformation. For most functions that return objects, however, switching to a different function is not an option and there is no way to avoid the construction and destruction of the return value. At least, there's no way to avoid it *conceptually*. Between concept and reality, however, lies a murky zone called *optimization*, and sometimes you can write your object-returning functions in a way that allows — nay, *encourages* — your compilers to optimize temporary objects out of existence. Of these optimizations, the most common and useful is the *return value optimization*, which is the subject of Item 20. All you need to know here is that it relies on the fact that C++ gives compilers more latitude to optimize temporary (unnamed) objects out of existence than named objects.

The bottom line is that temporary objects can be costly, so you want to eliminate them whenever you can. At the same time, unnamed objects offer compilers more flexibility in optimization than named objects, so if you must create an object and you have a choice between using a named object or creating a temporary, you should create the temporary and hope your compilers find a way to eliminate it.

More important than this, however, is to train yourself to look for places where temporary objects may be created. Anytime you see a reference-to-const parameter, the possibility exists that a temporary will be created to bind to that parameter. Anytime you see a function returning an object, a temporary will be created (and later destroyed). Learn to look for such constructs, and your insight into the cost of "behind the scenes" compiler actions will markedly improve.

Item 20: Facilitate the return value optimization

A function that returns an object is frustrating to efficiency aficionados, because the by-value return, including the constructor and destructor calls it implies (see Item 19), cannot be eliminated. The problem is simple: a function either has to return an object in order to offer correct behavior or it doesn't. If it does, there's no way to get rid of the object being returned. Period.

Consider the operator* function for rational numbers:

```
class Rational {
public:
  Rational(int numerator = 0, int denominator = 1);
  ...
  int numerator() const;
  int denominator() const;
};

// For an explanation of why the return value is const,
// see Item 6
const Rational operator*(const Rational& lhs,
                         const Rational& rhs);
```

Without even looking at the code for operator*, we know it must return an object, because it returns the product of two arbitrary numbers. These are *arbitrary* numbers. How can operator* possibly avoid creating a new object to hold their product? It can't, so it must create a new object and return it. C++ programmers have nevertheless expended Herculean efforts in a search for the legendary elimination of the by-value return.

Sometimes people return pointers, which leads to this syntactic travesty:

```
// an unreasonable way to avoid returning an object
const Rational * operator*(const Rational& lhs,
                           const Rational& rhs);

Rational a = 10;
Rational b(1, 2);

Rational c = *(a * b);          // Does this look "natural"
                                // to you?
```

It also raises a question. Should the caller delete the pointer returned by the function? The answer is usually yes, and that usually leads to resource leaks.

Other developers return references. That yields an acceptable syntax,

```
// a dangerous (and incorrect) way to avoid returning
// an object
const Rational& operator*(const Rational& lhs,
                          const Rational& rhs);

Rational a = 10;
Rational b(1, 2);

Rational c = a * b;             // looks perfectly reasonable
```

but such functions can't be implemented in a way that behaves correctly. A common attempt looks like this:

```
// another dangerous (and incorrect) way to avoid
// returning an object
const Rational& operator*(const Rational& lhs,
                          const Rational& rhs)
{
  Rational result(lhs.numerator() * rhs.numerator(),
                  lhs.denominator() * rhs.denominator());
  return result;
}
```

This function returns a reference to an object that no longer exists. In particular, it returns a reference to the local object result, but result is automatically destroyed when operator* is exited. Returning a reference to an object that's been destroyed is hardly useful.

Trust me on this: some functions (operator* among them) just have to return objects. That's the way it is. Don't fight it. You can't win.

That is, you can't win in your effort to eliminate by-value returns from functions that require them. But that's the wrong war to wage. From an efficiency point of view, you shouldn't care that a function returns an object, you should only care about the *cost* of that object. What you need to do is channel your efforts into finding a way to reduce the *cost* of returned objects, not to eliminate the objects themselves (which we now recognize is a futile quest). If no cost is associated with such objects, who cares how many get created?

It is frequently possible to write functions that return objects in such a way that compilers can eliminate the cost of the temporaries. The trick is to return *constructor arguments* instead of objects, and you can do it like this:

```
// an efficient and correct way to implement a
// function that returns an object
const Rational operator*(const Rational& lhs,
                         const Rational& rhs)
{
  return Rational(lhs.numerator() * rhs.numerator(),
                  lhs.denominator() * rhs.denominator());
}
```

Look closely at the expression being returned. It looks like you're calling a Rational constructor, and in fact you are. You're creating a temporary Rational object through this expression,

```
Rational(lhs.numerator() * rhs.numerator(),
         lhs.denominator() * rhs.denominator());
```

and it is this temporary object the function is copying for its return value.

This business of returning constructor arguments instead of local objects doesn't appear to have bought you a lot, because you still have to pay for the construction and destruction of the temporary created inside the function, and you still have to pay for the construction and destruction of the object the function returns. But you have gained something. The rules for C++ allow compilers to optimize temporary objects out of existence. As a result, if you call `operator*` in a context like this,

```
Rational a = 10;
Rational b(1, 2);

Rational c = a * b;              // operator* is called here
```

your compilers are allowed to eliminate both the temporary inside `operator*` *and* the temporary returned by `operator*`. They can construct the object defined by the `return` expression *inside the memory allotted for the object c*. If your compilers do this, the total cost of temporary objects as a result of your calling `operator*` is zero: no temporaries are created. Instead, you pay for only one constructor call — the one to create `c`. Furthermore, you can't do any better than this, because `c` is a named object, and named objects can't be eliminated (see also Item 22). You can, however, eliminate the overhead of the call to `operator*` by declaring that function `inline`:

```
// the most efficient way to write a function returning
// an object
inline const Rational operator*(const Rational& lhs,
                                const Rational& rhs)
{
  return Rational(lhs.numerator() * rhs.numerator(),
                  lhs.denominator() * rhs.denominator());
}
```

"Yeah, yeah," you mutter, "optimization, schmoptimization. Who cares what compilers *can* do? I want to know what they *do* do. Does any of this nonsense work with real compilers?" It does. This particular optimization — eliminating a local temporary by using a function's return location (and possibly replacing that with an object at the function's call site) — is both well-known and commonly implemented. It even has a name: the *return value optimization*. In fact, the existence of a name for this optimization may explain why it's so widely available. Programmers looking for a C++ compiler can ask vendors whether the return value optimization is implemented. If one vendor says yes and another says "The what?," the first vendor has a notable competitive advantage. Ah, capitalism. Sometimes you just gotta love it.

Item 21: Overload to avoid implicit type conversions

Here's some code that looks nothing if not eminently reasonable:

```
class UPInt {                    // class for unlimited
public:                          // precision integers
  UPInt();
  UPInt(int value);
  ...

};

// For an explanation of why the return value is const,
// see Item 6
const UPInt operator+(const UPInt& lhs, const UPInt& rhs);

UPInt upi1, upi2;

...

UPInt upi3 = upi1 + upi2;
```

There are no surprises here. upi1 and upi2 are both UPInt objects, so adding them together just calls operator+ for UPInts.

Now consider these statements:

```
upi3 = upi1 + 10;
upi3 = 10 + upi2;
```

These statements also succeed. They do so through the creation of temporary objects to convert the integer 10 into UPInts (see Item 19).

It is convenient to have compilers perform these kinds of conversions, but the temporary objects created to make the conversions work are a cost we may not wish to bear. Just as most people want government benefits without having to pay for them, most C++ programmers want implicit type conversions without incurring any cost for temporaries. But without the computational equivalent of deficit spending, how can we do it?

We can take a step back and recognize that our goal isn't really type conversion, it's being able to make calls to operator+ with a combination of UPInt and int arguments. Implicit type conversion happens to be a means to that end, but let us not confuse means and ends. There is another way to make mixed-type calls to operator+ succeed, and that's to eliminate the need for type conversions in the first place. If we want to be able to add UPInt and int objects, all we have to do is say so. We do it by declaring *several* functions, each with a different set of parameter types:

```
const UPInt operator+(const UPInt& lhs,     // add UPInt
                      const UPInt& rhs);     // and UPInt
```

```
const UPInt operator+(const UPInt& lhs,      // add UPInt
                      int rhs);              // and int

const UPInt operator+(int lhs,               // add int and
                      const UPInt& rhs);     // UPInt

UPInt upi1, upi2;

...

UPInt upi3 = upi1 + upi2;      // fine, no temporary for
                              // upi1 or upi2

upi3 = upi1 + 10;             // fine, no temporary for
                              // upi1 or 10

upi3 = 10 + upi2;            // fine, no temporary for
                            // 10 or upi2
```

Once you start overloading to eliminate type conversions, you run the risk of getting swept up in the passion of the moment and declaring functions like this:

```
const UPInt operator+(int lhs, int rhs);      // error!
```

The thinking here is reasonable enough. For the types UPInt and int, we want to overload on all possible combinations for operator+. Given the three overloadings above, the only one missing is operator+ taking two int arguments, so we want to add it.

Reasonable or not, there are rules to this C++ game, and one of them is that every overloaded operator must take at least one argument of a user-defined type. int isn't a user-defined type, so we can't overload an operator taking only arguments of that type. (If this rule didn't exist, programmers would be able to change the meaning of predefined operations, and that would surely lead to chaos. For example, the attempted overloading of operator+ above would change the meaning of addition on ints. Is that really something we want people to be able to do?)

Overloading to avoid temporaries isn't limited to operator functions. For example, in most programs, you'll want to allow a string object everywhere a char* is acceptable, and vice versa. Similarly, if you're using a numerical class like complex (see Item 35), you'll want types like int and double to be valid anywhere a numerical object is. As a result, any function taking arguments of type string, char*, complex, etc., is a reasonable candidate for overloading to eliminate type conversions.

Still, it's important to keep the 80-20 rule (see Item 16) in mind. There is no point in implementing a slew of overloaded functions unless you have good reason to believe that it will make a noticeable improvement in the overall efficiency of the programs that use them.

Item 22: Consider using *op=* instead of stand-alone *op*

Most programmers expect that if they can say things like these,

```
x = x + y;                          x = x - y;
```

they can also say things like these:

```
x += y;                             x -= y;
```

If x and y are of a user-defined type, there is no guarantee that this is so. As far as C++ is concerned, there is no relationship between operator+, operator=, and operator+=, so if you want all three operators to exist and to have the expected relationship, you must implement that yourself. Ditto for the operators -, *, /, etc.

A good way to ensure that the natural relationship between the assignment version of an operator (e.g., operator+=) and the stand-alone version (e.g., operator+) exists is to implement the latter in terms of the former (see also Item 6). This is easy to do:

```
class Rational {
public:
  ...
  Rational& operator+=(const Rational& rhs);
  Rational& operator-=(const Rational& rhs);
};

// operator+ implemented in terms of operator+=;
// see Item 6 for an explanation of why the return
// value is const
const Rational operator+(const Rational& lhs,
                         const Rational& rhs)
{
  return Rational(lhs) += rhs;
}

// operator- implemented in terms of operator -=
const Rational operator-(const Rational& lhs,
                         const Rational& rhs)
{
  return Rational(lhs) -= rhs;
}
```

In this example, operators += and -= are implemented (elsewhere) from scratch, and operator+ and operator- call them to provide their own functionality. With this design, only the assignment versions of these operators need to be maintained. Furthermore, assuming the assignment versions of the operators are in the class's public interface, there is never a need for the stand-alone operators to be friends of the class.

If you don't mind putting all stand-alone operators at global scope, you can use templates to eliminate the need to write the stand-alone functions:

```
template<class T>
const T operator+(const T& lhs, const T& rhs)
{
  return T(lhs) += rhs;          // see discussion below
}

template<class T>
const T operator-(const T& lhs, const T& rhs)
{
  return T(lhs) -= rhs;          // see discussion below
}

...
```

With these templates, as long as an assignment version of an operator is defined for some type T, the corresponding stand-alone operator will automatically be generated if it's needed.

All this is well and good, but so far we have failed to consider the issue of efficiency, and efficiency is, after all, the topic of this chapter. Three aspects of efficiency are worth noting here. The first is that, in general, assignment versions of operators are more efficient than stand-alone versions, because stand-alone versions must typically return a new object, and that costs us the construction and destruction of a temporary (see Items 19 and 20). Assignment versions of operators write to their left-hand argument, so there is no need to generate a temporary to hold the operator's return value.

The second point is that by offering assignment versions of operators as well as stand-alone versions, you allow *clients* of your classes to make the difficult trade-off between efficiency and convenience. That is, your clients can decide whether to write their code like this,

```
Rational a, b, c, d, result;
...
result = a + b + c + d;     // probably uses 3 temporary
                            // objects, one for each call
                            // to operator+
```

or like this:

```
result = a;         // no temporary needed
result += b;        // no temporary needed
result += c;        // no temporary needed
result += d;        // no temporary needed
```

The former is easier to write, debug, and maintain, and it offers acceptable performance about 80% of the time (see Item 16). The latter is more efficient, and, one supposes, more intuitive for assembly language programmers. By offering both options, you let clients develop and debug code using the easier-to-read stand-alone operators while still reserving the right to replace them with the more efficient assignment versions of the operators. Furthermore, by implementing the stand-alones in terms of the assignment versions, you ensure that when clients switch from one to the other, the semantics of the operations remain constant.

The final efficiency observation concerns implementing the stand-alone operators. Look again at the implementation for operator+:

```
template<class T>
const T operator+(const T& lhs, const T& rhs)
{
  return T(lhs) += rhs;
}
```

The expression T(lhs) is a call to T's copy constructor. It creates a temporary object whose value is the same as that of lhs. This temporary is then used to invoke operator+= with rhs, and the result of that operation is returned from operator+. This code seems unnecessarily cryptic. Wouldn't it be better to write it like this?

```
template<class T>
const T operator+(const T& lhs, const T& rhs)
{
  T result(lhs);           // copy lhs into result
  return result += rhs;    // add rhs to it and return
}
```

This template is almost equivalent to the one above, but there is a crucial difference. This second template contains a named object, result. The fact that this object is named means that the return value optimization (see Item 20) is not available for operator+. The first implementation *is* eligible for the return value optimization, so compilers can generate better code for it.

Now, truth in advertising compels me to point out that the expression

```
return T(lhs) += rhs;
```

is more complex than most compilers are willing to subject to the return value optimization. That being the case, the first implementation above may still cost you one temporary object within the function, just as you'd pay for using the named object result. However, the fact remains that unnamed objects are easier to eliminate than named objects, so when faced with a choice between named objects or temporary objects, you're better off using temporaries. In the worst case, they cost you no more than their named colleagues, and as compiler optimizations improve, they should cost you less.

All this talk of named objects, unnamed objects, and compiler optimizations is interesting, but let us not forget the big picture. The big picture is that assignment versions of operators (such as `operator+=`) tend to be more efficient than stand-alone versions of those operators (e.g. `operator+`). As a library designer, you should offer both, and as an application developer, you should consider using assignment versions of operators instead of stand-alone versions whenever performance is at a premium.

Item 23: Consider alternative libraries

Library design is an exercise in compromise. The ideal library is small, fast, powerful, flexible, extensible, intuitive, universally available, well supported, free of use restrictions, and bug-free. It is also nonexistent. Libraries optimized for size and speed are typically not portable. Libraries with rich functionality are rarely intuitive. Bug-free libraries are limited in scope. In the real world, you can't have everything; something always has to give.

Different designers assign different priorities to these criteria. They thus sacrifice different things in their designs. As a result, it is not uncommon for two libraries offering similar functionality to have quite different performance profiles.

As an example, consider the iostream and stdio libraries, both of which should be available to every C++ programmer. The iostream library has several advantages over its C counterpart. It's type-safe, for example, and it's extensible. In terms of efficiency, however, the iostream library generally suffers in comparison with stdio, because stdio usually results in executables that are both smaller and faster than those arising from iostreams.

Consider first the speed issue. One way to get a feel for the difference in performance between iostreams and stdio is to run benchmark applications using both libraries. Now, it's important to bear in mind that benchmarks lie. Not only is it difficult to come up with a set of inputs that correspond to "typical" usage of a program or library, it's also useless unless you have a reliable way of determining how "typical" you or your clients are. Nevertheless, benchmarks can provide *some* insight into the comparative performance of different approaches to a problem, so though it would be foolish to rely on them completely, it would also be foolish to ignore them.

Let's examine a simple-minded benchmark program that exercises only the most rudimentary I/O functionality. This program reads 30,000 floating point numbers from standard input and writes them to standard output in a fixed format. The choice between the iostream and stdio libraries is made during compilation and is determined by the preprocessor symbol STDIO. If this symbol is defined, the stdio library is used, otherwise the iostream library is employed.

```cpp
#ifdef STDIO
#include <stdio.h>
#else
#include <iostream.h>
#include <iomanip.h>
#endif

#include <math.h>

const int VALUES = 30000;          // # of values to read/write

int main()
{
  double d;

  for (int n = 1; n <= VALUES; n++) {
#ifdef STDIO
    scanf("%lf", &d);
    printf("%10.5f", d);
#else
    cin >> d;
    cout << setw(10)                      // set field width
         << setprecision(5)               // set decimal places
         << setiosflags(ios::showpoint)   // keep trailing 0s
         << setiosflags(ios::fixed)       // use these settings
         << d;
#endif

    if (n % 5 == 0) {
#ifdef STDIO
      printf("\n");
#else
      cout << '\n';
#endif
    }
  }

  return 0;
}
```

When this program is given the (base 10) logarithms of the positive integers as input, it produces output like this:

```
0.00000    0.69315    1.09861    1.38629    1.60944
1.79176    1.94591    2.07944    2.19722    2.30259
2.39790    2.48491    2.56495    2.63906    2.70805
2.77259    2.83321    2.89037    2.94444    2.99573
3.04452    3.09104    3.13549    3.17805    3.21888
```

Such output demonstrates, if nothing else, that it's possible to produce fixed-format I/O using iostreams. Of course,

```
cout << setw(10)
     << setprecision(5)
     << setiosflags(ios::showpoint)
     << setiosflags(ios::fixed)
     << d;
```

is nowhere near as easy to type as

```
printf("%10.5f", d);
```

but operator<< is both type-safe and extensible, and printf is neither.

I have run this program on several combinations of machines, operating systems, and compilers, and in every case the stdio version has been faster. Sometimes it's been only a little faster (about 20%), sometimes it's been substantially faster (nearly 200%), but I've never come across an iostream implementation that was as fast as the corresponding stdio implementation. In addition, the size of this trivial program's executable using stdio tends to be smaller (sometimes *much* smaller) than the corresponding program using iostreams. (For programs of a realistic size, this difference is rarely significant.)

Bear in mind that any efficiency advantages of stdio are highly implementation-dependent, so future implementations of systems I've tested or existing implementations of systems I haven't tested may show a negligible performance difference between iostreams and stdio. In fact, one can reasonably hope to discover an iostream implementation that's *faster* than stdio, because iostreams determine the types of their operands during compilation, while stdio functions typically parse a format string at runtime.

The contrast in performance between iostreams and stdio is just an example, however, it's not the main point. The main point is that different libraries offering similar functionality often feature different performance trade-offs, so once you've identified the bottlenecks in your software (via profiling — see Item 16), you should see if it's possible to remove those bottlenecks by replacing one library with another. If your program has an I/O bottleneck, for example, you might consider replacing iostreams with stdio, but if it spends a significant portion of its time on dynamic memory allocation and deallocation, you might see if there are alternative implementations of operator new and operator delete available (see Item 8). Because different libraries embody different design decisions regarding efficiency, extensibility, portability, type safety, and other issues, you can sometimes significantly improve the efficiency of your software by switching to libraries whose designers gave more weight to performance considerations than to other factors.

Item 24: Understand the costs of virtual functions, multiple inheritance, virtual base classes, and RTTI

C++ compilers must find a way to implement each feature in the language. Such implementation details are, of course, compiler-dependent, and different compilers implement language features in different ways. For the most part, you need not concern yourself with such matters. However, the implementation of some features can have a noticeable impact on the size of objects and the speed at which member functions execute, so for those features, it's important to have a basic understanding of what compilers are likely to be doing under the hood. The foremost example of such a feature is virtual functions.

When a virtual function is called, the code executed must correspond to the dynamic type of the object on which the function is invoked; the type of the pointer or reference to the object is immaterial. How can compilers provide this behavior efficiently? Most implementations use *virtual tables* and *virtual table pointers*. Virtual tables and virtual table pointers are commonly referred to as *vtbls* and *vptrs*, respectively.

A vtbl is usually an array of pointers to (non-member) functions. (Some compilers use a form of linked list instead of an array, but the fundamental strategy is the same.) Each class in a program has its own vtbl, and the entries in a class's vtbl are pointers to the implementations of the virtual functions for that class. For example, given a class definition like this,

```
class C1 {
public:
  C1();

  virtual ~C1();
  virtual void f1();
  virtual int f2(char c) const;
  virtual void f3(const string& s);

  void f4() const;

  ...
};
```

C1's virtual table array will look something like this:

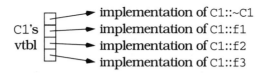

Note that the nonvirtual function f4 is not in the table, nor is C1's constructor. Nonvirtual functions — including constructors, which are by definition nonvirtual — are implemented just like ordinary C functions, so there are no special performance considerations surrounding their use.

If a class C2 inherits from C1, redefines some of the virtual functions it inherits, and adds some new ones of its own,

```
class C2: public C1 {
public:
  C2();                       // nonvirtual function
  virtual ~C2();              // redefined function
  virtual void f1();          // redefined function
  virtual void f5(char *str); // new virtual function
  ...
};
```

its virtual table entries point to the functions that are appropriate for objects of its type. These entries include pointers to the C1 virtual functions that C2 chose not to redefine:

This discussion brings out the first cost of virtual functions: you have to set aside space for a virtual table for each class that contains virtual functions. The size of a class's vtbl is proportional to the number of virtual functions defined for that class. There should be only one virtual table per class, so the total amount of space required for virtual tables is not usually significant, but if you have a large number of classes or a large number of virtual functions in each class, you may find that the vtbls take a significant bite out of your address space.

In general, abstract classes yield no vtbls. As we'll soon see, vtbls are referenced only by objects. Abstract classes can never be instantiated, so vtbls are unnecessary for such classes.

Because you need only one copy of a class's vtbl in your programs, compilers must address a tricky problem: where to put it. Most programs and libraries are created by linking together many object files, but each object file is generated independently of the others. Which object file should contain the vtbl for any given class? You might think to put it in the object file containing `main`, but libraries have no `main`, and at any rate the source file containing `main` may make no mention of many of the classes requiring vtbls. How could compilers then know which vtbls they were supposed to create?

A different strategy must be adopted, and compiler vendors tend to fall into two camps. For vendors who provide an integrated environment containing both compiler and linker, a brute-force strategy is to generate a copy of the vtbl in each object file that might need it. The linker then strips out duplicate copies, leaving only a single instance of each vtbl in the final executable or library.

A more common design is to employ a heuristic to determine which object file should contain the vtbl for a class. Usually this heuristic is as follows: a class's vtbl is generated in the object file containing the definition (i.e., the body) of the first non-inline virtual function in that class. Thus, the vtbl for class C1 above would be placed in the object file containing the definition of `C1::f1` (provided that function wasn't `inline`), and the vtbl for class C2 would be placed in the object file containing the definition of `C2::~C2` (again, provided that function wasn't `inline`).

In practice, this heuristic works well, but you can get into trouble if you go overboard on declaring virtual functions `inline`. If all virtual functions in a class are declared `inline`, the heuristic fails, and most heuristic-based implementations then generate a copy of the class's vtbl in *every object file* that uses it. In large systems, this can lead to programs containing hundreds or thousands of copies of a class's vtbl! Most compilers following this heuristic give you some way to control vtbl generation manually, but a better solution to this problem is to avoid declaring virtual functions `inline`. As we'll see below, there are good reasons why present compilers typically ignore the `inline` directive for virtual functions, anyway.

Virtual tables are half the implementation machinery for virtual functions, but by themselves they are useless. They become useful only when there is some way of indicating which vtbl corresponds to each object, and it is the job of the virtual table pointer to establish that correspondence.

Each object whose class declares virtual functions carries with it a hidden data member that points to the virtual table for that class. This hidden data member — the *vptr* — is added by compilers at a location in the object known only to the compilers. Conceptually, we can think of the layout of an object that has virtual functions as looking like this:

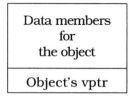

This picture shows the vptr at the end of the object, but don't be fooled: different compilers put them in different places. In the presence of inheritance, an object's vptr is often surrounded by data members. Multiple inheritance complicates this picture, but we'll deal with that a bit later. At this point, simply note the second cost of virtual functions: you have to pay for an extra pointer inside each object that is of a class containing virtual functions.

If your objects are small, this can be a significant cost. If your objects contain, on average, four bytes of member data, for example, the addition of a vptr can *double* their size (assuming four bytes are devoted to the vptr). On systems with limited memory, this means the number of objects you can create is reduced. Even on systems with unconstrained memory, you may find that the performance of your software decreases, because larger objects mean fewer fit on each cache or virtual memory page, and that means your paging activity will probably increase.

Suppose we have a program with several objects of types C1 and C2. Given the relationships among objects, vptrs, and vtbls that we have just seen, we can envision the objects in our program like this:

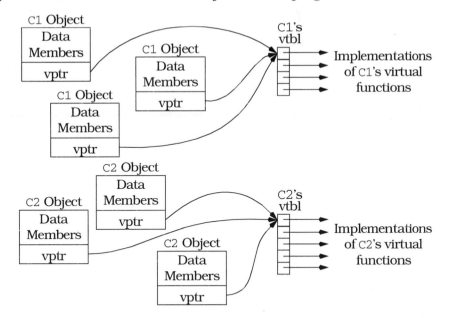

Now consider this program fragment:

```
void makeACall(C1 *pC1)
{
  pC1->f1();
}
```

This is a call to the virtual function f1 through the pointer pC1. By looking only at this code, there is no way to know which f1 function — C1::f1 or C2::f1 — should be invoked, because pC1 might point to a C1 object or to a C2 object. Your compilers must nevertheless generate code for the call to f1 inside makeACall, and they must ensure that the correct function is called, no matter what pC1 points to. They do this by generating code to do the following:

1. Follow the object's vptr to its vtbl. This is a simple operation, because the compilers know where to look inside the object for the vptr. (After all, they put it there.) As a result, this costs only an offset adjustment (to get to the vptr) and a pointer indirection (to get to the vtbl).

2. Find the pointer in the vtbl that corresponds to the function being called (f1 in this example). This, too, is simple, because compilers assign each virtual function a unique index within the table. This cost of this step is just an offset into the vtbl array.

3. Invoke the function pointed to by the pointer located in step 2.

If we imagine that each object has a hidden member called vptr and
that the vtbl index of function f1 is i, the code generated for the statement

```
    pC1->f1();
```

is

```
    (*pC1->vptr[i])();    // call the function pointed to by
                          // the i-th entry in the vtbl pointed
                          // to by pC1->vptr
```

This is almost as efficient as a non-virtual function call: on most machines it executes only a few more instructions. The cost of calling a
virtual function is thus basically the same as that of calling a function
through a function pointer. Virtual functions *per se* are not usually a
performance bottleneck.

The real runtime cost of virtual functions has to do with their interaction with inlining. For all practical purposes, virtual functions aren't
inlined. That's because "inline" means "during compilation, replace the
call site with the body of the called function," but "virtual" means "wait
until runtime to see which function is called." If your compilers don't
know which function will be called at a particular call site, you can understand why they won't inline that function call. This is the third cost
of virtual functions: you effectively give up inlining. (Virtual functions
can be inlined when invoked through *objects*, but most virtual function
calls are made through *pointers* or *references* to objects, and such calls
are not inlined. Because such calls are the norm, virtual functions are
effectively not inlined.)

Everything we've seen so far applies to both single and multiple inheritance, but when multiple inheritance enters the picture, things get
more complex. There is no point in dwelling on details, but with multiple inheritance, offset calculations to find vptrs within objects become
more complicated; there are multiple vptrs within a single object (one
per base class); and special vtbls must be generated for base classes in
addition to the stand-alone vtbls we have discussed. As a result, both
the per-class and the per-object space overhead for virtual functions
increases, and the runtime invocation cost grows slightly, too.

Multiple inheritance often leads to the need for virtual base classes.
Without virtual base classes, if a derived class has more than one inheritance path to a base class, the data members of that base class are
replicated within each derived class object, one copy for each path between the derived class and the base class. Such replication is almost
never what programmers want, and making base classes virtual eliminates the replication. Virtual base classes incur a cost of their own,

however, because implementations of virtual base classes generally use pointers to virtual base class parts as the means for avoiding the replication, and those pointers have to be stored inside your objects.

For example, consider this, which I generally call "the dreaded multiple inheritance diamond:"

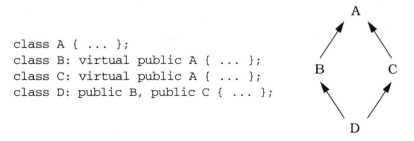

```
class A { ... };
class B: virtual public A { ... };
class C: virtual public A { ... };
class D: public B, public C { ... };
```

Here A is a virtual base class because B and C virtually inherit from it. The layout for an object of type D is likely to look like this:

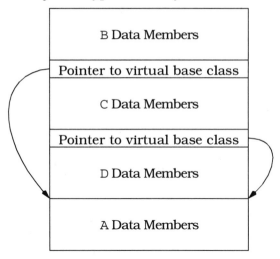

It seems a little strange to place the base class data members at the end of the object, but that's often how it's done. Of course, implementations are free to organize memory any way they like, so you should never rely on this picture for anything more than a conceptual overview of how virtual base classes generally lead to the addition of hidden pointers to your objects.

If we combine this picture with the earlier one showing how virtual table pointers are added to objects, we realize that if the base class A in the hierarchy on page 119 has any virtual functions, the memory layout for an object of type D will look more or less like this:

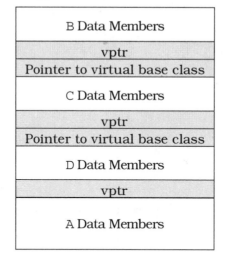

| B Data Members |
| vptr |
| Pointer to virtual base class |
| C Data Members |
| vptr |
| Pointer to virtual base class |
| D Data Members |
| vptr |
| A Data Members |

Here I've shaded the parts of the object that are added by compilers. The picture may be misleading, because the ratio of shaded to unshaded areas is determined by the amount of data in your classes. For small classes, the relative overhead is large. For classes with more data, the relative overhead is less significant, though it is typically noticeable.

An oddity in the above diagram is that there are only three vptrs even though four classes are involved. Implementations are free to generate four vptrs if they like, but three suffice (it turns out that B and D can share a vptr), and most implementations take advantage of this opportunity to reduce the compiler-generated overhead.

We've now seen how virtual functions make objects larger and preclude inlining, and we've examined how multiple inheritance and virtual base classes also increase the size of objects. Let us therefore turn to our final topic, the cost of runtime type identification (RTTI).

RTTI lets us discover information about objects and classes at runtime, so there has to be a place to store the information we're allowed to query. That information is stored in an object of type type_info, and you can access the type_info object for a class by using the typeid operator.

There only needs to be a single copy of the RTTI information for each class, but there must be a way to get to that information for any object. Actually, that's not quite true. The language specification states that we're guaranteed accurate information on an object's dynamic type only if that type has at least one virtual function. This makes RTTI data sound a lot like a virtual function table. We need only one copy of the information per class, and we need a way to get to the appropriate information from any object containing a virtual function. This parallel between RTTI and virtual function tables is no accident: RTTI was designed to be implementable in terms of a class's vtbl.

For example, index 0 of a vtbl array might contain a pointer to the type_info object for the class corresponding to that vtbl. The vtbl for class C1 on page 114 would then look like this:

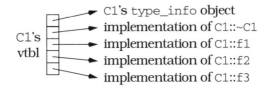

With this implementation, the space cost of RTTI is an additional entry in each class vtbl plus the cost of the storage for the type_info object for each class. Just as the memory for virtual tables is unlikely to be noticeable for most applications, however, you're unlikely to run into problems due to the size of type_info objects.

The following table summarizes the primary costs of virtual functions, multiple inheritance, virtual base classes, and RTTI:

Feature	Increases Size of Objects	Increases Per-Class Data	Reduces Inlining
Virtual Functions	Yes	Yes	Yes
Multiple Inheritance	Yes	Yes	No
Virtual Base Classes	Yes	No	No
RTTI	No	Yes	No

Some people look at this table and are aghast. "I'm sticking with C!", they declare. Fair enough. But remember that each of these features offers functionality you'd otherwise have to code by hand. In most cases, your manual approximation would probably be less efficient and less robust than the compiler-generated code. Using nested switch statements or cascading if-then-elses to emulate virtual function calls, for example, yields more code than virtual function calls do, and the code runs more slowly, too. Furthermore, you must manually track object types yourself, which means your objects carry around type tags of their own; you thus fail to gain even the benefit of smaller objects.

It is important to understand the costs of virtual functions, multiple inheritance, virtual base classes, and RTTI, but it is equally important to understand that if you need the functionality these features offer, you *will* pay for it, one way or another. Sometimes you have legitimate reasons for bypassing the compiler-generated services. For example, hidden vptrs and pointers to virtual base classes can make it difficult to store C++ objects in databases or to move them across process boundaries, so you may wish to emulate these features in a way that makes it easier to accomplish these other tasks. From the point of view of efficiency, however, you are unlikely to do better than the compiler-generated implementations by coding these features yourself.

Techniques

Most of this book is concerned with programming guidelines. Such guidelines are important, but no programmer lives by guidelines alone. According to the old TV show *Felix the Cat*, "Whenever he gets in a fix, he reaches into his bag of tricks." Well, if a cartoon character can have a bag of tricks, so too can C++ programmers. Think of this chapter as a starter set for your bag of tricks.

Some problems crop up repeatedly when designing C++ software. How can you make constructors and non-member functions act like virtual functions? How can you limit the number of instances of a class? How can you prevent objects from being created on the heap? How can you guarantee that they will be created there? How can you create objects that automatically perform some actions anytime some other class's member functions are called? How can you have different objects share data structures while giving clients the illusion that each has its own copy? How can you distinguish between read and write usage of `operator[]`? How can you create a virtual function whose behavior depends on the dynamic types of more than one object?

All these questions (and more) are answered in this chapter, in which I describe proven solutions to problems commonly encountered by C++ programmers. I call such solutions *techniques*, but they're also known as *idioms* and, when documented in a stylized fashion, *patterns*. Regardless of what you call them, the information that follows will serve you well as you engage in the day-to-day skirmishes of practical software development. It should also convince you that no matter what you want to do, there is almost certainly a way to do it in C++.

Item 25: Virtualizing constructors and non-member functions

On the face of it, it doesn't make much sense to talk about "virtual constructors." You call a virtual function to achieve type-specific behavior when you have a pointer or reference to an object but you don't know what the real type of the object is. You call a constructor only when you don't yet have an object but you know exactly what type you'd like to have. How, then, can one talk of *virtual* constructors?

It's easy. Though virtual constructors may seem nonsensical, they are remarkably useful. (If you think nonsensical ideas are never useful, how do you explain the success of modern physics?) For example, suppose you write applications for working with newsletters, where a newsletter consists of components that are either textual or graphical. You might organize things this way:

```
class NLComponent {          // abstract base class for
public:                      // newsletter components

  ...                        // contains at least one
};                           // pure virtual function

class TextBlock: public NLComponent {
public:
  ...                        // contains no pure virtual
};                           // functions

class Graphic: public NLComponent {
public:
  ...                        // contains no pure virtual
};                           // functions

class NewsLetter {           // a newsletter object
public:                      // consists of a list of
  ...                        // NLComponent objects

private:
  list<NLComponent*> components;
};
```

The classes relate in this way:

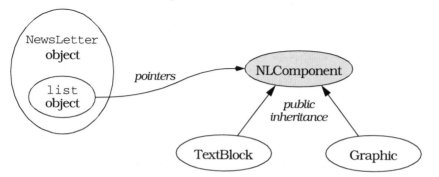

The list class used inside NewsLetter is part of the Standard Template Library, which is part of the standard C++ library (see Item 35).

Objects of type `list` behave like doubly linked lists, though they need not be implemented in that way.

`NewsLetter` objects, when not being worked on, would likely be stored on disk. To support the creation of a `Newsletter` from its on-disk representation, it would be convenient to give `NewsLetter` a constructor that takes an `istream`. The constructor would read information from the stream as it created the necessary in-core data structures:

```
class NewsLetter {
public:
  NewsLetter(istream& str);
  ...
};
```

Pseudocode for this constructor might look like this,

```
NewsLetter::NewsLetter(istream& str)
{
  while (str) {
    read the next component object from str;

    add the object to the list of this
    newsletter's components;
  }
}
```

or, after moving the tricky stuff into a separate function called read-Component, like this:

```
class NewsLetter {
public:
  ...

private:
  // read the data for the next NLComponent from str,
  // create the component and return a pointer to it
  static NLComponent * readComponent(istream& str);
  ...
};

NewsLetter::NewsLetter(istream& str)
{
  while (str) {
    // add the pointer returned by readComponent to the
    // end of the components list; "push_back" is a list
    // member function that inserts at the end of the list
    components.push_back(readComponent(str));
  }
}
```

Consider what `readComponent` does. It creates a new object, either a `TextBlock` or a `Graphic`, depending on the data it reads. Because it creates new objects, it acts much like a constructor, but because it can create different types of objects, we call it a *virtual constructor*. A virtual constructor is a function that creates different types of objects depending on the input it is given. Virtual constructors are useful in many contexts, only one of which is reading object information from disk (or off a network connection or from a tape, etc.).

A particular kind of virtual constructor — the *virtual copy constructor* — is also widely useful. A virtual copy constructor returns a pointer to a new copy of the object invoking the function. Because of this behavior, virtual copy constructors are typically given names like `copySelf`, `cloneSelf`, or, as shown below, just plain `clone`. Few functions are implemented in a more straightforward manner:

```
class NLComponent {
public:
  // declaration of virtual copy constructor
  virtual NLComponent * clone() const = 0;
  ...
};

class TextBlock: public NLComponent {
public:
  virtual TextBlock * clone() const        // virtual copy
  { return new TextBlock(*this); }         // constructor
  ...
};

class Graphic: public NLComponent {
public:
  virtual Graphic * clone() const          // virtual copy
  { return new Graphic(*this); }           // constructor
  ...
};
```

As you can see, a class's virtual copy constructor just calls its real copy constructor. The meaning of "copy" is hence the same for both functions. If the real copy constructor performs a shallow copy, so does the virtual copy constructor. If the real copy constructor performs a deep copy, so does the virtual copy constructor. If the real copy constructor does something fancy like reference counting or copy-on-write (see Item 29), so does the virtual copy constructor. Consistency — what a wonderful thing.

Notice that the above implementation takes advantage of a relaxation in the rules for virtual function return types that was adopted relatively recently. No longer must a derived class's redefinition of a base class's virtual function declare the same return type. Instead, if the function's return type is a pointer (or a reference) to a base class, the derived class's function may return a pointer (or reference) to a class derived from that base class. This opens no holes in C++'s type system, and it makes it possible to accurately declare functions such as virtual copy constructors. That's why TextBlock's clone can return a Text-Block* and Graphic's clone can return a Graphic*, even though the return type of NLComponent's clone is NLComponent*.

The existence of a virtual copy constructor in NLComponent makes it easy to implement a (normal) copy constructor for NewsLetter:

```cpp
class NewsLetter {
public:
  NewsLetter(const NewsLetter& s);
  ...

private:
  list<NLComponent*> components;
};

NewsLetter::NewsLetter(const NewsLetter& rhs)
{
  // iterate over rhs's list, using each element's
  // virtual copy constructor to copy the element into
  // the components list for this object. For details on
  // how the following code works, see Item 35.
  for (list<NLComponent*>::const_iterator it =
          rhs.components.begin();
       it != rhs.components.end();
       ++it) {

    // "it" points to the current element of rhs.components,
    // so call that element's clone function to get a copy
    // of the element, and add that copy to the end of
    // this object's list of components
    components.push_back((*it)->clone());
  }
}
```

Unless you are familiar with the Standard Template Library, this code looks bizarre, I know, but the idea is simple: just iterate over the list of components for the NewsLetter object being copied, and for each component in the list, call its virtual copy constructor. We need a virtual copy constructor here, because the list contains pointers to NLComponent objects, but we know each pointer really points to a TextBlock or a Graphic. We want to copy whatever the pointer really points to, and the virtual copy constructor does that for us.

Making Non-Member Functions Act Virtual

Just as constructors can't really be virtual, neither can non-member functions. However, just as it makes sense to conceive of functions that construct new objects of different types, it makes sense to conceive of non-member functions whose behavior depends on the dynamic types of their parameters. For example, suppose you'd like to implement output operators for the TextBlock and Graphic classes. The obvious approach to this problem is to make the output operator virtual. However, the output operator is operator<<, and that function takes an ostream& as its left-hand argument; that effectively rules out the possibility of making it a member function of the TextBlock or Graphic classes.

(It can be done, but then look what happens:

```
class NLComponent {
public:
  // unconventional declaration of output operator
  virtual ostream& operator<<(ostream& str) const = 0;
  ...
};

class TextBlock: public NLComponent {
public:
  // virtual output operator (also unconventional)
  virtual ostream& operator<<(ostream& str) const;
};

class Graphic: public NLComponent {
public:
  // virtual output operator (still unconventional)
  virtual ostream& operator<<(ostream& str) const;
};

TextBlock t;
Graphic g;

...

t << cout;                        // print t on cout via
                                  // virtual operator<<; note
                                  // unconventional syntax

g << cout;                        // print g on cout via
                                  // virtual operator<<; note
                                  // unconventional syntax
```

Clients must place the stream object on the *right-hand side* of the "<<" symbol, and that's contrary to the convention for output operators. To get back to the normal syntax, we must move operator<< out of the TextBlock and Graphic classes, but if we do that, we can no longer declare it virtual.)

An alternate approach is to declare a virtual function for printing (e.g., print) and define it for the TextBlock and Graphic classes. But if we do that, the syntax for printing TextBlock and Graphic objects is inconsistent with that for the other types in the language, all of which rely on operator<< as their output operator.

Neither of these solutions is very satisfying. What we want is a non-member function called operator<< that exhibits the behavior of a virtual function like print. This description of what we want is in fact very close to a description of how to get it. We define *both* operator<< and print and have the former call the latter!

```
class NLComponent {
public:
  virtual ostream& print(ostream& s) const = 0;
  ...
};

class TextBlock: public NLComponent {
public:
  virtual ostream& print(ostream& s) const;
  ...
};

class Graphic: public NLComponent {
public:
  virtual ostream& print(ostream& s) const;
  ...
};

inline
ostream& operator<<(ostream& s, const NLComponent& c)
{
  return c.print(s);
}
```

Virtual-acting non-member functions, then, are easy. You write virtual functions to do the work, then write a non-virtual function that does nothing but call the virtual function. To avoid incurring the cost of a function call for this syntactic sleight-of-hand, of course, you inline the non-virtual function.

Now that you know how to make non-member functions act virtually on one of their arguments, you may wonder if it's possible to make them act virtually on more than one of their arguments. It is, but it's not easy. How hard is it? Turn to Item 31; it's devoted to that question.

Item 26: Limiting the number of objects of a class

Okay, you're crazy about objects, but sometimes you'd like to bound your insanity. For example, you've got only one printer in your system, so you'd like to somehow limit the number of printer objects to one. Or you've got only 16 file descriptors you can hand out, so you've got to make sure there are never more than that many file descriptor objects in existence. How can you do such things? How can you limit the number of objects?

If this were a proof by mathematical induction, we might start with $n = 1$, then build from there. Fortunately, this is neither a proof nor an induction. Moreover, it turns out to be instructive to begin with $n = 0$, so we'll start there instead. How do you prevent objects from being instantiated at all?

Allowing Zero or One Objects

Each time an object is instantiated, we know one thing for sure: a constructor will be called. That being the case, the easiest way to prevent objects of a particular class from being created is to declare the constructors of that class *private*:

```
class CantBeInstantiated {
private:
  CantBeInstantiated();
  CantBeInstantiated(const CantBeInstantiated&);

  ...

};
```

Having thus removed everybody's right to create objects, we can selectively loosen the restriction. If, for example, we want to create a class for printers, but we also want to abide by the constraint that there is only one printer available to us, we can encapsulate the printer object inside a function so that everybody has access to the printer, but only a single printer object is created:

```
class PrintJob;                    // forward declaration

class Printer {
public:
  void submitJob(const PrintJob& job);
  void reset();
  void performSelfTest();

  ...

friend Printer& thePrinter();
```

```
private:
  Printer();
  Printer(const Printer& rhs);

  ...

};

Printer& thePrinter()
{
  static Printer p;              // the single printer object
  return p;
}
```

There are three separate components to this design. First, the constructors of the Printer class are private. That suppresses object creation. Second, the global function thePrinter is declared a friend of the class. That lets thePrinter escape the restriction imposed by the private constructors. Finally, thePrinter contains a *static* Printer object. That means only a single object will be created.

Client code refers to thePrinter whenever it wishes to interact with the system's lone printer. By returning a reference to a Printer object, thePrinter can be used in any context where a Printer object itself could be:

```
class PrintJob {
public:
  PrintJob(const string& whatToPrint);
  ...

};

string buffer;

...                                        // put stuff in buffer

thePrinter().reset();
thePrinter().submitJob(buffer);
```

It's possible, of course, that thePrinter strikes you as a needless addition to the global namespace. "Yes," you may say, "as a global function it looks more like a global variable, but global variables are gauche, and I'd prefer to localize all printer-related functionality inside the Printer class." Well, far be it from me to argue with someone who uses words like gauche. thePrinter can just as easily be made a static member function of Printer, and that puts it right where you want it. It also eliminates the need for a friend declaration, which many regard as tacky in its own right. Using a static member function, Printer looks like this:

```
class Printer {
public:
  static Printer& thePrinter();
  ...

private:
  Printer();
  Printer(const Printer& rhs);
  ...

};

Printer& Printer::thePrinter()
{
  static Printer p;
  return p;
}
```

Clients must now be a bit wordier when they refer to the printer:

```
Printer::thePrinter().reset();
Printer::thePrinter().submitJob(buffer);
```

Another approach is to move `Printer` and `thePrinter` out of the global scope and into a *namespace*. Namespaces are a recent addition to C++. Anything that can be declared at global scope can also be declared in a namespace. This includes classes, structs, functions, variables, objects, typedefs, etc. The fact that something is in a namespace doesn't affect its behavior, but it does prevent name conflicts between entities in different namespaces. By putting the `Printer` class and the `thePrinter` function into a namespace, we don't have to worry about whether anybody else happened to choose the names `Printer` or `thePrinter` for themselves; our namespace prevents name conflicts.

Syntactically, namespaces look much like classes, but there are no public, protected, or private sections; everything is public. This is how we'd put `Printer` and `thePrinter` into a namespace called `PrintingStuff`:

```
namespace PrintingStuff {
  class Printer {                    // this class is in the
  public:                            // PrintingStuff namespace

    void submitJob(const PrintJob& job);
    void reset();
    void performSelfTest();
    ...

  friend Printer& thePrinter();
```

```
private:
  Printer();
  Printer(const Printer& rhs);
  ...

};

Printer& thePrinter()              // so is this function
{
  static Printer p;
  return p;
}
}                                  // this is the end of the
                                   // namespace
```

Given this namespace, clients can refer to `thePrinter` using a fully-qualified name (i.e., one that includes the name of the namespace),

```
PrintingStuff::thePrinter().reset();
PrintingStuff::thePrinter().submitJob(buffer);
```

but they can also employ a *using declaration* to save themselves keystrokes:

```
using PrintingStuff::thePrinter; // import the name
                                 // "thePrinter" from the
                                 // namespace "PrintingStuff"
                                 // into the current scope

thePrinter().reset();            // now thePrinter can be
thePrinter().submitJob(buffer);  // used as if it were a
                                 // local name
```

There are two subtleties in the implementation of `thePrinter` that are worth exploring. First, it's important that the single `Printer` object be static in a *function* and not in a class. An object that's static in a class is, for all intents and purposes, *always* constructed (and destructed), even if it's never used. In contrast, an object that's static in a function is created the first time through the function, so if the function is never called, the object is never created. (You do, however, pay for a check each time the function is called to see whether the object needs to be created.) One of the philosophical pillars on which C++ was built is the idea that you shouldn't pay for things you don't use, and defining an object like our printer as a static object in a function is one way of adhering to this philosophy. It's a philosophy you should adhere to whenever you can.

There is another drawback to making the printer a class static versus a function static, and that has to do with its time of initialization. We know exactly when a function static is initialized: the first time through the function at the point where the static is defined. The situation with a class static (or, for that matter, a global static, should you be so gauche as to use one) is less well defined. C++ offers certain guarantees regarding the order of initialization of statics within a particular translation unit (i.e., a body of source code that yields a single object file), but it says *nothing* about the initialization order of static objects in different translation units. In practice, this turns out to be a source of countless headaches. Function statics, when they can be made to suffice, allow us to avoid these headaches. In our example here, they can, so why suffer?

The second subtlety has to do with the interaction of inlining and static objects inside functions. Look again at the code for the non-member version of thePrinter:

```
Printer& thePrinter()
{
  static Printer p;
  return p;
}
```

Except for the first time through this function (when p must be constructed), this is a one-line function — it consists entirely of the statement "return p;". If ever there were a good candidate for inlining, this function would certainly seem to be the one. Yet it's not declared inline. Why not?

Consider for a moment why you'd declare an object to be static. It's usually because you want only a single copy of that object, right? Now consider what inline means. Conceptually, it means compilers should replace each call to the function with a copy of the function body, but for non-member functions, it also means something else. It means the functions in question have *internal linkage.*

You don't ordinarily need to worry about such linguistic mumbo jumbo, but there is one thing you must remember: functions with internal linkage may be duplicated within a program (i.e., the object code for the program may contain more than one copy of each function with internal linkage), and *this duplication includes static objects contained within the functions.* The result? If you create an inline non-member function containing a local static object, you may end up with *more than one copy* of the static object in your program! So don't create inline non-member functions that contain local static data.

But maybe you think this business of creating a function to return a reference to a hidden object is the wrong way to go about limiting the number of objects in the first place. Perhaps you think it's better to simply count the number of objects in existence and throw an exception in a constructor if too many objects are requested. In other words, maybe you think we should handle printer creation like this:

```
class Printer {
public:
  class TooManyObjects{};        // exception class for use
                                 // when too many objects
                                 // are requested

  Printer();
  ~Printer();

  ...

private:
  static unsigned int numObjects;

  Printer(const Printer& rhs);   // there is a limit of 1
                                 // printer, so never allow
  };                             // copying
```

The idea is to use `numObjects` to keep track of how many `Printer` objects are in existence. This value will be incremented in the class constructor and decremented in its destructor. If an attempt is made to construct too many `Printer` objects, we throw an exception of type `TooManyObjects`:

```
// Obligatory definition of the class static
unsigned int Printer::numObjects = 0;

Printer::Printer()
{
  if (numObjects >= 1) {
    throw TooManyObjects();
  }

  proceed with normal construction here;

  ++numObjects;
}

Printer::~Printer()
{
  perform normal destruction here;

  --numObjects;
}
```

This approach to limiting object creation is attractive for a couple of reasons. For one thing, it's straightforward — everybody should be able to understand what's going on. For another, it's easy to generalize so that the maximum number of objects is some number other than one.

Contexts for Object Construction

There is also a problem with this strategy. Suppose we have a special kind of printer, say, a color printer. The class for such printers would have much in common with our generic printer class, so of course we'd inherit from it:

```
class ColorPrinter: public Printer {
  ...
};
```

Now suppose we have one generic printer and one color printer in our system:

```
Printer p;
ColorPrinter cp;
```

How many Printer objects result from these object definitions? The answer is two: one for p and one for the Printer part of cp. At run-time, a TooManyObjects exception will be thrown during the construction of the base class part of cp. For many programmers, this is neither what they want nor what they expect. (Designs that avoid having concrete classes inherit from other concrete classes do not suffer from this problem. For details on this design philosophy, see Item 33.)

A similar problem occurs when Printer objects are contained inside other objects:

```
class CPFMachine {        // for machines that can
private:                  // copy, print, and fax

  Printer p;              // for printing capabilities
  FaxMachine f;           // for faxing capabilities
  CopyMachine c;          // for copying capabilities

  ...

};

CPFMachine m1;            // fine

CPFMachine m2;            // throws TooManyObjects exception
```

The problem is that Printer objects can exist in three different contexts: on their own, as base class parts of more derived objects, and embedded inside larger objects. The presence of these different contexts significantly muddies the waters regarding what it means to keep track of the "number of objects in existence," because what you consider to be the existence of an object may not jibe with your compilers'.

Often you will be interested only in allowing objects to exist on their own, and you will wish to limit the number of *those* kinds of instantiations. That restriction is easy to satisfy if you adopt the strategy exemplified by our original `Printer` class, because the `Printer` constructors are private, and (in the absence of `friend` declarations) classes with private constructors can't be used as base classes, nor can they be embedded inside other objects.

The fact that you can't derive from classes with private constructors leads to a general scheme for preventing derivation, one that doesn't necessarily have to be coupled with limiting object instantiations. Suppose, for example, you have a class, `FSA`, for representing finite state automata. (Such state machines are useful in many contexts, among them user interface design.) Further suppose you'd like to allow any number of `FSA` objects to be created, but you'd also like to ensure that no class ever inherits from `FSA`. (One reason for doing this might be to justify the presence of a nonvirtual destructor in `FSA`. As Item 24 explains, classes without virtual functions yield smaller objects than do equivalent classes with virtual functions.) Here's how you can design `FSA` to satisfy both criteria:

```
class FSA {
public:
  // pseudo-constructors
  static FSA * makeFSA();
  static FSA * makeFSA(const FSA& rhs);
  ...

private:
  FSA();
  FSA(const FSA& rhs);
  ...
};

FSA * FSA::makeFSA()
{ return new FSA(); }

FSA * FSA::makeFSA(const FSA& rhs)
{ return new FSA(rhs); }
```

Unlike the `thePrinter` function that always returned a reference to a single object, each `makeFSA` pseudo-constructor returns a pointer to a unique object. That's what allows an unlimited number of FSA objects to be created.

This is nice, but the fact that each pseudo-constructor calls `new` implies that callers will have to remember to call `delete`. Otherwise a resource leak will be introduced. Callers who wish to have `delete` called automatically when the current scope is exited can store the pointer returned from `makeFSA` in an `auto_ptr` object (see Item 9); such objects automatically delete what they point to when they themselves go out of scope:

```
// indirectly call default FSA constructor
auto_ptr<FSA> pfsa1(FSA::makeFSA());

// indirectly call FSA copy constructor
auto_ptr<FSA> pfsa2(FSA::makeFSA(*pfsa1));
```

```
...              // use pfsa1 and pfsa2 as normal pointers,
                 // but don't worry about deleting them
```

Allowing Objects to Come and Go

We now know how to design a class that allows only a single instantiation, we know that keeping track of the number of objects of a particular class is complicated by the fact that object constructors are called
in three different contexts, and we know that we can eliminate the con-
fusion surrounding object counts by making constructors private. It is
worthwhile to make one final observation. Our use of the thePrinter
function to encapsulate access to a single object limits the number of
Printer objects to one, but it also limits us to a single Printer object
for each run of the program. As a result, it's not possible to write code
like this:

```
create Printer object p1;

use p1;

destroy p1;

create Printer object p2;

use p2;

destroy p2;

...
```

This design never instantiates more than a single Printer object at a
time, but it does use different Printer objects in different parts of the
program. It somehow seems unreasonable that this isn't allowed. After
all, at no point do we violate the constraint that only one printer may
exist. Isn't there a way to make this legal?

There is. All we have to do is combine the object-counting code we used
earlier with the pseudo-constructors we just saw:

```
class Printer {
public:
  class TooManyObjects{};

  // pseudo-constructor
  static Printer * makePrinter();

  ~Printer();
```

```
    void submitJob(const PrintJob& job);
    void reset();
    void performSelfTest();
    ...

  private:
    static unsigned int numObjects;

    Printer();

    Printer(const Printer& rhs);   // we don't define this
  };                               // function, because we'll
                                   // never allow copying

  // Obligatory definition of class static
  unsigned int Printer::numObjects = 0;

  Printer::Printer()
  {
    if (numObjects >= 1) {
      throw TooManyObjects();
    }

    proceed with normal object construction here;

    ++numObjects;
  }

  Printer * Printer::makePrinter()
  { return new Printer; }
```

If the notion of throwing an exception when too many objects are requested strikes you as unreasonably harsh, you could have the
pseudo-constructor return a null pointer instead. Clients would then
have to check for this before doing anything with it, of course.

Clients use this Printer class just as they would any other class, except they must call the pseudo-constructor function instead of the real
constructor:

```
  Printer p1;                    // error! default ctor is
                                 // private

  Printer *p2 =
    Printer::makePrinter();      // fine, indirectly calls
                                 // default ctor

  Printer p3 = *p2;              // error! copy ctor is
                                 // private

  p2->performSelfTest();         // all other functions are
  p2->reset();                   // called as usual

  ...

  delete p2;                     // avoid resource leak; this
                                 // would be unnecessary if
                                 // p2 were an auto_ptr
```

This technique is easily generalized to any number of objects. All we
have to do is replace the hard-wired constant 1 with a class-specific
value, then lift the restriction against copying objects. For example, the
following revised implementation of our `Printer` class allows up to 10
`Printer` objects to exist:

```
class Printer {
public:
  class TooManyObjects{};

  // pseudo-constructors
  static Printer * makePrinter();
  static Printer * makePrinter(const Printer& rhs);

  ...

private:
  static unsigned int numObjects;
  static const int maxObjects = 10;

  Printer();
  Printer(const Printer& rhs);
};
// Obligatory definitions of class statics
unsigned int Printer::numObjects = 0;
const int Printer::maxObjects;

Printer::Printer()
{
  if (numObjects >= maxObjects) {
    throw TooManyObjects();
  }

  ...

}

Printer::Printer(const Printer& rhs)
{
  if (numObjects >= maxObjects) {
    throw TooManyObjects();
  }

  ...

}

Printer * Printer::makePrinter()
{ return new Printer; }

Printer * Printer::makePrinter(const Printer& rhs)
{ return new Printer(rhs); }
```

Don't be surprised if your compilers get all upset about the declaration
of Printer::maxObjects in the class definition above. In particular, be

prepared for them to complain about the specification of 10 as an initial value for that variable. The ability to specify initial values for static const members (of integral type, e.g., ints, chars, enums, etc.) inside a class definition was added to C++ only recently, so many compilers don't yet allow it. If your compilers are as-yet-unupdated, pacify them by declaring maxObjects to be an enumerator inside a private anonymous enum,

```
class Printer {
private:
  enum { maxObjects = 10 };      // within this class,
  ...                            // maxObjects is the
};                               // constant 10
```

or by initializing the constant static like a non-const static member:

```
class Printer {
private:
  static const int maxObjects;    // no initial value given

  ...

};

// this goes in a single implementation file
const int Printer::maxObjects = 10;
```

This latter approach has the same effect as the original code above, but explicitly specifying the initial value is easier for other programmers to understand. When your compilers support the specification of initial values for const static members in class definitions, you should take advantage of that capability.

An Object-Counting Base Class

Initialization of statics aside, the approach above works like the proverbial charm, but there is one aspect of it that continues to nag. If we had a lot of classes like Printer whose instantiations needed to be limited, we'd have to write this same code over and over, once per class. That would be mind-numbingly dull. Given a fancy-pants language like C++, it somehow seems we should be able to automate the process. Isn't there a way to encapsulate the notion of counting instances and bundle it into a class?

We can easily come up with a base class for counting object instances and have classes like Printer inherit from that, but it turns out we can do even better. We can actually come up with a way to encapsulate the whole counting kit and kaboodle, by which I mean not only the functions to manipulate the instance count, but also the instance count itself. (We'll see the need for a similar trick when we examine reference counting in Item 29.)

The counter in the `Printer` class is the static variable `numObjects`, so we need to move that variable into an instance-counting class. However, we also need to make sure that each class for which we're counting instances has a *separate* counter. Use of a counting class *template* lets us automatically generate the appropriate number of counters, because we can make the counter a static member of the classes generated from the template:

```
template<class BeingCounted>
class Counted {
public:
  class TooManyObjects{};        // for throwing exceptions

  static int objectCount() { return numObjects; }

protected:
  Counted();
  Counted(const Counted& rhs);

  ~Counted() { --numObjects; }

private:
  static int numObjects;
  static int maxObjects;

  void init();                   // to avoid ctor code
};                               // duplication

template<class BeingCounted>
Counted<BeingCounted>::Counted()
{ init(); }

template<class BeingCounted>
Counted<BeingCounted>::Counted(const Counted<BeingCounted>&)
{ init(); }

template<class BeingCounted>
void Counted<BeingCounted>::init()
{
  if (numObjects >= maxObjects) throw TooManyObjects();
  ++numObjects;
}
```

The classes generated from this template are designed to be used only as base classes, hence the protected constructors and destructor. Note the use of the private member function `init` to avoid duplicating the statements in the two `Counted` constructors.

We can now modify the `Printer` class to use the `Counted` template:

```
class Printer: private Counted<Printer> {
public:
  // pseudo-constructors
  static Printer * makePrinter();
  static Printer * makePrinter(const Printer& rhs);

  ~Printer();

  void submitJob(const PrintJob& job);
  void reset();
  void performSelfTest();
  ...

  using Counted<Printer>::objectCount;      // see below
  using Counted<Printer>::TooManyObjects;   // see below
private:
  Printer();
  Printer(const Printer& rhs);
};
```

The fact that Printer uses the Counted template to keep track of how many Printer objects exist is, frankly, nobody's business but the author of Printer's. Such implementation details are best kept private, and that's why private inheritance is used here. The alternative would be to use public inheritance between Printer and Counted<Printer>, but then we'd be obliged to give the Counted classes a virtual destructor. (Otherwise we'd risk incorrect behavior if somebody deleted a Printer object through a Counted<Printer>* pointer.) As Item 24 makes clear, the presence of a virtual function in Counted would almost certainly affect the size and layout of objects of classes inheriting from Counted. We don't want to absorb that overhead, and the use of private inheritance lets us avoid it.

Quite properly, most of what Counted does is hidden from Printer's clients, but those clients might reasonably want to find out how many Printer objects exist. The Counted template offers the objectCount function to provide this information, but that function becomes private in Printer due to our use of private inheritance. To restore the public accessibility of that function, we employ a using declaration:

```
class Printer: private Counted<Printer> {
public:
  ...
  using Counted<Printer>::objectCount;  // make this function
                                        // public for clients
  ...                                   // of Printer
};
```

This is perfectly legitimate, but if your compilers don't yet support namespaces, they won't allow it. If they don't, you can use the older access declaration syntax:

```
class Printer: private Counted<Printer> {
public:
  ...
  Counted<Printer>::objectCount;        // make objectCount
                                        // public in Printer
  ...
};
```

This more traditional syntax has the same meaning as the using declaration, but it's deprecated. The class TooManyObjects is handled in the same fashion as objectCount, because clients of Printer must have access to TooManyObjects if they are to be able to catch exceptions of that type.

When Printer inherits from Counted<Printer>, it can forget about counting objects. The class can be written as if somebody else were doing the counting for it, because somebody else (Counted<Printer>) is. A Printer constructor now looks like this:

```
Printer::Printer()
{
  proceed with normal object construction;
}
```

What's interesting here is not what you see, it's what you don't. No checking of the number of objects to see if the limit is about to be exceeded, no incrementing the number of objects in existence once the constructor is done. All that is now handled by the Counted<Printer> constructors, and because Counted<Printer> is a base class of Printer, we know that a Counted<Printer> constructor will always be called before a Printer constructor. If too many objects are created, a Counted<Printer> constructor throws an exception, and the Printer constructor won't even be invoked. Nifty, huh?

Nifty or not, there's one loose end that demands to be tied, and that's the mandatory definitions of the statics inside Counted. It's easy enough to take care of numObjects — we just put this in Counted's implementation file:

```
template<class BeingCounted>                  // defines numObjects
int Counted<BeingCounted>::numObjects;        // and automatically
                                              // initializes it to 0
```

The situation with maxObjects is a bit trickier. To what value should we initialize this variable? If we want to allow up to 10 printers, we should initialize Counter<Printer>::maxObjects to 10. If, on the other hand, we want to allow up to 16 file descriptor objects, we should initialize Counted<FileDescriptor>::maxObjects to 16. What to do?

We take the easy way out: we do nothing. We provide no initialization at all for maxObjects. Instead, we require that *clients* of the class provide the appropriate initialization. The author of Printer must add this to an implementation file:

```
int Counted<Printer>::maxObjects = 10;
```

Similarly, the author of FileDescriptor must add this:

```
int Counted<FileDescriptor>::maxObjects = 16;
```

What will happen if these authors forget to provide a suitable definition for maxObjects? Simple: they'll get an error during linking, because maxObjects will be undefined. Provided we've adequately documented this requirement for clients of Counted, they can then say "Duh" to themselves and go back and add the requisite initialization.

Item 27: Requiring or prohibiting heap-based objects

Sometimes you want to arrange things so that objects of a particular type can commit suicide, i.e., can "delete this." Such an arrangement clearly requires that objects of that type be allocated on the heap. Other times you'll want to bask in the certainty that there can be no memory leaks for a particular class, because none of the objects could have been allocated on the heap. This might be the case if you are working on an embedded system, where memory leaks are especially troublesome and heap space is at a premium. Is it possible to produce code that requires or prohibits heap-based objects? Often it is, but it also turns out that the notion of being "on the heap" is more nebulous than you might think.

Requiring Heap-Based Objects

Let us begin with the prospect of limiting object creation to the heap. To enforce such a restriction, you've got to find a way to prevent clients from creating objects other than by calling new. This is easy to do. Non-heap objects are automatically constructed at their point of definition and automatically destructed at the end of their lifetime, so it suffices to simply make these implicit constructions and destructions illegal.

The straightforward way to make these calls illegal is to declare the constructors and the destructor private. This is overkill. There's no reason why they *both* need to be private. Better to make the destructor private and the constructors public. Then, in a process that should be familiar from Item 26, you can introduce a privileged pseudo-destructor function that has access to the real destructor. Clients then call the pseudo-destructor to destroy the objects they've created.

If, for example, we want to ensure that objects representing unlimited precision numbers are created only on the heap, we can do it like this:

```
class UPNumber {
public:
  UPNumber();
  UPNumber(int initValue);
  UPNumber(double initValue);
  UPNumber(const UPNumber& rhs);

  // pseudo-destructor
  void destroy() { delete this; }

  ...

private:
  ~UPNumber();
};
```

Clients would then program like this:

```
UPNumber n;                       // error! (legal here, but
                                  // illegal when n goes out
                                  // of scope)

UPNumber *p = new UPNumber;       // fine

...

delete p;                         // error! attempt to call
                                  // private destructor

p->destroy();                     // fine
```

An alternative is to declare all the constructors private. The drawback to that idea is that a class often has many constructors, and the class's author must remember to declare each of them private. This includes the copy constructor, and it may include a default constructor, too, if these functions would otherwise be generated by compilers; compiler-generated functions are always public. As a result, it's easier to declare only the destructor private, because a class can have only one of those.

Restricting access to a class's destructor or its constructors prevents the creation of non-heap objects, but, in a story that is told in Item 26, it also prevents both inheritance and containment:

```
class UPNumber { ... };           // declares dtor or ctors
                                  // private

class NonNegativeUPNumber:
  public UPNumber { ... };        // error! dtor or ctors
                                  // won't compile
```

```
class Asset {
private:
  UPNumber value;
  ...                            // error! dtor or ctors
                                 // won't compile
};
```

Neither of these difficulties is insurmountable. The inheritance problem can be solved by making UPNumber's destructor protected (while keeping its constructors public), and classes that need to contain objects of type UPNumber can be modified to contain *pointers* to UPNumber objects instead:

```
class UPNumber { ... };          // declares dtor protected

class NonNegativeUPNumber:
  public UPNumber { ... };        // now okay; derived
                                   // classes have access to
                                   // protected members

class Asset {
public:
  Asset(int initValue);
  ~Asset();
  ...

private:
  UPNumber *value;
};

Asset::Asset(int initValue)
: value(new UPNumber(initValue))   // fine
{ ... }

Asset::~Asset()
{ value->destroy(); }              // also fine
```

Determining Whether an Object is On The Heap

If we adopt this strategy, we must reexamine what it means to be "on the heap." Given the class definition sketched above, it's legal to define a non-heap NonNegativeUPNumber object:

```
NonNegativeUPNumber n;             // fine
```

Now, the UPNumber part of the NonNegativeUPNumber object n is not on the heap. Is that okay? The answer depends on the details of the class's design and implementation, but let us suppose it is *not* okay, that all UPNumber objects — even base class parts of more derived objects — *must* be on the heap. How can we enforce this restriction?

There is no easy way. It is not possible for a UPNumber constructor to determine whether it's being invoked as the base class part of a heap-based object. That is, there is no way for the UPNumber constructor to detect that the following contexts are different:

```
NonNegativeUPNumber *n1 =
    new NonNegativeUPNumber;           // on heap

NonNegativeUPNumber n2;                // not on heap
```

But perhaps you don't believe me. Perhaps you think you can play games with the interaction among the new operator, operator new and the constructor that the new operator calls (see Item 8). Perhaps you think you can outsmart them all by modifying UPNumber as follows:

```
class UPNumber {
public:
  // exception to throw if a non-heap object is created
  class HeapConstraintViolation {};

  static void * operator new(size_t size);

  UPNumber();
  ...

private:
  static bool onTheHeap;        // inside ctors, whether
                                // the object being
  ...                           // constructed is on heap

};
// obligatory definition of class static
bool UPNumber::onTheHeap = false;

void *UPNumber::operator new(size_t size)
{
  onTheHeap = true;
  return ::operator new(size);
}
UPNumber::UPNumber()
{
  if (!onTheHeap) {
    throw HeapConstraintViolation();
  }

  proceed with normal construction here;

  onTheHeap = false;            // clear flag for next obj.
}
```

There's nothing deep going on here. The idea is to take advantage of the fact that when an object is allocated on the heap, operator new is called to allocate the raw memory, then a constructor is called to initialize an object in that memory. In particular, operator new sets onTheHeap to true, and each constructor checks onTheHeap to see if the raw memory of the object being constructed was allocated by operator new. If not, an exception of type HeapConstraintViolation is thrown. Otherwise, construction proceeds as usual, and when construction is finished, onTheHeap is set to false, thus resetting the default value for the next object to be constructed.

This is a nice enough idea, but it won't work. Consider this potential client code:

```
UPNumber *numberArray = new UPNumber[100];
```

The first problem is that the memory for the array is allocated by operator new[], not operator new, but (provided your compilers support it) you can write the former function as easily as the latter. What is more troublesome is the fact that numberArray has 100 elements, so there will be 100 constructor calls. But there is only one call to allocate memory, so onTheHeap will be set to true for only the first of those 100 constructors. When the second constructor is called, an exception is thrown, and woe is you.

Even without arrays, this bit-setting business may fail. Consider this statement:

```
UPNumber *pn = new UPNumber(*new UPNumber);
```

Here we create two UPNumbers on the heap and make pn point to one of them; it's initialized with the value of the second one. This code has a resource leak, but let us ignore that in favor of an examination of what happens during execution of this expression:

```
new UPNumber(*new UPNumber)
```

This contains two calls to the new operator, hence two calls to operator new and two calls to UPNumber constructors (see Item 8). Programmers typically expect these function calls to be executed in this order,

1. Call operator new for first object
2. Call constructor for first object
3. Call operator new for second object
4. Call constructor for second object

but the language makes no guarantee that this is how it will be done. Some compilers generate the function calls in this order instead:

1. Call operator new for first object
2. Call operator new for second object
3. Call constructor for first object
4. Call constructor for second object

There is nothing wrong with compilers that generate this kind of code, but the set-a-bit-in-operator-new trick fails with such compilers. That's because the bit set in steps 1 and 2 is cleared in step 3, thus making the object constructed in step 4 think it's not on the heap, even though it is.

These difficulties don't invalidate the basic idea of having each constructor check to see if *this is on the heap. Rather, they indicate that checking a bit set inside operator new (or operator new[]) is not a reliable way to determine this information. What we need is a better way to figure it out.

If you're desperate enough, you might be tempted to descend into the realm of the unportable. For example, you might decide to take advantage of the fact that on many systems, a program's address space is organized as a linear sequence of addresses, with the program's stack growing down from the top of the address space and the heap rising up from the bottom:

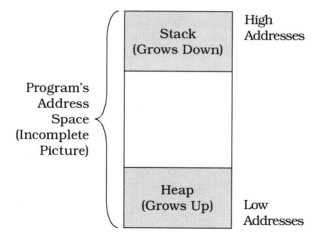

On systems that organize a program's memory in this way (many do, but many do not), you might think you could use the following function to determine whether a particular address is on the heap:

```
// incorrect attempt to determine whether an address
// is on the heap
bool onHeap(const void *address)
{
  char onTheStack;                    // local stack variable

  return address < &onTheStack;
}
```

The thinking behind this function is interesting. Inside onHeap, onTheStack is a local variable. As such, it is, well, it's on the stack.

When onHeap is called, its stack frame (i.e., its activation record) will be placed at the top of the program's stack, and because the stack grows down (toward lower addresses) in this architecture, the address of onTheStack must be less than the address of any other stack-based variable or object. If the parameter address is less than the location of onTheStack, it can't be on the stack, so it must be on the heap.

Such logic is fine, as far as it goes, but it doesn't go far enough. The fundamental problem is that there are *three* places where objects may be allocated, not two. Yes, the stack and the heap hold objects, but let us not forget about *static* objects. Static objects are those that are initialized only once during a program run. Static objects comprise not only those objects explicitly declared static, but also objects at global and namespace scope. Such objects have to go somewhere, and that somewhere is neither the stack nor the heap.

Where they go is system-dependent, but on many of the systems that have the stack and heap grow toward one another, they go below the heap. The earlier picture of memory organization, while telling the truth and nothing but the truth for many systems, failed to tell the whole truth for those systems. With static objects added to the picture, it looks like this:

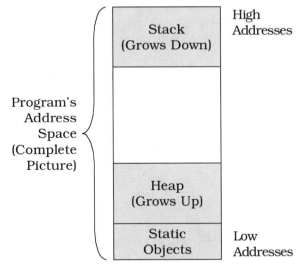

Suddenly it becomes clear why onHeap won't work, not even on systems where it's purported to: it fails to distinguish between heap objects and static objects:

```
void allocateSomeObjects()
{
  char *pc = new char;          // heap object: onHeap(pc)
                                // will return true
```

```
char c;                        // stack object: onHeap(&c)
                               // will return false

static char sc;                // static object: onHeap(&sc)
                               // will return true

...

}
```

Now, you may be desperate for a way to tell heap objects from stack objects, and in your desperation you may be willing to strike a deal with the portability Devil, but are you so desperate that you'll strike a deal that fails to guarantee you the right answers? Surely not, so I know you'll reject this seductive but unreliable compare-the-addresses trick.

The sad fact is there's not only no portable way to determine whether an object is on the heap, there isn't even a semi-portable way that works most of the time. If you absolutely, positively have to tell whether an address is on the heap, you're going to have to turn to unportable, implementation-dependent system calls, and that's that. As such, you're better off trying to redesign your software so you don't need to determine whether an object is on the heap in the first place.

If you find yourself obsessing over whether an object is on the heap, the likely cause is that you want to know if it's safe to invoke delete on it. Often such deletion will take the form of the infamous "delete this." Knowing whether it's safe to delete a pointer, however, is not the same as simply knowing whether that pointer points to something on the heap, because not all pointers to things on the heap can be safely deleted. Consider again an Asset object that contains a UPNumber object:

```
class Asset {
private:
  UPNumber value;
  ...

};

Asset *pa = new Asset;
```

Clearly *pa (including its member value) is on the heap. Equally clearly, it's not safe to invoke delete on a pointer to pa->value, because no such pointer was ever returned from new.

As luck would have it, it's easier to determine whether it's safe to delete a pointer than to determine whether a pointer points to something on the heap, because all we need to answer the former question is a collection of addresses that have been returned by operator new. Since we can write operator new ourselves, it's easy to construct such a collection. Here's how we might approach the problem:

```
void *operator new(size_t size)
{
  void *p = getMemory(size);        // call some function to
                                    // allocate memory and
                                    // handle out-of-memory
                                    // conditions

  add p to the collection of allocated addresses;

  return p;

}
void operator delete(void *ptr)
{
  releaseMemory(ptr);               // return memory to
                                    // free store

  remove ptr from the collection of allocated addresses;
}
bool isSafeToDelete(const void *address)
{
  return whether address is in collection of
  allocated addresses;
}
```

This is about as simple as it gets. operator new adds entries to a collection of allocated addresses, operator delete removes entries, and isSafeToDelete does a lookup in the collection to see if a particular address is there. If the operator new and operator delete functions are at global scope, this should work for all types, even the built-ins.

In practice, three things are likely to dampen our enthusiasm for this design. The first is our extreme reluctance to define anything at global scope, especially functions with predefined meanings like operator new and operator delete. Knowing as we do that there is but one global scope and but a single version of operator new and operator delete with the "normal" signatures (i.e., sets of parameter types) within that scope, the last thing we want to do is seize those function signatures for ourselves. Doing so would render our software incompatible with any other software that also implements global versions of operator new and operator delete (such as many object-oriented database systems).

Our second consideration is one of efficiency: why burden all heap allocations with the bookkeeping overhead necessary to keep track of returned addresses if we don't need to?

Our final concern is pedestrian, but important. It turns out to be essentially impossible to implement isSafeToDelete so that it always works. The difficulty has to do with the fact that objects with multiple or virtual base classes have multiple addresses, so there's no guarantee that the address passed to isSafeToDelete is the same as the one returned from operator new, even if the object in question was allocated on the heap. For details, see Items 24 and 31.

What we'd like is the functionality provided by these functions without the concomitant pollution of the global namespace, the mandatory overhead, and the correctness problems. Fortunately, C++ gives us exactly what we need in the form of an abstract mixin base class.

An abstract base class is a base class that can't be instantiated, i.e., one with at least one pure virtual function. A mixin ("mix in") class is one that provides a single well-defined capability and is designed to be compatible with any other capabilities an inheriting class might provide. Such classes are nearly always abstract. We can therefore come up with an abstract mixin base class that offers derived classes the ability to determine whether a pointer was allocated from operator new. Here's such a class:

```cpp
class HeapTracked {              // mixin class; keeps track of
public:                         // ptrs returned from op. new

  class MissingAddress{};       // exception class; see below

  virtual ~HeapTracked() = 0;

  static void *operator new(size_t size);
  static void operator delete(void *ptr);

  bool isOnHeap() const;

private:
  typedef const void* RawAddress;
  static list<RawAddress> addresses;
};
```

This class uses the list data structure that's part of the standard C++ library (see Item 35) to keep track of all pointers returned from operator new. That function allocates memory and adds entries to the list; operator delete deallocates memory and removes entries from the list; and isOnHeap returns whether an object's address is in the list.

Implementation of the HeapTracked class is simple, because the global operator new and operator delete functions are called to perform the real memory allocation and deallocation, and the list class has functions to make insertion, removal, and lookup single-statement operations. Here's the full implementation of HeapTracked:

```cpp
// mandatory definition of static class member
list<RawAddress> HeapTracked::addresses;
```

```
// HeapTracked's destructor is pure virtual to make the
// class abstract. The destructor must still be
// defined, however, so we provide this empty definition.
HeapTracked::~HeapTracked() {}


void * HeapTracked::operator new(size_t size)
{
  void *memPtr = ::operator new(size);  // get the memory

  addresses.push_front(memPtr);         // put its address at
                                        // the front of the list

  return memPtr;
}

void HeapTracked::operator delete(void *ptr)
{
  // get an "iterator" that identifies the list
  // entry containing ptr; see Item 35 for details
  list<RawAddress>::iterator it =
    find(addresses.begin(), addresses.end(), ptr);

  if (it != addresses.end()) {    // if an entry was found
    addresses.erase(it);          // remove the entry
    ::operator delete(ptr);       // deallocate the memory
  } else {                        // otherwise
    throw MissingAddress();       // ptr wasn't allocated by
  }                               // op. new, so throw an
}                                 // exception

bool HeapTracked::isOnHeap() const
{
  // get a pointer to the beginning of the memory
  // occupied by ptr; see below for details
  const void *rawAddress = dynamic_cast<const void*>(this);

  // look up the pointer in the list of addresses
  // returned by operator new
  list<RawAddress>::iterator it =
    find(addresses.begin(), addresses.end(), rawAddress);

  return it != addresses.end();  // return whether it was
}                                // found
```

This code is straightforward, though it may not look that way if you are
unfamiliar with the list class and the other components of the Standard Template Library. Item 35 explains everything, but the comments
in the code above should be sufficient to explain what's happening in
this example.

The only other thing that may confound you is this statement (in
isOnHeap):

```
const void *rawAddress = dynamic_cast<const void*>(this);
```

I mentioned earlier that writing the global function isSafeToDelete is complicated by the fact that objects with multiple or virtual base classes have several addresses. That problem plagues us in isOnHeap, too, but because isOnHeap applies only to HeapTracked objects, we can exploit a special feature of the dynamic_cast operator (see Item 2) to eliminate the problem. Simply put, dynamic_casting a pointer to void* (or const void* or volatile void* or, for those who can't get enough modifiers in their usual diet, const volatile void*) yields a pointer to the beginning of the memory for the object pointed to by the pointer. But dynamic_cast is applicable only to pointers to objects that have at least one virtual function. Our ill-fated isSafeToDelete function had to work with *any* type of pointer, so dynamic_cast wouldn't help it. isOnHeap is more selective (it tests only pointers to HeapTracked objects), so dynamic_casting this to const void* gives us a pointer to the beginning of the memory for the current object. That's the pointer that HeapTracked::operator new must have returned if the memory for the current object was allocated by Heap-Tracked::operator new in the first place. Provided your compilers support the dynamic_cast operator, this technique is completely portable.

Given this class, even BASIC programmers could add to a class the ability to track pointers to heap allocations. All they'd need to do is have the class inherit from HeapTracked. If, for example, we want to be able to determine whether a pointer to an Asset object points to a heap-based object, we'd modify Asset's class definition to specify HeapTracked as a base class:

```
class Asset: public HeapTracked {
private:
  UPNumber value;
  ...

};
```

We could then query Asset* pointers as follows:

```
void inventoryAsset(const Asset *ap)
{
  if (ap->isOnHeap()) {
    ap is a heap-based asset — inventory it as such;
  }
  else {
    ap is a non-heap-based asset — record it that way;
  }
}
```

A disadvantage of a mixin class like HeapTracked is that it can't be used with the built-in types, because types like int and char can't inherit from anything. Still, the most common reason for wanting to use a class like HeapTracked is to determine whether it's okay to "delete this," and you'll never want to do that with a built-in type because such types have no this pointer.

Prohibiting Heap-Based Objects

Thus ends our examination of determining whether an object is on the heap. At the opposite end of the spectrum is *preventing* objects from being allocated on the heap. Here the outlook is a bit brighter. There are, as usual, three cases: objects that are directly instantiated, objects instantiated as base class parts of derived class objects, and objects embedded inside other objects. We'll consider each in turn.

Preventing clients from directly instantiating objects on the heap is easy, because such objects are always created by calls to new and you can make it impossible for clients to call new. Now, you can't affect the availability of the new operator (that's built into the language), but you can take advantage of the fact that the new operator always calls operator new (see Item 8), and that function is one you can declare yourself. In particular, it is one you can declare private. If, for example, you want to keep clients from creating UPNumber objects on the heap, you could do it this way:

```
class UPNumber {
private:
  static void *operator new(size_t size);
  static void operator delete(void *ptr);
  ...
};
```

Clients can now do only what they're supposed to be able to do:

```
UPNumber n1;                  // okay

static UPNumber n2;           // also okay

UPNumber *p = new UPNumber;   // error! attempt to call
                              // private operator new
```

It suffices to declare operator new private, but it looks strange to have operator new be private and operator delete be public, so unless there's a compelling reason to split up the pair, it's best to declare them in the same part of a class. If you'd like to prohibit heap-based arrays of UPNumber objects, too, you could declare operator new[] and operator delete[] (see Item 8) private as well.

Interestingly, declaring operator new private often also prevents UP-Number objects from being instantiated as base class parts of heap-based derived class objects. That's because operator new and operator delete are inherited, so if these functions aren't declared public in a derived class, that class inherits the private versions declared in its base(s):

```
class UPNumber { ... };              // as above

class NonNegativeUPNumber:           // assume this class
  public UPNumber {                  // declares no operator new
  ...
};

NonNegativeUPNumber n1;              // okay

static NonNegativeUPNumber n2;       // also okay

NonNegativeUPNumber *p =             // error! attempt to call
  new NonNegativeUPNumber;           // private operator new
```

If the derived class declares an operator new of its own, that function will be called when allocating derived class objects on the heap, and a different way will have to be found to prevent UPNumber base class parts from winding up there. Similarly, the fact that UPNumber's operator new is private has no effect on attempts to allocate objects containing UPNumber objects as members:

```
class Asset {
public:
  Asset(int initValue);
  ...

private:
  UPNumber value;
};

Asset *pa = new Asset(100);         // fine, calls
                                    // Asset::operator new or
                                    // ::operator new, not
                                    // UPNumber::operator new
```

For all practical purposes, this brings us back to where we were when we wanted to throw an exception in the UPNumber constructors if a UP-Number object was being constructed in memory that wasn't on the heap. This time, of course, we want to throw an exception if the object in question *is* on the heap. Just as there is no portable way to determine if an address is on the heap, however, there is no portable way to determine that it is not on the heap, so we're out of luck. This should be no surprise. After all, if we could tell when an address *is* on the heap, we could surely tell when an address is *not* on the heap. But we can't, so we can't. Oh well.

Item 28: Smart pointers

Smart pointers are objects that are designed to look, act, and feel like built-in pointers, but to offer greater functionality. They have a variety of applications, including resource management (see Items 9, 10, 25, and 31) and the automation of repetitive coding tasks (see Items 17 and 29).

When you use smart pointers in place of C++'s built-in pointers (i.e., *dumb* pointers), you gain control over the following aspects of pointer behavior:

- **Construction and destruction**. You determine what happens when a smart pointer is created and destroyed. It is common to give smart pointers a default value of 0 to avoid the headaches associated with uninitialized pointers. Some smart pointers are made responsible for deleting the object they point to when the last smart pointer pointing to the object is destroyed. This can go a long way toward eliminating resource leaks.

- **Copying and assignment**. You control what happens when a smart pointer is copied or is involved in an assignment. For some smart pointer types, the desired behavior is to automatically copy or make an assignment to what is pointed to, i.e., to perform a deep copy. For others, only the pointer itself should be copied or assigned. For still others, these operations should not be allowed at all. Regardless of what behavior you consider "right," the use of smart pointers lets you call the shots.

- **Dereferencing**. What should happen when a client refers to the object pointed to by a smart pointer? You get to decide. You could, for example, use smart pointers to help implement the lazy fetching strategy outlined in Item 17.

Smart pointers are generated from templates because, like built-in pointers, they must be strongly typed; the template parameter specifies the type of object pointed to. Most smart pointer templates look something like this:

```
template<class T>                    // template for smart
class SmartPtr {                     // pointer objects
public:
  SmartPtr(T* realPtr = 0);          // create a smart ptr to an
                                     // obj given a dumb ptr to
                                     // it; uninitialized ptrs
                                     // default to 0 (null)

  SmartPtr(const SmartPtr& rhs);     // copy a smart ptr

  ~SmartPtr();                       // destroy a smart ptr

  // make an assignment to a smart ptr
  SmartPtr& operator=(const SmartPtr& rhs);

  T* operator->() const;             // dereference a smart ptr
                                     // to get at a member of
                                     // what it points to

  T& operator*() const;              // defererence a smart ptr
private:
  T *pointee;                        // what the smart ptr
};                                   // points to
```

The copy constructor and assignment operator are both shown public
here. For smart pointer classes where copying and assignment are not
allowed, they would typically be declared private. The two dereferencing operators are declared const, because dereferencing a pointer
doesn't modify it (though it may lead to modification of what the
pointer points to). Finally, each smart pointer-to-T object is implemented by containing a dumb pointer-to-T within it. It is this dumb
pointer that does the actual pointing.

Before going into the details of smart pointer implementation, it's
worth seeing how clients might use smart pointers. Consider a distributed system in which some objects are local and some are remote. Access to local objects is generally simpler and faster than access to
remote objects, because remote access may require remote procedure
calls or some other way of communicating with a distant machine.

For clients writing application code, the need to handle local and remote objects differently is a nuisance. It is more convenient to have all
objects appear to be located in the same place. Smart pointers allow a
library to offer this illusion:

```
template<class T>                    // template for smart ptrs
class DBPtr {                        // to objects in a
public:                              // distributed DB

  DBPtr(T *realPtr = 0);             // create a smart ptr to a
                                     // DB object given a local
                                     // dumb pointer to it
```

```
    DBPtr(DataBaseID id);           // create a smart ptr to a
                                    // DB object given its
                                    // unique DB identifier

    ...                             // other smart ptr
};                                  // functions as above

class Tuple {                       // class for database
public:                             // tuples
    ...
    void displayEditDialog();       // present a graphical
                                    // dialog box allowing a
                                    // user to edit the tuple

    bool isValid() const;           // return whether *this
};                                  // passes validity check

// template class for making log entries whenever a T
// object is modified; see below for details
template<class T>
class LogEntry {
public:
    LogEntry(const T& objectToBeModified);
    ~LogEntry();
};

void editTuple(DBPtr<Tuple>& pt)
{
    LogEntry<Tuple> entry(*pt);    // make log entry for this
                                   // editing operation; see
                                   // below for details

    // repeatedly display edit dialog until valid values
    // are provided
    do {
        pt->displayEditDialog();
    } while (pt->isValid() == false);
}
```

The tuple to be edited inside editTuple may be physically located on a remote machine, but the programmer writing editTuple need not be concerned with such matters; the smart pointer class hides that aspect of the system. As far as the programmer is concerned, all tuples are accessed through objects that, except for how they're declared, act just like run-of-the-mill built-in pointers.

Notice the use of a LogEntry object in editTuple. A more conventional design would have been to surround the call to displayEditDialog with calls to begin and end the log entry. In the approach shown here, the LogEntry's constructor begins the log entry and its destructor ends the log entry. As Item 9 explains, using an object to begin and end logging is more robust in the face of exceptions than explicitly calling functions, so you should accustom yourself to using classes like LogEntry. Besides, it's easier to create a single LogEntry object than to add separate calls to start and stop an entry.

As you can see, using a smart pointer isn't much different from using the dumb pointer it replaces. That's testimony to the effectiveness of encapsulation. Clients of smart pointers are *supposed* to be able to treat them as dumb pointers. As we shall see, sometimes the substitution is more transparent than others.

Construction, Assignment, and Destruction of Smart Pointers

Construction of a smart pointer is usually straightforward: locate an object to point to (typically by using the smart pointer's constructor arguments), then make the smart pointer's internal dumb pointer point there. If no object can be located, set the internal pointer to 0 or signal an error (possibly by throwing an exception).

Implementing a smart pointer's copy constructor, assignment operator(s) and destructor is complicated somewhat by the issue of *ownership*. If a smart pointer *owns* the object it points to, it is responsible for deleting that object when it (the smart pointer) is destroyed. This assumes the object pointed to by the smart pointer is dynamically allocated. Such an assumption is common when working with smart pointers. (For ideas on how to make sure the assumption is true, see Item 27.)

Consider the auto_ptr template from the standard C++ library. As Item 9 explains, an auto_ptr object is a smart pointer that points to a heap-based object until it (the auto_ptr) is destroyed. When that happens, the auto_ptr's destructor deletes the pointed-to object. The auto_ptr template might be implemented like this:

```
template<class T>
class auto_ptr {
public:
  auto_ptr(T *ptr = 0): pointee(ptr) {}
  ~auto_ptr() { delete pointee; }
  ...

private:
  T *pointee;
};
```

This works fine provided only one auto_ptr owns an object. But what should happen when an auto_ptr is copied or assigned?

```
auto_ptr<TreeNode> ptn1(new TreeNode);

auto_ptr<TreeNode> ptn2 = ptn1;     // call to copy ctor;
                                    // what should happen?
```

```
auto_ptr<TreeNode> ptn3;

ptn3 = ptn2;                        // call to operator=;
                                    // what should happen?
```

If we just copied the internal dumb pointer, we'd end up with two auto_ptrs pointing to the same object. This would lead to grief, because each auto_ptr would delete what it pointed to when the auto_ptr was destroyed. That would mean we'd delete an object more than once. The results of such double-deletes are undefined (and are frequently disastrous).

An alternative would be to create a new copy of what was pointed to by calling new. That would guarantee we didn't have too many auto_ptrs pointing to a single object, but it might engender an unacceptable performance hit for the creation (and later destruction) of the new object. Furthermore, we wouldn't necessarily know what type of object to create, because an auto_ptr<T> object need not point to an object of type T; it might point to an object of a type *derived* from T. Virtual constructors (see Item 25) can help solve this problem, but it seems inappropriate to require their use in a lightweight, general-purpose class like auto_ptr.

The problems would vanish if auto_ptr prohibited copying and assignment, but a more flexible solution was adopted for the auto_ptr classes: object ownership is *transferred* when an auto_ptr is copied or assigned:

```
template<class T>
class auto_ptr {
public:
  ...

  auto_ptr(auto_ptr<T>& rhs);         // copy constructor

  auto_ptr<T>&                        // assignment
  operator=(auto_ptr<T>& rhs);        // operator

  ...
};
template<class T>
auto_ptr<T>::auto_ptr(auto_ptr<T>& rhs)
{
  pointee = rhs.pointee;              // transfer ownership of
                                      // *pointee to *this

  rhs.pointee = 0;                    // rhs no longer owns
}                                     // anything
```

```
template<class T>
auto_ptr<T>& auto_ptr<T>::operator=(auto_ptr<T>& rhs)
{
  if (this == &rhs)              // do nothing if this
    return *this;                // object is being assigned
                                 // to itself

  delete pointee;                // delete currently owned
                                 // object

  pointee = rhs.pointee;         // transfer ownership of
  rhs.pointee = 0;               // *pointee from rhs to *this

  return *this;
}
```

Notice that the assignment operator must delete the object it owns before assuming ownership of a new object. If it failed to do this, the object would never be deleted. Remember, nobody but the auto_ptr object owns the object the auto_ptr points to.

Because object ownership is transferred when auto_ptr's copy constructor is called, passing auto_ptrs by value is often a *very* bad idea. Here's why:

```
// this function will often lead to disaster
void printTreeNode(ostream& s, auto_ptr<TreeNode> p)
{ s << *p; }

int main()
{
  auto_ptr<TreeNode> ptn(new TreeNode);

  ...

  printTreeNode(cout, ptn);      // pass auto_ptr by value

  ...

}
```

When printTreeNode's parameter p is initialized (by calling auto_ptr's copy constructor), ownership of the object pointed to by ptn is transferred to p. When printTreeNode finishes executing, p goes out of scope and its destructor deletes what it points to (which is what ptn used to point to). ptn, however, no longer points to anything (its underlying dumb pointer is null), so just about any attempt to use it after the call to printTreeNode will yield undefined behavior. Passing auto_ptrs by value, then, is something to be done only if you're *sure* you want to transfer ownership of an object to a (transient) function parameter. Only rarely will you want to do this.

This doesn't mean you can't pass auto_ptrs as parameters, it just means that pass-by-value is not the way to do it. Pass-by-reference-to-const is:

```
// this function behaves much more intuitively
void printTreeNode(ostream& s,
                   const auto_ptr<TreeNode>& p)
{ s << *p; }
```

In this function, p is a reference, not an object, so no constructor is called to initialize p. When ptn is passed to this version of print-TreeNode, it retains ownership of the object it points to, and ptn can safely be used after the call to printTreeNode. Thus, passing auto_ptrs by reference-to-const avoids the hazards arising from pass-by-value.

The notion of transferring ownership from one smart pointer to another during copying and assignment is interesting, but you may have been at least as interested in the unconventional declarations of the copy constructor and assignment operator. These functions normally take const parameters, but above they do not. In fact, the code above *changes* these parameters during the copy or the assignment. In other words, auto_ptr objects are modified if they are copied or are the source of an assignment!

Yes, that's exactly what's happening. Isn't it nice that C++ is flexible enough to let you do this? If the language required that copy constructors and assignment operators take const parameters, you'd probably have to cast away the parameters' constness or play other games to implement ownership transferral. Instead, you get to say exactly what you want to say: when an object is copied or is the source of an assignment, that object is changed. This may not seem intuitive, but it's simple, direct, and, in this case, accurate.

If you find this examination of auto_ptr member functions interesting, you may wish to see a complete implementation. You'll find one on pages 291-294, where you'll also see that the auto_ptr template in the standard C++ library has copy constructors and assignment operators that are more flexible than those described here. In the standard auto_ptr template, those functions are member function *templates*, not just member functions. (Member function templates are described later in this Item.)

A smart pointer's destructor often looks like this:

```
template<class T>
SmartPtr<T>::~SmartPtr()
{
  if (*this owns *pointee) {
    delete pointee;
  }
}
```

Sometimes there is no need for the test. An `auto_ptr` always owns what it points to, for example. At other times the test is a bit more complicated. A smart pointer that employs reference counting (see Item 29) must adjust a reference count before determining whether it has the right to delete what it points to.

Implementing the Dereferencing Operators

Let us now turn our attention to the very heart of smart pointers, the `operator*` and `operator->` functions. The former returns the object pointed to. Conceptually, this is simple:

```
template<class T>
T& SmartPtr<T>::operator*() const
{
  perform "smart pointer" processing;

  return *pointee;
}
```

First the function does whatever processing is needed to initialize or otherwise make `pointee` valid. For example, if lazy fetching is being used (see Item 17), the function may have to conjure up a new object for `pointee` to point to. Once `pointee` is valid, the `operator*` function just returns a reference to the pointed-to object.

Note that the return type is a *reference*. It would be disastrous to return an *object* instead, though compilers will let you do it. Bear in mind that `pointee` need not point to an object of type T; it may point to an object of a class *derived* from T. If that is the case and your operator* function returns a T object instead of a reference to the actual derived class object, your function will return an object of the wrong type! Virtual functions invoked on the object returned from your star-crossed `operator*` will not invoke the function corresponding to the dynamic type of the pointed-to object. In essence, your smart pointer will not properly support virtual functions, and how smart is a pointer like that? Besides, returning a reference is more efficient anyway, because there is no need to construct a temporary object (see Item 19). This is one of those happy occasions when correctness and efficiency go hand in hand.

If you're the kind who likes to worry, you may wonder what you should do if somebody invokes operator* on a null smart pointer, i.e., one whose embedded dumb pointer is null. Relax. You can do anything you want. The result of dereferencing a null pointer is undefined, so there is no "wrong" behavior. Wanna throw an exception? Go ahead, throw it. Wanna call abort (possibly by having an assert call fail)? Fine, call it. Wanna walk through memory setting every byte to your birth date modulo 256? That's okay, too. It's not nice, but as far as the language is concerned, you are completely unfettered.

The story with operator-> is similar to that for operator*, but before examining operator->, let us remind ourselves of the unusual meaning of a call to this function. Consider again the editTuple function that uses a smart pointer-to-Tuple object:

```
void editTuple(DBPtr<Tuple> pt)
{
  LogEntry<Tuple> entry(*pt);

  do {
    pt->displayEditDialog();
  } while (pt->isValid() == false);
}
```

The statement

```
pt->displayEditDialog();
```

is interpreted by compilers as:

```
(pt.operator->())->displayEditDialog();
```

That means that whatever operator-> returns, it must be legal to apply the member-selection operator (->) to it. There are thus only two things operator-> can return: a dumb pointer to an object or another smart pointer object. Most of the time, you'll want to return an ordinary dumb pointer. In those cases, you implement operator-> as follows:

```
template<class T>
T* SmartPtr<T>::operator->() const
{
  perform "smart pointer" processing;

  return pointee;
}
```

This will work fine. Because this function returns a pointer, virtual function calls via operator-> will behave the way they're supposed to.

For many applications, this is all you need to know about smart pointers. The reference-counting code of Item 29, for example, draws on no more functionality than we've discussed here. If you want to push your smart pointers further, however, you must know more about dumb pointer behavior and how smart pointers can and cannot emulate it. If your motto is "Most people stop at the Z — but not me!", the material that follows is for you.

Testing Smart Pointers for Nullness

With the functions we have discussed so far, we can create, destroy, copy, assign, and dereference smart pointers. One of the things we cannot do, however, is find out if a smart pointer is null:

```
SmartPtr<TreeNode> ptn;

...

if (ptn == 0) ...              // error!

if (ptn) ...                   // error!

if (!ptn) ...                  // error!
```

This is a serious limitation.

It would be easy to add an isNull member function to our smart pointer classes, but that wouldn't address the problem that smart pointers don't act like dumb pointers when testing for nullness. A different approach is to provide an implicit conversion operator that allows the tests above to compile. The conversion traditionally employed for this purpose is to void*:

```
template<class T>
class SmartPtr {
public:
  ...
  operator void*();            // returns 0 if the smart
  ...                          // ptr is null, nonzero
};                             // otherwise

SmartPtr<TreeNode> ptn;

...

if (ptn == 0) ...              // now fine

if (ptn) ...                   // also fine

if (!ptn) ...                  // fine
```

This is similar to a conversion provided by the iostream classes, and it explains why it's possible to write code like this:

```
ifstream inputFile("datafile.dat");
```

```
if (inputFile) ...              // test to see if inputFile
                                // was successfully
                                // opened
```

Like all type conversion functions, this one has the drawback of letting function calls succeed that most programmers would expect to fail (see Item 5). In particular, it allows comparisons of smart pointers of completely different types:

```
SmartPtr<Apple> pa;
SmartPtr<Orange> po;

...

if (pa == po) ...               // this compiles!
```

Even if there is no operator== taking a SmartPtr<Apple> and a SmartPtr<Orange>, this compiles, because both smart pointers can be implicitly converted into void* pointers, and there is a built-in comparison function for built-in pointers. This kind of behavior makes implicit conversion functions dangerous. (Again, see Item 5, and keep seeing it over and over until you can see it in the dark.)

There are variations on the conversion-to-void* motif. Some designers advocate conversion to const void*, others embrace conversion to bool. Neither of these variations eliminates the problem of allowing mixed-type comparisons.

There is a middle ground that allows you to offer a reasonable syntactic form for testing for nullness while minimizing the chances of accidentally comparing smart pointers of different types. It is to overload operator! for your smart pointer classes so that operator! returns true if and only if the smart pointer on which it's invoked is null:

```
template<class T>
class SmartPtr {
public:
  ...
  bool operator!() const;       // returns true iff the
  ...                           // smart ptr is null

};
```

This lets your clients program like this,

```
SmartPtr<TreeNode> ptn;

...

if (!ptn) {                     // fine
  ...                           // ptn is null
}
else {
  ...                           // ptn is not null
}
```

but not like this:

```
if (ptn == 0) ...               // still an error

if (ptn) ...                    // also an error
```

The only risk for mixed-type comparisons is statements such as these:

```
SmartPtr<Apple> pa;
SmartPtr<Orange> po;

...

if (!pa == !po) ...             // alas, this compiles
```

Fortunately, programmers don't write code like this very often. Interestingly, iostream library implementations provide an operator! in addition to the implicit conversion to void*, but these two functions typically test for slightly different stream states. (In the C++ library standard (see Item 35), the implicit conversion to void* has been replaced by an implicit conversion to bool, and operator bool always returns the negation of operator!.)

Converting Smart Pointers to Dumb Pointers

Sometimes you'd like to add smart pointers to an application or library that already uses dumb pointers. For example, your distributed database system may not originally have been distributed, so you may have some old library functions that aren't designed to use smart pointers:

```
class Tuple { ... };            // as before

void normalize(Tuple *pt);      // put *pt into canonical
                                // form; note use of dumb
                                // pointer
```

Consider what will happen if you try to call normalize with a smart pointer-to-Tuple:

```
DBPtr<Tuple> pt;

...

normalize(pt);                  // error!
```

The call will fail to compile, because there is no way to convert a DBPtr<Tuple> to a Tuple*. You can make it work by doing this,

```
normalize(&*pt);                    // gross, but legal
```

but I hope you'll agree this is repugnant.

The call can be made to succeed by adding to the smart pointer-to-T template an implicit conversion operator to a dumb pointer-to-T:

```
template<class T>                   // as before
class DBPtr {
public:
  ...
  operator T*() { return pointee; }
  ...
};

DBPtr<Tuple> pt;

...

normalize(pt);                      // this now works
```

Addition of this function also eliminates the problem of testing for nullness:

```
if (pt == 0) ...                    // fine, converts pt to a
                                    // Tuple*

if (pt) ...                         // ditto

if (!pt) ...                        // ditto (reprise)
```

However, there is a dark side to such conversion functions. (There almost always is. Have you been seeing Item 5?) They make it easy for clients to program directly with dumb pointers, thus bypassing the smarts your pointer-like objects are designed to provide:

```
void processTuple(DBPtr<Tuple>& pt)
{
  Tuple *rawTuplePtr = pt;          // converts DBPtr<Tuple> to
                                    // Tuple*

  use rawTuplePtr to modify the tuple;
}
```

Usually, the "smart" behavior provided by a smart pointer is an essential component of your design, so allowing clients to use dumb pointers typically leads to disaster. For example, if DBPtr implements the reference-counting strategy of Item 29, allowing clients to manipulate dumb pointers directly will almost certainly lead to bookkeeping errors that corrupt the reference-counting data structures.

Even if you provide an implicit conversion operator to go from a smart pointer to the dumb pointer it's built on, your smart pointer will never be truly interchangeable with the dumb pointer. That's because the conversion from a smart pointer to a dumb pointer is a user-defined conversion, and compilers are forbidden from applying more than one such conversion at a time. For example, suppose you have a class representing all the clients who have accessed a particular tuple:

```
class TupleAccessors {
public:
  TupleAccessors(const Tuple *pt);   // pt identifies the
  ...                                // tuple whose accessors
};                                   // we care about
```

As usual, TupleAccessors' single-argument constructor also acts as a type-conversion operator from Tuple* to TupleAccessors (see Item 5). Now consider a function for merging the information in two Tuple-Accessors objects:

```
TupleAccessors merge(const TupleAccessors& ta1,
                     const TupleAccessors& ta2);
```

Because a Tuple* may be implicitly converted to a TupleAccessors, calling merge with two dumb Tuple* pointers is fine:

```
Tuple *pt1, *pt2;

...

merge(pt1, pt2);        // fine, both pointers are converted
                        // to TupleAccessors objects
```

The corresponding call with smart DBPtr<Tuple> pointers, however, fails to compile:

```
DBPtr<Tuple> pt1, pt2;

...

merge(pt1, pt2);        // error! No way to convert pt1 and
                        // pt2 to TupleAccessors objects
```

That's because a conversion from DBPtr<Tuple> to TupleAccessors calls for *two* user-defined conversions (one from DBPtr<Tuple> to Tuple* and one from Tuple* to TupleAccessors), and such sequences of conversions are prohibited by the language.

Smart pointer classes that provide an implicit conversion to a dumb pointer open the door to a particularly nasty bug. Consider this code:

```
DBPtr<Tuple> pt = new Tuple;

...

delete pt;
```

This should not compile. After all, pt is not a pointer, it's an object, and you can't delete an object. Only pointers can be deleted, right?

Right. But remember from Item 5 that compilers use implicit type conversions to make function calls succeed whenever they can, and recall from Item 8 that use of the delete operator leads to calls to a destructor and to operator delete, both of which are functions. Compilers want these function calls to succeed, so in the delete statement above, they implicitly convert pt to a Tuple*, then they delete that. This will almost certainly break your program.

If pt owns the object it points to, that object is now deleted twice, once at the point where delete is called, a second time when pt's destructor is invoked. If pt doesn't own the object, somebody else does. That somebody may be the person who deleted pt, in which case all is well. If, however, the owner of the object pointed to by pt is not the person who deleted pt, we can expect the rightful owner to delete that object again later. The first and last of these scenarios leads to an object being deleted twice, and deleting an object more than once yields undefined behavior.

This bug is especially pernicious because the whole idea behind smart pointers is to make them look and feel as much like dumb pointers as possible. The closer you get to this ideal, the more likely your clients are to forget they are using smart pointers. If they do, who can blame them if they continue to think that in order to avoid resource leaks, they must call delete if they called new?

The bottom line is simple: don't provide implicit conversion operators to dumb pointers unless there is a compelling reason to do so.

Smart Pointers and Inheritance-Based Type Conversions

Suppose we have a public inheritance hierarchy modeling consumer products for storing music:

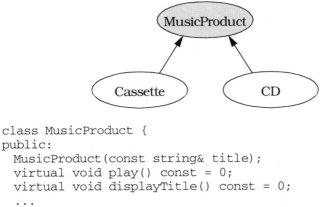

```
class MusicProduct {
public:
  MusicProduct(const string& title);
  virtual void play() const = 0;
  virtual void displayTitle() const = 0;
  ...
};
```

```
class Cassette: public MusicProduct {
public:
  Cassette(const string& title);
  virtual void play() const;
  virtual void displayTitle() const;
  ...
};

class CD: public MusicProduct {
public:
  CD(const string& title);
  virtual void play() const;
  virtual void displayTitle() const;
  ...
};
```

Further suppose we have a function that, given a MusicProduct object, displays the title of the product and then plays it:

```
void displayAndPlay(const MusicProduct* pmp, int numTimes)
{
  for (int i = 1; i <= numTimes; ++i) {
    pmp->displayTitle();
    pmp->play();
  }
}
```

Such a function might be used like this:

```
Cassette *funMusic = new Cassette("Alapalooza");
CD *nightmareMusic = new CD("Disco Hits of the 70s");

displayAndPlay(funMusic, 10);
displayAndPlay(nightmareMusic, 0);
```

There are no surprises here, but look what happens if we replace the dumb pointers with their allegedly smart counterparts:

```
void displayAndPlay(const SmartPtr<MusicProduct>& pmp,
                    int numTimes);

SmartPtr<Cassette> funMusic(new Cassette("Alapalooza"));
SmartPtr<CD> nightmareMusic(new CD("Disco Hits of the 70s"));

displayAndPlay(funMusic, 10);           // error!
displayAndPlay(nightmareMusic, 0);      // error!
```

If smart pointers are so brainy, why won't these compile?

They won't compile because there is no conversion from a SmartPtr<CD> or a SmartPtr<Cassette> to a SmartPtr<MusicProduct>. As far as compilers are concerned, these are three separate classes — they have no relationship to one another. Why should compilers think otherwise? After all, it's not like SmartPtr<CD> or SmartPtr<Cassette> inherits from SmartPtr<MusicProduct>. With no inheritance relationship between these classes, we can hardly expect compilers to run around converting objects of one type to objects of other types.

Fortunately, there is a way to get around this limitation, and the idea (if not the practice) is simple: give each smart pointer class an implicit type conversion operator (see Item 5) for each smart pointer class to which it should be implicitly convertible. For example, in the music hierarchy, you'd add an `operator SmartPtr<MusicProduct>` to the smart pointer classes for `Cassette` and `CD`:

```
class SmartPtr<Cassette> {
public:
  operator SmartPtr<MusicProduct>()
  { return SmartPtr<MusicProduct>(pointee); }

  ...

private:
  Cassette *pointee;
};
class SmartPtr<CD> {
public:
  operator SmartPtr<MusicProduct>()
  { return SmartPtr<MusicProduct>(pointee); }

  ...

private:
  CD *pointee;
};
```

The drawbacks to this approach are twofold. First, you must manually specialize the `SmartPtr` class instantiations so you can add the necessary implicit type conversion operators, but that pretty much defeats the purpose of templates. Second, you may have to add many such conversion operators, because your pointed-to object may be deep in an inheritance hierarchy, and you must provide a conversion operator for *each* base class from which that object directly or indirectly inherits. (If you think you can get around this by providing only an implicit type conversion operator for each direct base class, think again. Because compilers are prohibited from employing more than one user-defined type conversion function at a time, they can't convert a smart pointer-to-T to a smart pointer-to-indirect-base-class-of-T unless they can do it in a single step.)

It would be quite the time-saver if you could somehow get compilers to write all these implicit type conversion functions for you. Thanks to a recent language extension, you can. The extension in question is the ability to declare (nonvirtual) *member function templates* (usually just called *member templates*), and you use it to generate smart pointer conversion functions like this:

```
template<class T>              // template class for smart
class SmartPtr {               // pointers-to-T objects
public:
  SmartPtr(T* realPtr = 0);

  T* operator->() const;
  T& operator*() const;

  template<class newType>        // template function for
  operator SmartPtr<newType>()   // implicit conversion ops.
  {
    return SmartPtr<newType>(pointee);
  }

  ...
};
```

Now hold on to your headlights, this isn't magic — but it's close. It works as follows. (I'll give a specific example in a moment, so don't despair if the remainder of this paragraph reads like so much gobbledygook. After you've seen the example, it'll make more sense, I promise.) Suppose a compiler has a smart pointer-to-T object, and it's faced with the need to convert that object into a smart pointer-to-base-class-of-T. The compiler checks the class definition for SmartPtr<T> to see if the requisite conversion operator is declared, but it is not. (It can't be: no conversion operators are declared in the template above.) The compiler then checks to see if there's a member function template it can instantiate that would let it perform the conversion it's looking for. It finds such a template (the one taking the formal type parameter newType), so it instantiates the template with newType bound to the base class of T that's the target of the conversion. At that point, the only question is whether the code for the instantiated member function will compile. In order for it to compile, it must be legal to pass the (dumb) pointer pointee to the constructor for the smart pointer-to-base-of-T. pointee is of type T, so it is certainly legal to convert it into a pointer to its (public or protected) base classes. Hence, the code for the type conversion operator will compile, and the implicit conversion from smart pointer-to-T to smart pointer-to-base-of-T will succeed.

An example will help. Let us return to the music hierarchy of CDs, cassettes, and music products. We saw earlier that the following code wouldn't compile, because there was no way for compilers to convert the smart pointers to CDs or cassettes into smart pointers to music products:

```
void displayAndPlay(const SmartPtr<MusicProduct>& pmp,
                    int howMany);

SmartPtr<Cassette> funMusic(new Cassette("Alapalooza"));
SmartPtr<CD> nightmareMusic(new CD("Disco Hits of the 70s"));

displayAndPlay(funMusic, 10);        // used to be an error
displayAndPlay(nightmareMusic, 0);   // used to be an error
```

With the revised smart pointer class containing the member function template for implicit type conversion operators, this code will succeed. To see why, look at this call:

```
displayAndPlay(funMusic, 10);
```

The object `funMusic` is of type `SmartPtr<Cassette>`. The function `displayAndPlay` expects a `SmartPtr<MusicProduct>` object. Compilers detect the type mismatch and seek a way to convert `funMusic` into a `SmartPtr<MusicProduct>` object. They look for a single-argument constructor (see Item 5) in the `SmartPtr<MusicProduct>` class that takes a `SmartPtr<Cassette>`, but they find none. They look for an implicit type conversion operator in the `SmartPtr<Cassette>` class that yields a `SmartPtr<MusicProduct>` class, but that search also fails. They then look for a member function template they can instantiate to yield one of these functions. They discover that the template inside `SmartPtr<Cassette>`, when instantiated with `newType` bound to `MusicProduct`, generates the necessary function. They instantiate the function, yielding the following code:

```
SmartPtr<Cassette>::operator SmartPtr<MusicProduct>()
{
  return SmartPtr<MusicProduct>(pointee);
}
```

Will this compile? For all intents and purposes, nothing is happening here except the calling of the `SmartPtr<MusicProduct>` constructor with `pointee` as its argument, so the real question is whether one can construct a `SmartPtr<MusicProduct>` object with a `Cassette*` pointer. The `SmartPtr<MusicProduct>` constructor expects a `MusicProduct*` pointer, but now we're on the familiar ground of conversions between dumb pointer types, and it's clear that `Cassette*` can be passed in where a `MusicProduct*` is expected. The construction of the `SmartPtr<MusicProduct>` is therefore successful, and the conversion of the `SmartPtr<Cassette>` to `SmartPtr<MusicProduct>` is equally successful. *Voilà!* Implicit conversion of smart pointer types. What could be simpler?

Furthermore, what could be more powerful? Don't be misled by this example into assuming that this works only for pointer conversions up an inheritance hierarchy. The method shown succeeds for *any* legal implicit conversion between pointer types. If you've got a dumb pointer type T1 and another dumb pointer type T2, you can implicitly convert a smart pointer-to-T1 to a smart pointer-to-T2 if and only if you can implicitly convert a T1 to a T2.

This technique gives you exactly the behavior you want — almost. Suppose we augment our MusicProduct hierarchy with a new class, CasSingle, for representing cassette singles. The revised hierarchy looks like this:

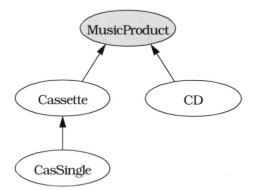

Now consider this code:

```
template<class T>          // as above, including member tem-
class SmartPtr { ... };    // plate for conversion operators

void displayAndPlay(const SmartPtr<MusicProduct>& pmp,
                    int howMany);

void displayAndPlay(const SmartPtr<Cassette>& pc,
                    int howMany);

SmartPtr<CasSingle> dumbMusic(new CasSingle("Achy Breaky Heart"));

displayAndPlay(dumbMusic, 1);   // error!
```

In this example, displayAndPlay is overloaded, with one function taking a SmartPtr<MusicProduct> object and the other taking a SmartPtr<Cassette> object. When we invoke displayAndPlay with a SmartPtr<CasSingle>, we expect the SmartPtr<Cassette> function to be chosen, because CasSingle inherits directly from Cassette and only indirectly from MusicProduct. Certainly that's how it would work with dumb pointers. Alas, our smart pointers aren't that smart. They employ member functions as conversion operators, and as far as C++ compilers are concerned, all calls to conversion functions are equally good. As a result, the call to displayAndPlay is ambiguous, because the conversion from SmartPtr<CasSingle> to

`SmartPtr<Cassette>` is no better than the conversion to `SmartPtr<MusicProduct>`.

Implementing smart pointer conversions through member templates has two additional drawbacks. First, support for member templates is rare, so this technique is currently anything but portable. In the future, that will change, but nobody knows just how far in the future that will be. Second, the mechanics of why this works are far from transparent, relying as they do on a detailed understanding of argument-matching rules for function calls, implicit type conversion functions, implicit instantiation of template functions, and the existence of member function templates. Pity the poor programmer who has never seen this trick before and is then asked to maintain or enhance code that relies on it. The technique is clever, that's for sure, but too much cleverness can be a dangerous thing.

Let's stop beating around the bush. What we really want to know is how we can make smart pointer classes behave just like dumb pointers for purposes of inheritance-based type conversions. The answer is simple: we can't. As Daniel Edelson has noted, smart pointers are smart, but they're not pointers. The best we can do is to use member templates to generate conversion functions, then use casts (see Item 2) in those cases where ambiguity results. This isn't a perfect state of affairs, but it's pretty good, and having to cast away ambiguity in a few cases is a small price to pay for the sophisticated functionality smart pointers can provide.

Smart Pointers and const

Recall that for dumb pointers, `const` can refer to the thing pointed to, to the pointer itself, or both:

```
CD goodCD("Flood");

const CD *p;                     // p is a non-const pointer
                                 // to a const CD object

CD * const p = &goodCD;          // p is a const pointer to
                                 // a non-const CD object;
                                 // because p is const, it
                                 // must be initialized

const CD * const p = &goodCD;    // p is a const pointer to
                                 // a const CD object
```

Naturally, we'd like to have the same flexibility with smart pointers. Unfortunately, there's only one place to put the const, and there it applies to the pointer, not to the object pointed to:

```
const SmartPtr<CD> p =           // p is a const smart ptr
    &goodCD;                     // to a non-const CD object
```

This seems simple enough to remedy — just create a smart pointer to a *const* CD:

```
SmartPtr<const CD> p =           // p is a non-const smart ptr
    &goodCD;                     // to a const CD object
```

Now we can create the four combinations of const and non-const objects and pointers we seek:

```
SmartPtr<CD> p;                         // non-const object,
                                        // non-const pointer

SmartPtr<const CD> p;                   // const object,
                                        // non-const pointer

const SmartPtr<CD> p = &goodCD;         // non-const object,
                                        // const pointer

const SmartPtr<const CD> p = &goodCD;   // const object,
                                        // const pointer
```

Like most C++ ointments, this one has a fly in it. Using dumb pointers, we can assign non-const pointers to const pointers and we can assign pointers to non-const objects to pointers to consts. For example:

```
CD *pCD = new CD("Famous Movie Themes");

const CD * pConstCD = pCD;              // fine
```

But look what happens if we try the same thing with smart pointers:

```
SmartPtr<CD> pCD = new CD("Famous Movie Themes");

SmartPtr<const CD> pConstCD = pCD;     // fine?
```

SmartPtr<CD> and SmartPtr<const CD> are completely different types. As far as your compilers know, they are unrelated, so they have no reason to believe they are assignment-compatible. In what must be an old story by now, the only way these two types will be considered assignment-compatible is if you've provided a function to convert objects of type SmartPtr<CD> to objects of type SmartPtr<const CD>. If you've got a compiler that supports member templates, you can use the technique shown above for automatically generating the implicit type conversion operators you need. (I remarked earlier that the technique worked anytime the corresponding conversion for dumb pointers would work, and I wasn't kidding. Conversions involving const are no exception.) If you don't have such a compiler, you have to jump through one more hoop.

Conversions involving const are a one-way street: it's safe to go from non-const to const, but it's not safe to go from const to non-const. Furthermore, anything you can do with a const pointer you can do with a non-const pointer, but with non-const pointers you can do other things, too (for example, assignment). Similarly, anything you can do with a pointer-to-const is legal for a pointer-to-non-const, but you can do some things (such as assignment) with pointers-to-non-consts that you can't do with pointers-to-consts.

These rules sound like the rules for public inheritance. You can convert from a derived class object to a base class object, but not vice versa, and you can do anything to a derived class object you can do to a base class object, but you can typically do additional things to a derived class object, as well. We can take advantage of this similarity when implementing smart pointers by having each smart pointer-to-T class publicly inherit from a corresponding smart pointer-to-const-T class:

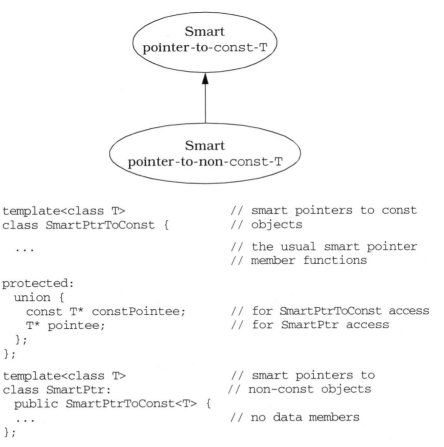

```
template<class T>              // smart pointers to const
class SmartPtrToConst {        // objects

   ...                         // the usual smart pointer
                               // member functions

protected:
  union {
    const T* constPointee;     // for SmartPtrToConst access
    T* pointee;                // for SmartPtr access
  };
};

template<class T>              // smart pointers to
class SmartPtr:                // non-const objects
  public SmartPtrToConst<T> {
   ...                         // no data members
};
```

With this design, the smart pointer-to-non-const-T object needs to contain a dumb pointer-to-non-const-T, and the smart pointer-to-const-T needs to contain a dumb pointer-to-const-T. The naive way to handle this would be to put a dumb pointer-to-const-T in the base class and a dumb pointer-to-non-const-T in the derived class. That would be wasteful, however, because SmartPtr objects would contain two dumb pointers: the one they inherited from SmartPtrToConst and the one in SmartPtr itself.

This problem is resolved by employing that old battle axe of the C world, a union, which can be as useful in C++ as it is in C. The union is protected, so both classes have access to it, and it contains both of the necessary dumb pointer types. SmartPtrToConst<T> objects use the constPointee pointer, SmartPtr<T> objects use the pointee pointer. We therefore get the advantages of two different pointers without having to allocate space for more than one. Such is the beauty of a union. Of course, the member functions of the two classes must constrain themselves to using only the appropriate pointer, and you'll get no help from compilers in enforcing that constraint. Such is the risk of a union.

With this new design, we get the behavior we want:

```
SmartPtr<CD> pCD = new CD("Famous Movie Themes");

SmartPtrToConst<CD> pConstCD = pCD;    // fine
```

Evaluation

That wraps up the subject of smart pointers, but before we leave the topic, we should ask this question: are they worth the trouble, especially if your compilers lack support for member function templates?

Often they are. The reference-counting code of Item 29, for example, is greatly simplified by using smart pointers. Furthermore, as that example demonstrates, some uses of smart pointers are sufficiently limited in scope that things like testing for nullness, conversion to dumb pointers, inheritance-based conversions, and support for pointers-to-consts are irrelevant. At the same time, smart pointers can be tricky to implement, understand, and maintain. Debugging code using smart pointers is more difficult than debugging code using dumb pointers. Try as you may, you will never succeed in designing a general-purpose smart pointer that can seamlessly replace its dumb pointer counterpart.

Smart pointers nevertheless make it possible to achieve effects in your code that would otherwise be difficult to implement. Smart pointers should be used judiciously, but every C++ programmer will find them useful at one time or another.

This rode on website

Item 29: Reference counting

Reference counting is a technique that allows multiple objects with the same value to share a single representation of that value. There are two common motivations for the technique. The first is to simplify the bookkeeping surrounding heap objects. Once an object is allocated by calling new, it's crucial to keep track of who *owns* that object, because the owner — and only the owner — is responsible for calling delete on it. But ownership can be transferred from object to object as a program runs (by passing pointers as parameters, for example), so keeping track of an object's ownership is hard work. Classes like auto_ptr (see Item 9) can help with this task, but experience has shown that most programs still fail to get it right. Reference counting eliminates the burden of tracking object ownership, because when an object employs reference counting, it owns itself. When nobody is using it any longer, it destroys itself automatically. Thus, reference counting constitutes a simple form of garbage collection.

The second motivation for reference counting is simple common sense. If many objects have the same value, it's silly to store that value more than once. Instead, it's better to let all the objects with that value *share* its representation. Doing so not only saves memory, it also leads to faster-running programs, because there's no need to construct and destruct redundant copies of the same object value.

Like most simple ideas, this one hovers above a sea of interesting details. God may or may not be in the details, but successful implementations of reference counting certainly are. Before delving into details, however, let us master basics. A good way to begin is by seeing how we might come to have many objects with the same value in the first place. Here's one way:

```
class String {          // the standard string class may
public:                 // employ the techniques in this
                        // Item, but that is not required

  String(const char *value = "");
  String& operator=(const String& rhs);
  ...

private:
  char *data;
};

String a, b, c, d, e;

a = b = c = d = e = "Hello";
```

It should be apparent that objects a through e all have the same value, namely "Hello". How that value is represented depends on how the

`String` class is implemented, but a common implementation would have each `String` object carry its own copy of the value. For example, `String`'s assignment operator might be implemented like this:

```
String& String::operator=(const String& rhs)
{
  if (this == &rhs) return *this;

  delete [] data;
  data = new char[strlen(rhs.data) + 1];
  strcpy(data, rhs.data);

  return *this;
}
```

Given this implementation, we can envision the five objects and their values as follows:

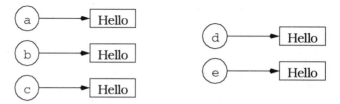

The redundancy in this approach is clear. In an ideal world, we'd like to change the picture to look like this:

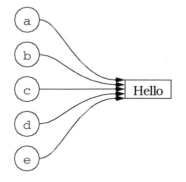

Here only one copy of the value "Hello" is stored, and all the `String` objects with that value share its representation.

In practice, it isn't possible to achieve this ideal, because we need to keep track of how many objects are sharing a value. If object a above is assigned a different value from "Hello", we can't destroy the value "Hello", because four other objects still need it. On the other hand, if only a single object had the value "Hello" and that object went out of scope, no object would have that value and we'd have to destroy the value to avoid a resource leak.

The need to store information on the number of objects currently sharing — *referring to* — a value means our ideal picture must be modified
somewhat to take into account the existence of a *reference count*:

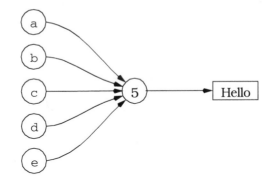

(Some people call this number a *use count*, but I am not one of them.
C++ has enough idiosyncrasies of its own; the last thing it needs is ter-
minological factionalism.)

Implementing Reference Counting

Creating a reference-counted String class isn't difficult, but it does
require attention to detail, so we'll walk through the implementation of
the most common member functions of such a class. Before we do
that, however, it's important to recognize that we need a place to store
the reference count for each String value. That place cannot be in a
String object, because we need one reference count per string *value*,
not one reference count per string *object*. That implies a coupling between values and reference counts, so we'll create a class to store reference counts and the values they track. We'll call this class
StringValue, and because its only *raison d'être* is to help implement
the String class, we'll nest it inside String's private section. Furthermore, it will be convenient to give all the member functions of String
full access to the StringValue data structure, so we'll declare
StringValue to be a struct. This is a trick worth knowing: nesting a
struct in the private part of a class is a convenient way to give access
to the struct to all the members of the class, but to deny access to everybody else (except, of course, friends of the class).

Our basic design looks like this:

```
class String {
public:
  ...                                    // the usual String member
                                         // functions go here

private:
  struct StringValue { ... };    // holds a reference count
                                 // and a string value

  StringValue *value;            // value of this String
};
```

We could give this class a different name (RCString, perhaps) to emphasize that it's implemented using reference counting, but the implementation of a class shouldn't be of concern to clients of that class.
Rather, clients should interest themselves only in a class's public interface. Our reference-counting implementation of the String interface supports exactly the same operations as a non-reference-counted
version, so why muddy the conceptual waters by embedding implementation decisions in the names of classes that correspond to abstract concepts? Why indeed? So we don't.

Here's StringValue:

```
class String {
private:
  struct StringValue {
    int refCount;
    char *data;

    StringValue(const char *initValue);
    ~StringValue();

  };

  ...

};
String::StringValue::StringValue(const char *initValue)
: refCount(1)
{
  data = new char[strlen(initValue) + 1];
  strcpy(data, initValue);
}
String::StringValue::~StringValue()
{
  delete [] data;
}
```

That's all there is to it, and it should be clear that's nowhere near
enough to implement the full functionality of a reference-counted
string. For one thing, there's neither a copy constructor nor an assign-

ment operator, and for another, there's no manipulation of the ref-
Count field. Worry not — the missing functionality will be provided by
the String class. The primary purpose of StringValue is to give us a
place to associate a particular value with a count of the number of
String objects sharing that value. StringValue gives us that, and
that's enough.

We're now ready to walk our way through String's member functions.
We'll begin with the constructors:

```
class String {
public:
  String(const char *initValue = "");
  String(const String& rhs);

    . . .

};
```

The first constructor is implemented about as simply as possible. We
just copy the passed-in char* string to a new StringValue object, set
the reference count for that object to 1, and make the String object
we're constructing point to the new StringValue object:

```
String::String(const char *initValue)
: value(new StringValue(initValue))
{}
```

For client code that looks like this,

```
String s("More Effective C++");
```

we end up with a data structure that looks like this:

String objects constructed separately, but with the same initial value
do not share a data structure, so client code of this form,

```
String s1("More Effective C++");
String s2("More Effective C++");
```

yields this data structure:

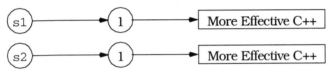

It is possible to eliminate such duplication by having String (or
StringValue) keep track of existing StringValue objects and create
new ones only for truly unique strings, but such refinements on refer-

ence counting are somewhat off the beaten path. As a result, I'll leave them in the form of the feared and hated exercise for the reader.

The String copy constructor is not only unfeared and unhated, it's also efficient: the newly created String object shares the same StringValue object as the String object that's being copied:

```
String::String(const String& rhs)
: value(rhs.value)
{
  value->++refCount;
}
```

Graphically, code like this,

```
String s1("More Effective C++");
String s2 = s1;
```

results in this data structure:

This is substantially more efficient than a conventional (non-reference-counted) String class, because there is no need to allocate memory for the second copy of the string value, no need to deallocate that memory later, and no need to copy the value that would go in that memory. Instead, we merely copy a pointer and increment a reference count.

The String destructor is also easy to implement, because most of the time it doesn't do anything. As long as the reference count for a StringValue is non-zero, at least one String object is using the value; it must therefore not be destroyed. Only when the String being destructed is the sole user of the value — i.e., when the value's reference count is 1 — should the String destructor destroy the StringValue object:

```
class String {
public:
  ~String();
  ...
};

String::~String()
{
  if (--value->refCount == 0) delete value;
}
```

Compare the efficiency of this function with that of the destructor for a non-reference-counted implementation. Such a function would always call `delete` and would almost certainly have a nontrivial runtime cost. Provided that different `String` objects do in fact sometimes have the same values, the implementation above will sometimes do nothing more than decrement a counter and compare it to zero.

If, at this point, the appeal of reference counting is not becoming apparent, you're just not paying attention.

That's all there is to `String` construction and destruction, so we'll move on to consideration of the `String` assignment operator:

```
class String {
public:
  String& operator=(const String& rhs);
  ...

};
```

When a client writes code like this,

```
s1 = s2;                 // s1 and s2 are both String objects
```

the result of the assignment should be that s1 and s2 both point to the same `StringValue` object. That object's reference count should therefore be incremented during the assignment. Furthermore, the `StringValue` object that s1 pointed to prior to the assignment should have its reference count decremented, because s1 will no longer have that value. If s1 was the only `String` with that value, the value should be destroyed. In C++, all that looks like this:

```
String& String::operator=(const String& rhs)
{
  if (value == rhs.value) {      // do nothing if the values
    return *this;                // are already the same; this
  }                              // subsumes the usual test of
                                 // this against &rhs

  if (--value->refCount == 0) {  // destroy *this's value if
    delete value;                // no one else is using it
  }

  value = rhs.value;             // have *this share rhs's
  value->refCount++;             // value

  return *this;
}
```

Copy-on-Write

To round out our examination of reference-counted strings, consider an array-bracket operator ([]), which allows individual characters within strings to be read and written:

```
class String {
public:
  char operator[](int index) const;  // for const Strings
  char& operator[](int index);       // for non-const Strings

  ...

};
```

Implementation of the const version of this function is straightforward, because it's a read-only operation; the value of the string can't be affected:

```
char String::operator[](int index) const
{
  return value->data[index];
}
```

(This function performs sanity checking on index in the grand C++ tradition, which is to say not at all. As usual, if you'd like a greater degree of parameter validation, it's easy to add.)

The non-const version of operator[] is a completely different story. This function may be called to read a character, but it might be called to write one, too:

```
String s;

...

cout << s[3];              // this is a read
s[5] = 'x';                // this is a write
```

We'd like to deal with reads and writes differently. A simple read can be dealt with in the same way as the const version of operator[] above, but a write must be implemented in quite a different fashion.

When we modify a String's value, we have to be careful to avoid modifying the value of other String objects that happen to be sharing the same StringValue object. Unfortunately, there is no way for C++ compilers to tell us whether a particular use of operator[] is for a read or a write, so we must be pessimistic and assume that *all* calls to the non-const operator[] are for writes. (Proxy classes can help us differentiate reads from writes — see Item 30.)

To implement the non-const operator[] safely, we must ensure that no other String object shares the StringValue to be modified by the presumed write. In short, we must ensure that the reference count for a String's StringValue object is exactly one any time we return a reference to a character inside that StringValue object. Here's how we do it:

```
char& String::operator[](int index)
{
  // if we're sharing a value with other String objects,
  // break off a separate copy of the value for ourselves
  if (value->refCount > 1) {
    value->refCount--;       // decrement current value's
                             // refcount, because we won't
                             // be using that value any more

    value =                          // make a copy of the
      new StringValue(value->data);  // value for ourselves
  }

  // return a reference to a character inside our
  // unshared StringValue object
  return value->data[index];
}
```

This idea — that of sharing a value with other objects until we have to write on our own copy of the value — has a long and distinguished history in Computer Science, especially in operating systems, where processes are routinely allowed to share pages until they want to modify data on their own copy of a page. The technique is common enough to have a name: *copy-on-write*. It's a specific example of a more general approach to efficiency, that of lazy evaluation (see Item 17).

Pointers, References, and Copy-on-Write

This implementation of copy-on-write allows us to preserve both efficiency and correctness — almost. There is one lingering problem. Consider this code:

```
String s1 = "Hello";

char *p = &s1[1];
```

Our data structure at this point looks like this:

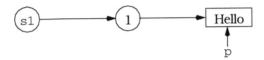

Now consider an additional statement:

```
String s2 = s1;
```

The `String` copy constructor will make s2 share s1's `StringValue`, so the resulting data structure will be this one:

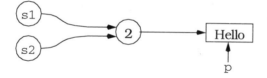

The implications of a statement such as the following, then, are not pleasant to contemplate:

```
*p = 'x';                          // modifies both s1 and s2!
```

There is no way the `String` copy constructor can detect this problem, because it has no way to know that a pointer into s1's `StringValue` object exists. And this problem isn't limited to pointers: it would exist if someone had saved a *reference* to the result of a call to `String`'s non-const `operator[]`.

There are at least three ways of dealing with this problem. The first is to ignore it, to pretend it doesn't exist. This approach turns out to be distressingly common in class libraries that implement reference-counted strings. If you have access to a reference-counted string class, try the above example and see if you're distressed, too. If you're not sure if you have access to a reference-counted string class, try the example anyway. Through the wonder of encapsulation, you may be using such a class without knowing it.

Not all implementations ignore such problems. A slightly more sophisticated way of dealing with such difficulties is to define them out of existence. Implementations adopting this strategy typically put something in their documentation that says, more or less, "Don't do that. If you do, results are undefined." If you then do it anyway — wittingly or no — and complain about the results, they respond, "Well, we *told* you not to do that." Such implementations are often efficient, but they leave much to be desired in the usability department.

There is a third solution, and that's to eliminate the problem. It's not difficult to implement, but it can reduce the amount of value sharing between objects. Its essence is this: add a flag to each `StringValue` object indicating whether that object is shareable. Turn the flag on initially (the object is shareable), but turn it off whenever the non-const `operator[]` is invoked on the value represented by that object. Once the flag is set to `false`, it stays that way forever.

Here's a modified version of `StringValue` that includes a shareability flag:

```
class String {
private:
  struct StringValue {
    int refCount;
    bool shareable;                       // add this
    char *data;

    StringValue(const char *initValue);
    ~StringValue();

  };

  ...

};

String::StringValue::StringValue(const char *initValue)
:  refCount(1),
   shareable(true)                        // add this
{
  data = new char[strlen(initValue) + 1];
  strcpy(data, initValue);
}

String::StringValue::~StringValue()
{
  delete [] data;
}
```

As you can see, not much needs to change; the two lines that require modification are flagged with comments. Of course, String's member functions must be updated to take the shareable field into account. Here's how the copy constructor would do that:

```
String::String(const String& rhs)
{
  if (rhs.value->shareable) {
    value = rhs.value;
    value->refCount++;
  }

  else {
    value = new StringValue(rhs.value->data);
  }
}
```

All the other String member functions would have to check the shareable field in an analogous fashion. The non-const version of operator[] would be the only function to set the shareable flag to false:

```
char& String::operator[](int index)
{
  if (value->refCount > 1) {
    value->refCount--;
    value = new StringValue(value->data);
  }

  value->shareable = false;        // add this

  return value->data[index];
}
```

If you use the proxy class technique of Item 30 to distinguish read usage from write usage in operator[], you can usually reduce the number of StringValue objects that must be marked unshareable.

A Reference-Counting Base Class

Reference counting is useful for more than just strings. Any class in which different objects may have values in common is a legitimate candidate for reference counting. Rewriting a class to take advantage of reference counting can be a lot of work, however, and most of us already have more than enough to do. Wouldn't it be nice if we could somehow write (and test and document) the reference counting code in a context-independent manner, then just graft it onto classes when needed? Of course it would. In a curious twist of fate, there's a way to do it (or at least to do most of it).

The first step is to create a base class, RCObject, for reference-counted objects. Any class wishing to take advantage of automatic reference counting must inherit from this class. RCObject encapsulates the reference count itself, as well as functions for incrementing and decrementing that count. It also contains the code for destroying a value when it is no longer in use, i.e., when its reference count becomes 0. Finally, it contains a field that keeps track of whether this value is shareable, and it provides functions to query this value and set it to false. There is no need for a function to set the shareability field to true, because all values are shareable by default. As noted above, once an object has been tagged unshareable, there is no way to make it shareable again.

RCObject's class definition looks like this:

```
class RCObject {
public:
  RCObject();
  RCObject(const RCObject& rhs);
  RCObject& operator=(const RCObject& rhs);
  virtual ~RCObject() = 0;
```

```
void addReference();
void removeReference();

void markUnshareable();
bool isShareable() const;

bool isShared() const;
private:
  int refCount;
  bool shareable;
};
```

RCObjects can be created (as the base class parts of more derived objects) and destroyed; they can have new references added to them and can have current references removed; their shareability status can be queried and can be disabled; and they can report whether they are currently being shared. That's all they offer. As a class encapsulating the notion of being reference-countable, that's really all we have a right to expect them to do. Note the tell-tale virtual destructor, a sure sign this class is designed for use as a base class. Note also how the destructor is a *pure* virtual function, a sure sign this class is designed to be used *only* as a base class.

The code to implement RCObject is, if nothing else, brief:

```
RCObject::RCObject()
: refCount(0), shareable(true) {}

RCObject::RCObject(const RCObject&)
: refCount(0), shareable(true) {}

RCObject& RCObject::operator=(const RCObject&)
{ return *this; }

RCObject::~RCObject() {}            // virtual dtors must always
                                   // be implemented, even if
                                   // they are pure virtual
                                   // and do nothing (see also
                                   // Item 33)

void RCObject::addReference() { ++refCount; }

void RCObject::removeReference()
{ if (--refCount == 0) delete this; }

void RCObject::markUnshareable()
{ shareable = false; }

bool RCObject::isShareable() const
{ return shareable; }

bool RCObject::isShared() const
{ return refCount > 1; }
```

Curiously, we set refCount to 0 inside both constructors. This seems counterintuitive. Surely at least the creator of the new RCObject is referring to it! As it turns out, it simplifies things for the creators of RCObjects to set refCount to 1 themselves, so we oblige them here by not getting in their way. We'll get a chance to see the resulting code simplification shortly.

Another curious thing is that the copy constructor always sets ref-Count to 0, regardless of the value of refCount for the RCObject we're copying. That's because we're creating a new object representing a value, and new values are always unshared and referenced only by their creator. Again, the creator is responsible for setting the refCount to its proper value.

The RCObject assignment operator looks downright subversive: it does *nothing*. Frankly, it's unlikely this operator will ever be called. RCObject is a base class for a shared *value* object, and in a system based on reference counting, such objects are not assigned to one another, objects *pointing* to them are. In our case, we don't expect StringValue objects to be assigned to one another, we expect only String objects to be involved in assignments. In such assignments, no change is made to the value of a StringValue — only the StringValue reference count is modified.

Nevertheless, it is conceivable that some as-yet-unwritten class might someday inherit from RCObject and might wish to allow assignment of reference-counted values (see Item 32). If so, RCObject's assignment operator should do the right thing, and the right thing is to do nothing. To see why, imagine that we wished to allow assignments between StringValue objects. Given StringValue objects sv1 and sv2, what should happen to sv1's and sv2's reference counts in an assignment?

```
sv1 = sv2;              // how are sv1's and sv2's reference
                        // counts affected?
```

Before the assignment, some number of String objects are pointing to sv1. That number is unchanged by the assignment, because only sv1's *value* changes. Similarly, some number of String objects are pointing to sv2 prior to the assignment, and after the assignment, exactly the same String objects point to sv2. sv2's reference count is also unchanged. When RCObjects are involved in an assignment, then, the number of objects pointing to those objects is unaffected, hence RCObject::operator= should change no reference counts. That's exactly what the implementation above does. Counterintuitive? Perhaps, but it's still correct.

The code for RCObject::removeReference is responsible not only for decrementing the object's refCount, but also for destroying the object if the new value of refCount is 0. It accomplishes this latter task by deleteing this, which, as Item 27 explains, is safe only if we know that *this is a heap object. For this class to be successful, we must engineer things so that RCObjects can be created only on the heap. General approaches to achieving that end are discussed in Item 27, but the specific measures we'll employ in this case are described at the conclusion of this Item.

To take advantage of our new reference-counting base class, we modify StringValue to inherit its reference counting capabilities from RCObject:

```
class String {
private:
  struct StringValue: public RCObject {
    char *data;

    StringValue(const char *initValue);
    ~StringValue();

  };

  ...

};

String::StringValue::StringValue(const char *initValue)
{
  data = new char[strlen(initValue) + 1];
  strcpy(data, initValue);
}

String::StringValue::~StringValue()
{
  delete [] data;
}
```

This version of StringValue is almost identical to the one we saw earlier. The only thing that's changed is that StringValue's member functions no longer manipulate the refCount field. RCObject now handles what they used to do.

Don't feel bad if you blanched at the sight of a nested class (StringValue) inheriting from a class (RCObject) that's unrelated to the nesting class (String). It looks weird to everybody at first, but it's perfectly kosher. A nested class is just as much a class as any other, so it has the freedom to inherit from whatever other classes it likes. In time, you won't think twice about such inheritance relationships.

Automating Reference Count Manipulations

The RCObject class gives us a place to store a reference count, and it gives us member functions through which that reference count can be manipulated, but the *calls* to those functions must still be manually inserted in other classes. It is still up to the String copy constructor and the String assignment operator to call addReference and removeReference on StringValue objects. This is clumsy. We'd like to move those calls out into a reusable class, too, thus freeing authors of classes like String from worrying about *any* of the details of reference counting. Can it be done? Isn't C++ supposed to support reuse?

It can, and it does. There's no easy way to arrange things so that *all* reference-counting considerations can be moved out of application classes, but there is a way to eliminate *most* of them for most classes. (In some application classes, you *can* eliminate all reference-counting code, but our String class, alas, isn't one of them. One member function spoils the party, and I suspect you won't be too surprised to hear it's our old nemesis, the non-const version of operator[]. Take heart, however; we'll tame that miscreant in the end.)

Notice that each String object contains a pointer to the StringValue object representing that String's value:

```
class String {
private:
  struct StringValue: public RCObject { ... };

  StringValue *value;              // value of this String

  ...

};
```

We have to manipulate the refCount field of the StringValue object anytime anything interesting happens to one of the pointers pointing to it. "Interesting happenings" include copying a pointer, reassigning one, and destroying one. If we could somehow make the *pointer itself* detect these happenings and automatically perform the necessary manipulations of the refCount field, we'd be home free. Unfortunately, pointers are rather dense creatures, and the chances of them detecting anything, much less automatically reacting to things they detect, are pretty slim. Fortunately, there's a way to smarten them up: replace them with objects that *act like* pointers, but that do more.

Such objects are called *smart pointers*, and you can read about them in more detail than you probably care to in Item 28. For our purposes here, it's enough to know that smart pointer objects support the member selection (->) and dereferencing (*) operations, just like real pointers (which, in this context, are generally referred to as *dumb pointers*), and, like dumb pointers, they are strongly typed: you can't make a smart pointer-to-T point to an object that isn't of type T.

Here's a template for objects that act as smart pointers to reference-counted objects:

```
template<class T>              // template class for smart
class RCPtr {                  // pointers-to-T objects; T
public:                        // must inherit from RCObject
  RCPtr(T* realPtr = 0);
  RCPtr(const RCPtr& rhs);
  ~RCPtr();

  RCPtr& operator=(const RCPtr& rhs);

  T* operator->() const;       // see Item 28
  T& operator*() const;        // see Item 28

private:
  T *pointee;                  // dumb pointer this
                               // object is emulating

  void init();                 // common initialization
};                             // code
```

This template gives smart pointer objects control over what happens during their construction, assignment, and destruction. When such events occur, these objects can automatically perform the appropriate manipulations of the refCount field in the objects to which they point.

For example, when an RCPtr is created, the object it points to needs to have its reference count increased. There's no need to burden application developers with the requirement to tend to this irksome detail manually, because RCPtr constructors can handle it themselves. The code in the two constructors is all but identical — only the member initialization lists differ — so rather than write it twice, we put it in a private member function called init and have both constructors call that:

```
template<class T>
RCPtr<T>::RCPtr(T* realPtr): pointee(realPtr)
{
  init();
}

template<class T>
RCPtr<T>::RCPtr(const RCPtr& rhs): pointee(rhs.pointee)
{
  init();
}
```

```
template<class T>
void RCPtr<T>::init()
{
  if (pointee == 0) {           // if the dumb pointer is
    return;                     // null, so is the smart one
  }

  if (pointee->isShareable() == false) {   // if the value
    pointee = new T(*pointee);              // isn't shareable,
  }                                         // copy it

  pointee->addReference();      // note that there is now a
}                               // new reference to the value
```

Moving common code into a separate function like init is exemplary
software engineering, but its luster dims when, as in this case, the
function won't compile. The problem is that when we instantiate RCPtr
to create a RCPtr<String::StringValue> class, that class's init
function will contain calls to StringValue's isShareable, addReference, and copy constructor functions, but those functions are private
in String. This was never a problem when String contained only
dumb pointers, because String's member functions did everything
that needed to be done, but now that the smart pointer class is doing
some of the work, it needs to have access to StringValue's members,
too. The solution is to make RCPtr<String::StringValue> a friend
of String::StringValue:

```
class String {
private:
  struct StringValue: public RCObject {
    ...

  friend class RCPtr<StringValue>;
  };

  RCPtr<StringValue> value;     // smart pointer to this
                                // string's value
  ...

};
```

This solves our compilation difficulties, but now there is another problem. The code executed in init when we have to create a new copy of
a value (because the existing copy isn't shareable) is

```
pointee = new T(*pointee);
```

The type of pointee is pointer-to-T, so the first line above creates a
new T object and initializes it by calling T's copy constructor. In the
case of the String class, T will be String::StringValue, so this will
be a call to String::StringValue's copy constructor. We haven't declared a copy constructor for that class, however, so our compilers will

generate one for us. The copy constructor so generated will, in accordance with the rules for automatically generated copy constructors in C++, copy only StringValue's data *pointer*; it will *not* copy the char* string data points to. Such behavior is disastrous in nearly *any* class (not just reference-counted classes), and that's why you should get into the habit of writing a copy constructor (and an assignment operator) for all your classes that contain pointers.

The correct behavior of the RCPtr<T> template depends on T containing a copy constructor that makes a truly independent copy (i.e., a *deep copy*) of the value represented by T. We must augment StringValue with such a constructor before we can use it with the RCPtr class:

```
class String {
private:
  struct StringValue: public RCObject {
    StringValue(const StringValue& rhs);
    ...
  };

  ...

};

String::StringValue::StringValue(const StringValue& rhs)
{
  data = new char[strlen(rhs.data) + 1];
  strcpy(data, rhs.data);
}
```

The existence of a deep-copying copy constructor is not the only assumption RCPtr<T> makes about T. It also requires that T inherit from RCObject, or at least that T provide all the functionality that RCObject does. In view of the fact that RCPtr objects are designed to point only to reference-counted objects, this is hardly an unreasonable assumption. Nevertheless, the assumption must be documented.

A final assumption in RCPtr<T> is that the type of the object pointed to is T. This seems obvious enough. After all, pointee is declared to be of type T*. But pointee might really point to a class *derived* from T. For example, if we had a class SpecialStringValue that inherited from String::StringValue,

```
class String {
private:
  struct StringValue: public RCObject { ... };

  struct SpecialStringValue: public StringValue { ... };

  ...

};
```

we could end up with a String containing a RCPtr<StringValue> pointing to a SpecialStringValue object. In that case, we'd want this part of init,

```
pointee = new T(*pointee);        // T is StringValue, but
                                  // pointee really points to
                                  // a SpecialStringValue
```

to call SpecialStringValue's copy constructor, not StringValue's. We can arrange for this to happen by using a virtual copy constructor (see Item 25). In the case of our String class, we don't expect classes to derive from StringValue, so we'll disregard this issue.

With RCPtr's constructors out of the way, the rest of the class's functions can be dispatched with considerably greater alacrity. Assignment of an RCPtr is straightforward, though the need to test whether the newly assigned value is shareable complicates matters slightly. Fortunately, such complications have already been handled by the init function that was created for RCPtr's constructors. We take advantage of that fact by using it again here:

```
template<class T>
RCPtr<T>& RCPtr<T>::operator=(const RCPtr& rhs)
{
  if (pointee != rhs.pointee) {     // skip assignments
                                    // where the value
                                    // doesn't change

    if (pointee) {
      pointee->removeReference();   // remove reference to
    }                               // current value

    pointee = rhs.pointee;          // point to new value
    init();                         // if possible, share it
  }                                 // else make own copy

  return *this;
}
```

The destructor is easier. When an RCPtr is destroyed, it simply removes its reference to the reference-counted object:

```
template<class T>
RCPtr<T>::~RCPtr()
{
  if (pointee) pointee->removeReference();
}
```

If the RCPtr that just expired was the last reference to the object, that object will be destroyed inside RCObject's removeReference member function. Hence RCPtr objects never need to worry about destroying the values they point to.

Finally, RCPtr's pointer-emulating operators are part of the smart pointer boilerplate you can read about in Item 28:

```
template<class T>
T* RCPtr<T>::operator->() const { return pointee; }

template<class T>
T& RCPtr<T>::operator*() const { return *pointee; }
```

Putting it All Together

Enough! *Finis!* At long last we are in a position to put all the pieces together and build a reference-counted String class based on the reusable RCObject and RCPtr classes. With luck, you haven't forgotten that that was our original goal.

Each reference-counted string is implemented via this data structure:

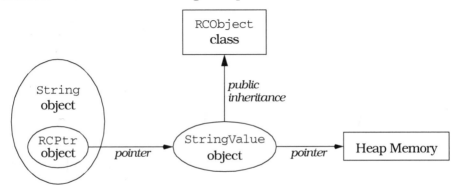

The classes making up this data structure are defined like this:

```
template<class T>                   // template class for smart
class RCPtr {                       // pointers-to-T objects; T
public:                             // must inherit from RCObject
  RCPtr(T* realPtr = 0);
  RCPtr(const RCPtr& rhs);
  ~RCPtr();

  RCPtr& operator=(const RCPtr& rhs);

  T* operator->() const;
  T& operator*() const;

private:
  T *pointee;

  void init();
};
```

```
class RCObject {                    // base class for reference-
public:                             // counted objects
  void addReference();
  void removeReference();

  void markUnshareable();
  bool isShareable() const;

  bool isShared() const;

protected:
  RCObject();
  RCObject(const RCObject& rhs);
  RCObject& operator=(const RCObject& rhs);
  virtual ~RCObject();

private:
  int refCount;
  bool shareable;
};

class String {                      // class to be used by
public:                             // application developers

  String(const char *value = "");

  char operator[](int index) const;
  char& operator[](int index);

private:
  // class representing string values
  struct StringValue: public RCObject {
    char *data;

    StringValue(const char *initValue);
    StringValue(const StringValue& rhs);
    void init(const char *initValue);
    ~StringValue();

  friend class RCPtr<StringValue>;
  };

  RCPtr<StringValue> value;
};
```

For the most part, this is just a recap of what we've already developed, so nothing should be much of a surprise. Close examination reveals we've added an init function to String::StringValue, but, as we'll see below, that serves the same purpose as the corresponding function in RCPtr: it prevents code duplication in the constructors.

There is a significant difference between the public interface of this String class and the one we used at the beginning of this Item. Where is the copy constructor? Where is the assignment operator? Where is the destructor? Something is definitely amiss here.

Actually, no. Nothing is amiss. In fact, some things are working perfectly. If you don't see what they are, prepare yourself for a C++ epiphany.

We don't need those functions anymore. Sure, copying of String objects is still supported, and yes, the copying will correctly handle the underlying reference-counted StringValue objects, but the String class doesn't have to provide a single line of code to make this happen. That's because the compiler-generated copy constructor for String will automatically call the copy constructor for String's RCPtr member, and the copy constructor for *that* class will perform all the necessary manipulations of the StringValue object, including its reference count. An RCPtr is a *smart* pointer, remember? We designed it to take care of the details of reference counting, so that's what it does. It also handles assignment and destruction, and that's why String doesn't need to write those functions, either. Our original goal was to move the unreusable reference-counting code out of our hand-written String class and into context-independent classes where it would be available for use with *any* class. Now we've done it (in the form of the RCObject and RCPtr classes), so don't be so surprised when it suddenly starts working. It's *supposed* to work.

Just so you have everything in one place, here's the implementation of RCObject:

```
RCObject::RCObject()
: refCount(0), shareable(true) {}

RCObject::RCObject(const RCObject&)
: refCount(0), shareable(true) {}

RCObject& RCObject::operator=(const RCObject&)
{ return *this; }

RCObject::~RCObject() {}

void RCObject::addReference() { ++refCount; }

void RCObject::removeReference()
{ if (--refCount == 0) delete this; }

void RCObject::markUnshareable()
{ shareable = false; }

bool RCObject::isShareable() const
{ return shareable; }

bool RCObject::isShared() const
{ return refCount > 1; }
```

And here's the implementation of RCPtr:

```cpp
template<class T>
void RCPtr<T>::init()
{
  if (pointee == 0) return;

  if (pointee->isShareable() == false) {
    pointee = new T(*pointee);
  }

  pointee->addReference();
}

template<class T>
RCPtr<T>::RCPtr(T* realPtr)
: pointee(realPtr)
{ init(); }

template<class T>
RCPtr<T>::RCPtr(const RCPtr& rhs)
: pointee(rhs.pointee)
{ init(); }

template<class T>
RCPtr<T>::~RCPtr()
{ if (pointee) pointee->removeReference(); }

template<class T>
RCPtr<T>& RCPtr<T>::operator=(const RCPtr& rhs)
{
  if (pointee != rhs.pointee) {
    if (pointee) pointee->removeReference();

    pointee = rhs.pointee;
    init();
  }

  return *this;
}

template<class T>
T* RCPtr<T>::operator->() const { return pointee; }

template<class T>
T& RCPtr<T>::operator*() const { return *pointee; }
```

The implementation of `String::StringValue` looks like this:

```cpp
void String::StringValue::init(const char *initValue)
{
  data = new char[strlen(initValue) + 1];
  strcpy(data, initValue);
}

String::StringValue::StringValue(const char *initValue)
{ init(initValue); }
```

```
String::StringValue::StringValue(const StringValue& rhs)
{ init(rhs.data); }

String::StringValue::~StringValue()
{ delete [] data; }
```

Ultimately, all roads lead to String, and that class is implemented this way:

```
String::String(const char *initValue)
: value(new StringValue(initValue)) {}

char String::operator[](int index) const
{ return value->data[index]; }

char& String::operator[](int index)
{
  if (value->isShared()) {
    value->removeReference();
    value = new StringValue(value->data);
  }

  value->markUnshareable();

  return value->data[index];
}
```

If you compare the code for this String class with that we developed for the String class using dumb pointers, you'll be struck by two things. First, there's a lot less of it here than there. That's because RCPtr has assumed much of the reference-counting burden that used to fall on String. Second, the code that remains in String is nearly unchanged: the smart pointer replaced the dumb pointer essentially seamlessly. In fact, the only change of any kind is that operator[] calls member functions to manipulate the reference count rather than manipulating the reference count directly.

This is all very nice, of course. Who can object to less code? Who can oppose encapsulation success stories? The bottom line, however, is determined more by the impact of this newfangled String class on its clients than by any of its implementation details, and it is here that things really shine. If no news is good news, the news here is very good indeed. *The String interface has not changed.* We added reference counting, we added the ability to mark individual string values as unshareable, we moved the notion of reference countability into a new base class, we added smart pointers to automate the manipulation of reference counts, yet not one line of client code needs to be changed. Sure, we changed the String class definition, so clients who want to take advantage of reference-counted strings must recompile and relink, but their investment in code is completely and utterly preserved. You see? Encapsulation really *is* a wonderful thing.

Adding Reference Counting to Existing Classes

Everything we've discussed so far assumes we have access to the source code of the classes we're interested in. But what if we'd like to apply the benefits of reference counting to some class Widget that's in a library we can't modify? There's no way to make Widget inherit from RCObject, so we can't use smart RCPtrs with it. Are we out of luck?

We're not. With some minor modifications to our design, we can add reference counting to *any* type.

First, let's consider what our design would look like if we could have Widget inherit from RCObject. In that case, we'd have to add a class, RCWidget, for clients to use, but everything would then be analogous to our String/StringValue example, with RCWidget playing the role of String and Widget playing the role of StringValue. The design would look like this:

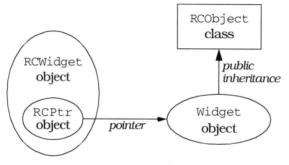

We can now apply the maxim that most problems in Computer Science can be solved with an additional level of indirection. We add a new class, CountHolder, to hold the reference count, and we have Count-Holder inherit from RCObject. We also have CountHolder contain a pointer to a Widget. We then replace the smart RCPtr template with an equally smart RCIPtr template that knows about the existence of the CountHolder class. (The "I" in RCIPtr stands for "indirect.") The modified design looks like this:

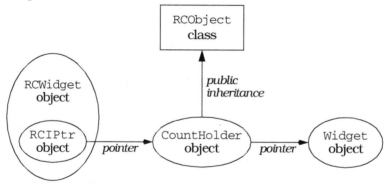

Just as StringValue was an implementation detail hidden from clients of String, CountHolder is an implementation detail hidden from clients of RCWidget. In fact, it's an implementation detail of RCIPtr, so it's nested inside that class. RCIPtr is implemented this way:

```
template<class T>
class RCIPtr {
public:
  RCIPtr(T* realPtr = 0);
  RCIPtr(const RCIPtr& rhs);
  ~RCIPtr();

  RCIPtr& operator=(const RCIPtr& rhs);

  T* operator->() const;
  T& operator*() const;

private:
  struct CountHolder: public RCObject {
    ~CountHolder() { delete pointee; }
    T *pointee;
  };

  CountHolder *counter;

  void init();
};

template<class T>
void RCIPtr<T>::init()
{
  if (counter == 0) return;

  if (counter->isShareable() == false) {
    counter = new CountHolder;
    counter->pointee = new T(*counter->pointee);
  }

  counter->addReference();
}

template<class T>
RCIPtr<T>::RCIPtr(T* realPtr)
: counter(new CountHolder)
{
  counter->pointee = realPtr;
  init();
}

template<class T>
RCIPtr<T>::RCIPtr(const RCIPtr& rhs)
: counter(rhs.counter)
{ init(); }

template<class T>
RCIPtr<T>::~RCIPtr()
{ if (counter) counter->removeReference(); }
```

```
template<class T>
RCIPtr<T>& RCIPtr<T>::operator=(const RCIPtr& rhs)
{
  if (counter != rhs.counter) {
    if (counter) counter->removeReference();
    counter = rhs.counter;
    init();
  }

  return *this;
}

template<class T>
T* RCIPtr<T>::operator->() const
{ return counter->pointee; }

template<class T>
T& RCIPtr<T>::operator*() const
{ return *(counter->pointee); }
```

If you compare this implementation with that of RCPtr, you'll see they are conceptually identical. They differ only in that RCPtr objects point to values directly, while RCIPtr objects point to values through an intervening CountHolder object.

Given RCIPtr, it's easy to implement RCWidget, because each function in RCWidget is implemented by forwarding the call through the underlying RCIPtr to a Widget object. For example, if Widget looks like this,

```
class Widget {
public:
  Widget(int size);
  Widget(const Widget& rhs);
  ~Widget();

  Widget& operator=(const Widget& rhs);

  void doThis();
  int showThat() const;
};
```

RCWidget will be defined this way:

```
class RCWidget {
public:
  RCWidget(int size)
   : value(new Widget(size)) {}

  void doThis() { value->doThis(); }
  int showThat() const { return value->showThat(); }

private:
  RCIPtr<Widget> value;
};
```

Note how the RCWidget constructor calls the Widget constructor (via the new operator — see Item 8) with the argument it was passed; how RCWidget's doThis calls doThis in the Widget class; and how RCWidget::showThat returns whatever its Widget counterpart returns. Notice also how RCWidget declares no copy constructor, no assignment operator, and no destructor. As with the String class, there is no need to write these functions. Thanks to the behavior of the RCIPtr class, the default versions do the right things.

If the thought occurs to you that creation of RCWidget is so mechanical, it could be automated, you're right. It would not be difficult to write a program that takes a class like Widget as input and produces a class like RCWidget as output. If you write such a program, please let me know.

Evaluation

Let us disentangle ourselves from the details of widgets, strings, values, smart pointers, and reference-counting base classes. That gives us an opportunity to step back and view reference counting in a broader context. In that more general context, we must address a higher-level question, namely, when is reference counting an appropriate technique?

Reference-counting implementations are not without cost. Each reference-counted value carries a reference count with it, and most operations require that this reference count be examined or manipulated in some way. Object values therefore require more memory, and we sometimes execute more code when we work with them. Furthermore, the underlying source code is considerably more complex for a reference-counted class than for a less elaborate implementation. An un-reference-counted string class typically stands on its own, while our final String class is useless unless it's augmented with three auxiliary classes (StringValue, RCObject, and RCPtr). True, our more complicated design holds out the promise of greater efficiency when values can be shared, it eliminates the need to track object ownership, and it promotes reusability of the reference counting idea and implementation. Nevertheless, that quartet of classes has to be written, tested, documented, and maintained, and that's going to be more work than writing, testing, documenting, and maintaining a single class. Even a manager can see that.

Reference counting is an optimization technique predicated on the assumption that objects will commonly share values (see also Item 18). If this assumption fails to hold, reference counting will use more memory than a more conventional implementation and it will execute more code. On the other hand, if your objects *do* tend to have common values, reference counting should save you both time and space. The bigger your object values and the more objects that can simultaneously share values, the more memory you'll save. The more you copy and assign values between objects, the more time you'll save. The more expensive it is to create and destroy a value, the more time you'll save there, too. In short, reference counting is most useful for improving efficiency under the following conditions:

- **Relatively few values are shared by relatively many objects**. Such sharing typically arises through calls to assignment operators and copy constructors. The higher the objects/values ratio, the better the case for reference counting.

- **Object values are expensive to create or destroy, or they use lots of memory**. Even when this is the case, reference counting still buys you nothing unless these values can be shared by multiple objects.

There is only one sure way to tell whether these conditions are satisfied, and that way is *not* to guess or rely on your programmer's intuition (see Item 16). The reliable way to find out whether your program can benefit from reference counting is to profile or instrument it. That way you can find out if creating and destroying values is a performance bottleneck, and you can measure the objects/values ratio. Only when you have such data in hand are you in a position to determine whether the benefits of reference counting (of which there are many) outweigh the disadvantages (of which there are also many).

Even when the conditions above are satisfied, a design employing reference counting may still be inappropriate. Some data structures (e.g., directed graphs) lead to self-referential or circular dependency structures. Such data structures have a tendency to spawn isolated collections of objects, used by no one, whose reference counts never drop to zero. That's because each object in the unused structure is pointed to by at least one other object in the same structure. Industrial-strength garbage collectors use special techniques to find such structures and eliminate them, but the simple reference-counting approach we've examined here is not easily extended to include such techniques.

Reference counting can be attractive even if efficiency is not your primary concern. If you find yourself weighed down with uncertainty over who's allowed to delete what, reference counting could be just the technique you need to ease your burden. Many programmers are devoted to reference counting for this reason alone.

Let us close this discussion on a technical note by tying up one remaining loose end. When RCObject::removeReference decrements an object's reference count, it checks to see if the new count is 0. If it is, removeReference destroys the object by deleteing this. This is a safe operation only if the object was allocated by calling new, so we need some way of ensuring that RCObjects are created only in that manner.

In this case we do it by convention. RCObject is designed for use as a base class of reference-counted value objects, and those value objects should be referred to only by smart RCPtr pointers. Furthermore, the value objects should be instantiated only by application objects that realize values are being shared; the classes describing the value objects should never be available for general use. In our example, the class for value objects is StringValue, and we limit its use by making it private in String. Only String can create StringValue objects, so it is up to the author of the String class to ensure that all such objects are allocated via new.

Our approach to the constraint that RCObjects be created only on the heap, then, is to assign responsibility for conformance to this constraint to a well-defined set of classes and to ensure that only that set of classes can create RCObjects. There is no possibility that random clients can accidently (or maliciously) create RCObjects in an inappropriate manner. We limit the right to create reference-counted objects, and when we do hand out the right, we make it clear that it's accompanied by the concomitant responsibility to follow the rules governing object creation.

Item 30: Proxy classes

Though your in-laws may be one-dimensional, the world, in general, is not. Unfortunately, C++ hasn't yet caught on to that fact. At least, there's little evidence for it in the language's support for arrays. You can create two-dimensional, three-dimensional — heck, you can create *n*-dimensional — arrays in FORTRAN, in BASIC, even in COBOL (okay, FORTRAN only allows up to seven dimensions, but let's not quibble), but can you do it in C++? Only sometimes, and even then only sort of.

This much is legal:

```
int data[10][20];              // 2D array: 10 by 20
```

The corresponding construct using variables as dimension sizes, however, is not:

```
void processInput(int dim1, int dim2)
{
  int data[dim1][dim2];        // error! array dimensions
  ...                          // must be known during
}                              // compilation
```

It's not even legal for a heap-based allocation:

```
int *data =
  new int[dim1][dim2];              // error!
```

Implementing Two-Dimensional Arrays

Multidimensional arrays are as useful in C++ as they are in any other language, so it's important to come up with a way to get decent support for them. The usual way is the standard one in C++: create a class to represent the objects we need but that are missing in the language proper. Hence we can define a class template for two-dimensional arrays:

```
template<class T>
class Array2D {
public:
  Array2D(int dim1, int dim2);
  ...

};
```

Now we can define the arrays we want:

```
Array2D<int> data(10, 20);              // fine

Array2D<float> *data =
  new Array2D<float>(10, 20);           // fine

void processInput(int dim1, int dim2)
{
  Array2D<int> data(dim1, dim2);        // fine
  ...
}
```

Using these array objects, however, isn't quite as straightforward. In keeping with the grand syntactic tradition of both C and C++, we'd like to be able to use brackets to index into our arrays,

```
cout << data[3][6];
```

but how do we declare the indexing operator in Array2D to let us do this?

Our first impulse might be to declare operator[][] functions, like this:

```
template<class T>
class Array2D {
public:

  // declarations that won't compile
  T& operator[][](int index1, int index2);
  const T& operator[][](int index1, int index2) const;

  ...

};
```

We'd quickly learn to rein in such impulses, however, because there is no such thing as operator[][], and don't think your compilers will forget it. (For a complete list of operators, overloadable and otherwise, see Item 7.) We'll have to do something else.

If you can stomach the syntax, you might follow the lead of the many programming languages that use parentheses to index into arrays. To use parentheses, you just overload operator():

```
template<class T>
class Array2D {
public:

  // declarations that will compile
  T& operator()(int index1, int index2);
  const T& operator()(int index1, int index2) const;

  ...

};
```

Clients then use arrays this way:

```
cout << data(3, 6);
```

This is easy to implement and easy to generalize to as many dimensions as you like. The drawback is that your Array2D objects don't look like built-in arrays any more. In fact, the above access to element (3, 6) of data looks, on the face of it, like a function call.

If you reject the thought of your arrays looking like FORTRAN refugees, you might turn again to the notion of using brackets as the indexing operator. Although there is no such thing as operator[][], it is nonetheless legal to write code that appears to use it:

```
int data[10][20];

...

cout << data[3][6];                    // fine
```

What gives?

What gives is that the variable data is not really a two-dimensional array at all, it's a 10-element one-dimensional array. Each of those 10 elements is itself a 20-element array, so the expression data[3][6] really means (data[3])[6], i.e., the seventh element of the array that is the fourth element of data. In short, the value yielded by the first application of the brackets is another array, so the second application of the brackets gets an element from that secondary array.

We can play the same game with our Array2D class by overloading operator[] to return an object of a new class, Array1D. We can then overload operator[] again in Array1D to return an element in our original two-dimensional array:

```
template<class T>
class Array2D {
public:
  class Array1D {
  public:
    T& operator[](int index);
    const T& operator[](int index) const;
    ...

  };

  Array1D operator[](int index);
  const Array1D operator[](int index) const;
  ...

};
```

The following then becomes legal:

```
Array2D<float> data(10, 20);
  .
  ...

cout << data[3][6];                // fine
```

Here, data[3] yields an Array1D object and the operator[] invocation on that object yields the float in position (3, 6) of the original two-dimensional array.

Clients of the Array2D class need not be aware of the presence of the Array1D class. Objects of this latter class stand for one-dimensional array objects that, conceptually, do not exist for clients of Array2D. Such clients program as if they were using real, live, honest-to-Allah two-dimensional arrays. It is of no concern to Array2D clients that those objects must, in order to satisfy the vagaries of C++, be syntactically compatible with one-dimensional arrays of other one-dimensional arrays.

Each Array1D object *stands for* a one-dimensional array that is absent from the conceptual model used by clients of Array2D. Objects that stand for other objects are often called *proxy objects*, and the classes that give rise to proxy objects are often called *proxy classes*. In this example, Array1D is a proxy class. Its instances stand for one-dimensional arrays that, conceptually, do not exist. (The terminology for proxy objects and classes is far from universal; objects of such classes are also sometimes known as *surrogates*.)

Distinguishing Reads from Writes via operator[]

The use of proxies to implement classes whose instances act like multidimensional arrays is common, but proxy classes are more flexible than that. Item 5, for example, shows how proxy classes can be employed to prevent single-argument constructors from being used to perform unwanted type conversions. Of the varied uses of proxy classes, however, the most heralded is that of helping distinguish reads from writes through operator[].

Consider a reference-counted string class that supports operator[]. Such a class is examined in detail in Item 29. If the concepts behind reference counting have slipped your mind, it would be a good idea to familiarize yourself with the material in that Item now.

A string class supporting operator[] allows clients to write code like this:

```
String s1, s2;             // a string-like class; the
                           // use of proxies keeps this
                           // class from conforming to
                           // the standard string
...                        // interface
cout << s1[5];             // read s1
s2[5] = 'x';               // write s2
s1[3] = s2[8];             // write s1, read s2
```

Note that operator[] can be called in two different contexts: to read a character or to write a character. Reads are known as *rvalue* usages; writes are known as *lvalue* usages. (The terms come from the field of compilers, where an lvalue goes on the left-hand side of an assignment and an rvalue goes on the right-hand side.) In general, using an object as an lvalue means using it such that it might be modified, and using it as an rvalue means using it such that it cannot be modified.

We'd like to distinguish between lvalue and rvalue usage of operator[] because, especially for reference-counted data structures, reads can be much less expensive to implement than writes. As Item 29 explains, writes of reference-counted objects may involve copying an entire data structure, but reads never require more than the simple returning of a value. Unfortunately, inside operator[], there is no way to determine the context in which the function was called; it is not possible to distinguish lvalue usage from rvalue usage within operator[].

"But wait," you say, "we don't need to. We can overload operator[] on the basis of its constness, and that will allow us to distinguish reads from writes." In other words, you suggest we solve our problem this way:

```
class String {
public:
  char operator[](int index) const;      // for reads
  char& operator[](int index);           // for writes
  ...

};
```

Alas, this won't work. Compilers choose between const and non-const member functions by looking only at whether the *object* invoking a function is const. No consideration is given to the context in which a call is made. Hence:

```
String s1, s2;

...

cout << s1[5];              // calls non-const operator[],
                            // because s1 isn't const

s2[5] = 'x';                // also calls non-const
                            // operator[]: s2 isn't const

s1[3] = s2[8];              // both calls are to non-const
                            // operator[], because both s1
                            // and s2 are non-const objects
```

Overloading operator[], then, fails to distinguish reads from writes.

In Item 29, we resigned ourselves to this unsatisfactory state of affairs and made the conservative assumption that all calls to operator[] were for writes. This time we shall not give up so easily. It may be impossible to distinguish lvalue from rvalue usage inside operator[], but we still want to do it. We will therefore find a way. What fun is life if you allow yourself to be limited by the possible?

Our approach is based on the fact that though it may be impossible to tell whether operator[] is being invoked in an lvalue or an rvalue context from within operator[], we can still treat reads differently from writes if we *delay* our lvalue-versus-rvalue actions until we see how the result of operator[] is used. All we need is a way to postpone our decision on whether our object is being read or written until *after* operator[] has returned. (This is an example of *lazy evaluation* — see Item 17.)

A proxy class allows us to buy the time we need, because we can modify operator[] to return a *proxy* for a string character instead of a string character itself. We can then wait to see how the proxy is used. If it's read, we can belatedly treat the call to operator[] as a read. If it's written, we must treat the call to operator[] as a write.

We will see the code for this in a moment, but first it is important to understand the proxies we'll be using. There are only three things you can do with a proxy:

- Create it, i.e., specify which string character it stands for.

- Use it as the target of an assignment, in which case you are really making an assignment to the string character it stands for. When used in this way, a proxy represents an lvalue use of the string on which operator[] was invoked.

- Use it in any other way. When used like this, a proxy represents an rvalue use of the string on which operator[] was invoked.

Here are the class definitions for a reference-counted String class using a proxy class to distinguish between lvalue and rvalue usages of operator[]:

```
class String {                  // reference-counted strings;
public:                         // see Item 29 for details

  class CharProxy {             // proxies for string chars
  public:
    CharProxy(String& str, int index);          // creation

    CharProxy& operator=(const CharProxy& rhs); // lvalue
    CharProxy& operator=(char c);               // uses

    operator char() const;                      // rvalue
                                                // use
  private:
    String& theString;      // string this proxy pertains to

    int charIndex;          // char within that string
                            // this proxy stands for
  };

  // continuation of String class
  const CharProxy
    operator[](int index) const;        // for const Strings
```

```
CharProxy operator[](int index);       // for non-const Strings
...

friend class CharProxy;

private:
  RCPtr<StringValue> value;
};
```

Other than the addition of the CharProxy class (which we'll examine
below), the only difference between this String class and the final
String class in Item 29 is that both operator[] functions now return
CharProxy objects. Clients of String can generally ignore this, however, and program as if the operator[] functions returned characters
(or references to characters — see Item 1) in the usual manner:

```
String s1, s2;              // reference-counted strings
                            // using proxies
...

cout << s1[5];              // still legal, still works

s2[5] = 'x';                // also legal, also works

s1[3] = s2[8];              // of course it's legal,
                            // of course it works
```

What's interesting is not that this works. What's interesting is *how* it
works.

Consider first this statement:

```
cout << s1[5];
```

The expression s1[5] yields a CharProxy object. No output operator
is defined for such objects, so your compilers labor to find an implicit
type conversion they can apply to make the call to operator<< succeed (see Item 5). They find one: the implicit conversion from Char-
Proxy to char declared in the CharProxy class. They automatically
invoke this conversion operator, and the result is that the string character represented by the CharProxy is printed. This is representative
of the CharProxy-to-char conversion that takes place for all Char-
Proxy objects used as rvalues.

Lvalue usage is handled differently. Look again at

```
s2[5] = 'x';
```

As before, the expression s2[5] yields a CharProxy object, but this
time that object is the target of an assignment. Which assignment operator is invoked? The target of the assignment is a CharProxy, the assignment operator that's called is in the CharProxy class. This is
crucial, because inside a CharProxy assignment operator, we know

that the CharProxy object being assigned to is being used as an lvalue. We therefore know that the string character for which the proxy stands is being used as an lvalue, and we must take whatever actions are necessary to implement lvalue access for that character.

Similarly, the statement

```
s1[3] = s2[8];
```

calls the assignment operator for two CharProxy objects, and inside that operator we know the object on the left is being used as an lvalue and the object on the right as an rvalue.

"Yeah, yeah, yeah," you grumble, "show me." Okay. Here's the code for String's operator[] functions:

```
const String::CharProxy String::operator[](int index) const
{
  return CharProxy(const_cast<String&>(*this), index);
}

String::CharProxy String::operator[](int index)
{
  return CharProxy(*this, index);
}
```

Each function just creates and returns a proxy for the requested character. No action is taken on the character itself: we defer such action until we know whether the access is for a read or a write.

Note that the const version of operator[] returns a const proxy. Because CharProxy::operator= isn't a const member function, such proxies can't be used as the target of assignments. Hence neither the proxy returned from the const version of operator[] nor the character for which it stands may be used as an lvalue. Conveniently enough, that's exactly the behavior we want for the const version of operator[].

Note also the use of a const_cast (see Item 2) on *this when creating the CharProxy object that the const operator[] returns. That's necessary to satisfy the constraints of the CharProxy constructor, which accepts only a non-const String. Casts are usually worrisome, but in this case the CharProxy object returned by operator[] is itself const, so there is no risk the String containing the character to which the proxy refers will be modified.

Each proxy returned by an operator[] function remembers which string it pertains to and, within that string, the index of the character it represents:

```
String::CharProxy::CharProxy(String& str, int index)
: theString(str), charIndex(index) {}
```

Conversion of a proxy to an rvalue is straightforward — we just return a copy of the character represented by the proxy:

```
String::CharProxy::operator char() const
{
  return theString.value->data[charIndex];
}
```

If you've forgotten the relationship among a String object, its value member, and the data member it points to, you can refresh your memory by turning to Item 29. Because this function returns a character by value, and because C++ limits the use of such by-value returns to rvalue contexts only, this conversion function can be used only in places where an rvalue is legal.

We thus turn to implementation of CharProxy's assignment operators, which is where we must deal with the fact that a character represented by a proxy is being used as the target of an assignment, i.e., as an lvalue. We can implement CharProxy's conventional assignment operator as follows:

```
String::CharProxy&
String::CharProxy::operator=(const CharProxy& rhs)
{
  // if the string is sharing a value with other String objects,
  // break off a separate copy of the value for this string only
  if (theString.value->isShared()) {
    theString.value->removeReference();
    theString.value = new StringValue(theString.value->data);
  }

  // now make the assignment: assign the value of the char
  // represented by rhs to the char represented by *this
  theString.value->data[charIndex] =
    rhs.theString.value->data[rhs.charIndex];

  return *this;
}
```

If you compare this with the implementation of the non-const String::operator[] in Item 29 on page 207, you'll see that they are strikingly similar. This is to be expected. In Item 29, we pessimistically assumed that all invocations of the non-const operator[] were writes, so we treated them as such. Here, we moved the code implementing a write into CharProxy's assignment operators, and that allows us to avoid paying for a write when the non-const operator[] is used only in an rvalue context. Note, by the way, that this function requires access to String's private data member value. That's why

CharProxy is declared a friend in the earlier class definition for String.

The second CharProxy assignment operator is almost identical:

```
String::CharProxy& String::CharProxy::operator=(char c)
{
  if (theString.value->isShared()) {
    theString.value->removeReference();
    theString.value = new StringValue(theString.value->data);
  }

  theString.value->data[charIndex] = c;

  return *this;
}
```

As an accomplished software engineer, you would, of course, banish the code duplication present in these two assignment operators to a private CharProxy member function that both would call. Aren't you the modular one?

Limitations

The use of a proxy class is a nice way to distinguish lvalue and rvalue usage of operator[], but the technique is not without its drawbacks. We'd like proxy objects to seamlessly replace the objects they stand for, but this ideal is difficult to achieve. That's because objects are used as lvalues in contexts other than just assignment, and using proxies in such contexts usually yields different behavior than using real objects.

Consider again the code fragment from Item 29 that motivated our decision to add a shareability flag to each StringValue object. If String::operator[] returns a CharProxy instead of a char&, that code will no longer compile:

```
String s1 = "Hello";

char *p = &s1[1];                    // error!
```

The expression s1[1] returns a CharProxy, so the type of the expression on the right-hand side of the "=" is CharProxy*. There is no conversion from a CharProxy* to a char*, so the initialization of p fails to compile. In general, taking the address of a proxy yields a different type of pointer than does taking the address of a real object.

To eliminate this difficulty, you'll need to overload the address-of operators for the CharProxy class:

```
class String {
public:

  class CharProxy {
  public:
    ...
    char * operator&();
    const char * operator&() const;
    ...
  };

  ...
};
```

These functions are easy to implement. The const function just returns a pointer to a const version of the character represented by the proxy:

```
const char * String::CharProxy::operator&() const
{
  return &(theString.value->data[charIndex]);
}
```

The non-const function is a bit more work, because it returns a pointer to a character that may be modified. This is analogous to the behavior of the non-const version of String::operator[] in Item 29, and the implementation is equally analogous:

```
char * String::CharProxy::operator&()
{
  // make sure the character to which this function returns
  // a pointer isn't shared by any other String objects
  if (theString.value->isShared()) {
    theString.value->removeReference();
    theString.value = new StringValue(theString.value->data);
  }

  // we don't know how long the pointer this function
  // returns will be kept by clients, so the StringValue
  // object can never be shared
  theString.value->markUnshareable();

  return &(theString.value->data[charIndex]);
}
```

Much of this code is common to other CharProxy member functions, so I know you'd encapsulate it in a private member function that all would call.

A second difference between chars and the CharProxys that stand for them becomes apparent if we have a template for reference-counted arrays that use proxy classes to distinguish lvalue and rvalue invocations of operator[]:

```
template<class T>              // reference-counted array
class Array {                  // using proxies
public:
  class Proxy {
  public:
    Proxy(Array<T>& array, int index);
    Proxy& operator=(const T& rhs);
    operator T() const;
    ...
  };

  const Proxy operator[](int index) const;
  Proxy operator[](int index);
  ...
};
```

Consider how these arrays might be used:

```
Array<int> intArray;

...

intArray[5] = 22;              // fine

intArray[5] += 5;              // error!

intArray[5]++;                 // error!
```

As expected, use of operator[] as the target of a simple assignment succeeds, but use of operator[] on the left-hand side of a call to operator+= or operator++ fails. That's because operator[] returns a proxy, and there is no operator+= or operator++ for Proxy objects. A similar situation exists for other operators that require lvalues, including operator*=, operator<<=, operator--, etc. If you want these operators to work with operator[] functions that return proxies, you must define each of these functions for the Array<T>::Proxy class. That's a lot of work, and you probably don't want to do it. Unfortunately, you either do the work or you do without. Them's the breaks.

A related problem has to do with invoking member functions on real objects through proxies. To be blunt about it, you can't. For example, suppose we'd like to work with reference-counted arrays of rational numbers. We could define a class Rational and then use the Array template we just saw:

```
class Rational {
public:
  Rational(int numerator = 0, int denominator = 1);
  int numerator() const;
  int denominator() const;
  ...
};

Array<Rational> array;
```

This is how we'd expect to be able to use such arrays, but, alas, we'd be disappointed:

```
cout << array[4].numerator();              // error!

int denom = array[22].denominator();       // error!
```

By now the difficulty is predictable; `operator[]` returns a proxy for a rational number, not an actual `Rational` object. But the `numerator` and `denominator` member functions exist only for `Rationals`, not their proxies. Hence the complaints by your compilers. To make proxies behave like the objects they stand for, you must overload each function applicable to the real objects so it applies to proxies, too.

Yet another situation in which proxies fail to replace real objects is when being passed to functions that take non-const references:

```
void swap(char& a, char& b);     // swaps the value of a and b

String s = "+C+";                // oops, should be "C++"

swap(s[0], s[1]);                // this should fix the
                                 // problem, but it won't
                                 // compile
```

`String::operator[]` returns a `CharProxy`, but `swap` demands that its arguments be of type `char&`. A `CharProxy` may be implicitly converted into a `char`, but there is no conversion function to a `char&`. Furthermore, the `char` to which it may be converted can't be bound to `swap`'s `char&` parameters, because that `char` is a temporary object (it's `operator char`'s return value) and, as Item 19 explains, there are good reasons for refusing to bind temporary objects to non-const reference parameters.

A final way in which proxies fail to seamlessly replace real objects has to do with implicit type conversions. When a proxy object is implicitly converted into the real object it stands for, a user-defined conversion function is invoked. For instance, a `CharProxy` can be converted into the `char` it stands for by calling `operator char`. As Item 5 explains, compilers may use only one user-defined conversion function when converting a parameter at a call site into the type needed by the corresponding function parameter. As a result, it is possible for function calls that succeed when passed real objects to fail when passed proxies. For example, suppose we have a `TVStation` class and a function, `watchTV`:

```
class TVStation {
public:
  TVStation(int channel);
  ...

};
```

```
void watchTV(const TVStation& station, float hoursToWatch);
```

Thanks to implicit type conversion from `int` to `TVStation` (see Item 5), we could then do this:

```
watchTV(10, 2.5);                    // watch channel 10 for
                                     // 2.5 hours
```

Using the template for reference-counted arrays that use proxy classes to distinguish lvalue and rvalue invocations of `operator[]`, however, we could not do this:

```
Array<int> intArray;

intArray[4] = 10;

watchTV(intArray[4], 2.5);           // error! no conversion
                                     // from Proxy<int> to
                                     // TVStation
```

Given the problems that accompany implicit type conversions, it's hard to get too choked up about this. In fact, a better design for the `TVStation` class would declare its constructor `explicit`, in which case even the first call to `watchTV` would fail to compile. For all the details on implicit type conversions and how `explicit` affects them, see Item 5.

Evaluation

Proxy classes allow you to achieve some types of behavior that are otherwise difficult or impossible to implement. Multidimensional arrays are one example, lvalue/rvalue differentiation is a second, suppression of implicit conversions (see Item 5) is a third.

At the same time, proxy classes have disadvantages. As function return values, proxy objects are temporaries (see Item 19), so they must be created and destroyed. That's not free, though the cost may be more than recouped through their ability to distinguish write operations from read operations. The very existence of proxy classes increases the complexity of software systems that employ them, because additional classes make things harder to design, implement, understand, and maintain, not easier.

Finally, shifting from a class that works with real objects to a class that works with proxies often changes the semantics of the class, because proxy objects usually exhibit behavior that is subtly different from that of the real objects they represent. Sometimes this makes proxies a poor choice when designing a system, but in many cases there is little need for the operations that would make the presence of proxies apparent to clients. For instance, few clients will want to take the address of an `Array1D` object in the two-dimensional array example we saw at the beginning of this Item, and there isn't much chance that an `ArrayIndex` object (see Item 5) would be passed to a function expecting a different type. In many cases, proxies can stand in for real objects perfectly acceptably. When they can, it is often the case that nothing else will do.

Item 31: Making functions virtual with respect to more than one object

Sometimes, to borrow a phrase from Jacqueline Susann, once is not enough. Suppose, for example, you're bucking for one of those high-profile, high-prestige, high-paying programming jobs at that famous software company in Redmond, Washington — by which of course I mean Nintendo. To bring yourself to the attention of Nintendo's management, you might decide to write a video game. Such a game might take place in outer space and involve space ships, space stations, and asteroids.

As the ships, stations, and asteroids whiz around in your artificial world, they naturally run the risk of colliding with one another. Let's assume the rules for such collisions are as follows:

- If a ship and a station collide at low velocity, the ship docks at the station. Otherwise the ship and the station sustain damage that's proportional to the speed at which they collide.

- If a ship and a ship or a station and a station collide, both participants in the collision sustain damage that's proportional to the speed at which they hit.

- If a small asteroid collides with a ship or a station, the asteroid is destroyed. If it's a big asteroid, the ship or the station is destroyed.

- If an asteroid collides with another asteroid, both break into pieces and scatter little baby asteroids in all directions.

This may sound like a dull game, but it suffices for our purpose here, which is to consider how to structure the C++ code that handles collisions between objects.

We begin by noting that ships, stations, and asteroids share some common features. If nothing else, they're all in motion, so they all have a direction and a velocity that describes that motion. Given this commonality, it is natural to define a base class from which they all inherit. In practice, such a class is almost invariably an abstract base class, and, if you heed the warning I give in Item 33, base classes are always abstract. The hierarchy might therefore look like this:

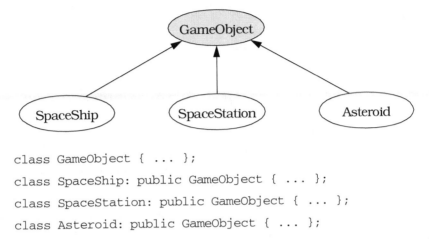

```
class GameObject { ... };

class SpaceShip: public GameObject { ... };

class SpaceStation: public GameObject { ... };

class Asteroid: public GameObject { ... };
```

Now, suppose you're deep in the bowels of your program, writing the code to check for and handle object collisions. You might come up with a function that looks something like this:

```
void checkForCollision(GameObject& object1,
                       GameObject& object2)
{
  if (theyJustCollided(object1, object2)) {
    processCollision(object1, object2);
  }
  else {
    ...
  }
}
```

This is where the programming challenge becomes apparent. When you call processCollision, you know that object1 and object2 just collided, and you know that what happens in that collision depends on what object1 really is and what object2 really is, but you don't know what kinds of objects they really are; all you know is that they're both GameObjects. If the collision processing depended only on the dynamic type of object1, you could make processCollision virtual in GameObject and call object1.processCollision(object2). You could do the same thing with object2 if the details of the collision depended only on its dynamic type. What happens in the collision, however, depends on *both* their dynamic types. A function call that's virtual on only one object, you see, is not enough.

What you need is a kind of function whose behavior is somehow virtual on the types of more than one object. C++ offers no such function. Nevertheless, you still have to implement the behavior required above. The question, then, is how you are going to do it.

One possibility is to scrap the use of C++ and choose another programming language. You could turn to CLOS, for example, the Common Lisp Object System. CLOS supports what is possibly the most general object-oriented function-invocation mechanism one can imagine: *multi-methods*. A multi-method is a function that's virtual on as many parameters as you'd like, and CLOS goes even further by giving you substantial control over how calls to overloaded multi-methods are resolved.

Let us assume, however, that you must implement your game in C++ — that you must come up with your own way of implementing what is commonly referred to as *double-dispatching*. (The name comes from the object-oriented programming community, where what C++ programmers know as a virtual function call is termed a "message dispatch." A call that's virtual on two parameters is implemented through a "double dispatch." The generalization of this — a function acting virtual on several parameters — is called *multiple dispatch*.) There are several approaches you might consider. None is without its disadvantages, but that shouldn't surprise you. C++ offers no direct support for double-dispatching, so you must yourself do the work compilers do when they implement virtual functions (see Item 24). If that were easy to do, we'd probably all be doing it ourselves and simply programming in C. We aren't and we don't, so fasten your seat-belts, it's going to be a bumpy ride.

Using Virtual Functions and RTTI

Virtual functions implement a single dispatch; that's half of what we need; and compilers do virtual functions for us, so we begin by declaring a virtual function `collide` in `GameObject`. This function is overridden in the derived classes in the usual manner:

```
class GameObject {
public:
  virtual void collide(GameObject& otherObject) = 0;
  ...
};

class SpaceShip: public GameObject {
public:
  virtual void collide(GameObject& otherObject);
  ...
};
```

Here I'm showing only the derived class `SpaceShip`, but `SpaceStation` and `Asteroid` are handled in exactly the same manner.

The most common approach to double-dispatching returns us to the unforgiving world of virtual function emulation via chains of if-then-elses. In this harsh world, we first discover the real type of otherObject, then we test it against all the possibilities:

```
// if we collide with an object of unknown type, we
// throw an exception of this type:
class CollisionWithUnknownObject {
public:
  CollisionWithUnknownObject(GameObject& whatWeHit);
  ...
};

void SpaceShip::collide(GameObject& otherObject)
{
  const type_info& objectType = typeid(otherObject);

  if (objectType == typeid(SpaceShip)) {
    SpaceShip& ss = static_cast<SpaceShip&>(otherObject);

    process a SpaceShip-SpaceShip collision;

  }
  else if (objectType == typeid(SpaceStation)) {
    SpaceStation& ss =
      static_cast<SpaceStation&>(otherObject);

    process a SpaceShip-SpaceStation collision;

  }
  else if (objectType == typeid(Asteroid)) {
    Asteroid& a = static_cast<Asteroid&>(otherObject);

    process a SpaceShip-Asteroid collision;

  }
  else {
    throw CollisionWithUnknownObject(otherObject);
  }
}
```

Notice how we need to determine the type of only one of the objects involved in the collision. The other object is *this, and its type is determined by the virtual function mechanism. We're inside a SpaceShip member function, so *this must be a SpaceShip object. Thus we only have to figure out the real type of otherObject.

There's nothing complicated about this code. It's easy to write. It's even easy to make work. That's one of the reasons RTTI is worrisome: it looks harmless. The true danger in this code is hinted at only by the final else clause and the exception that's thrown there.

We've pretty much bidden *adios* to encapsulation, because each col-lide function must be aware of each of its sibling classes, i.e., those classes that inherit from GameObject. In particular, if a new type of object — a new class — is added to the game, we must update each RTTI-based if-then-else chain in the program that might encounter the new object type. If we forget even a single one, the program will have a bug, and the bug will *not* be obvious. Furthermore, compilers are in no position to help us detect such an oversight, because they have no idea what we're doing.

This kind of type-based programming has a long history in C, and one of the things we know about it is that it yields programs that are essentially unmaintainable. Enhancement of such programs eventually becomes unthinkable. This is the primary reason why virtual functions were invented in the first place: to shift the burden of generating and maintaining type-based function calls from programmers to compilers. When we employ RTTI to implement double-dispatching, we are harking back to the bad old days.

The techniques of the bad old days led to errors in C, and they'll lead to errors in C++, too. In recognition of our human frailty, we've included a final else clause in the collide function, a clause where control winds up if we hit an object we don't know about. Such a situation is, in principle, impossible, but where were our principles when we decided to use RTTI? There are various ways to handle such unanticipated interactions, but none is very satisfying. In this case, we've chosen to throw an exception, but it's not clear how our callers can hope to handle the error any better than we can, since we've just run into something we didn't know existed.

Using Virtual Functions Only

There is a way to minimize the risks inherent in an RTTI approach to implementing double-dispatching, but before we look at that, it's convenient to see how to attack the problem using nothing but virtual functions. That strategy begins with the same basic structure as the RTTI approach. The collide function is declared virtual in GameObject and is redefined in each derived class. In addition, collide is overloaded in each class, one overloading for each derived class in the hierarchy:

```
class SpaceShip;                    // forward declarations
class SpaceStation;
class Asteroid;
```

```
class GameObject {
public:
  virtual void collide(GameObject&    otherObject) = 0;
  virtual void collide(SpaceShip&     otherObject) = 0;
  virtual void collide(SpaceStation&  otherObject) = 0;
  virtual void collide(Asteroid&      otherobject) = 0;
  ...

};
class SpaceShip: public GameObject {
public:
  virtual void collide(GameObject&    otherObject);
  virtual void collide(SpaceShip&     otherObject);
  virtual void collide(SpaceStation&  otherObject);
  virtual void collide(Asteroid&      otherobject);
  ...

};
```

The basic idea is to implement double-dispatching as two single dispatches, i.e., as two separate virtual function calls: the first determines the dynamic type of the first object, the second determines that
of the second object. As before, the first virtual call is to the collide
function taking a GameObject& parameter. That function's implementation now becomes startlingly simple:

```
void SpaceShip::collide(GameObject& otherObject)
{
  otherObject.collide(*this);
}
```

At first glance, this appears to be nothing more than a recursive call to
collide with the order of the parameters reversed, i.e., with other-
Object becoming the object calling the member function and *this
becoming the function's parameter. Glance again, however, because
this is *not* a recursive call. As you know, compilers figure out which of
a set of functions to call on the basis of the static types of the arguments passed to the function. In this case, four different collide
functions could be called, but the one chosen is based on the static
type of *this. What is that static type? Being inside a member function of the class SpaceShip, *this must be of type SpaceShip. The
call is therefore to the collide function taking a SpaceShip&, not the
collide function taking a GameObject&.

All the collide functions are virtual, so the call inside Space-
Ship::collide resolves to the implementation of collide corresponding to the real type of otherObject. Inside *that* implementation of
collide, the real types of both objects are known, because the left-
hand object is *this (and therefore has as its type the class imple-

menting the member function) and the right-hand object's real type is SpaceShip, the same as the declared type of the parameter.

All this may be clearer when you see the implementations of the other collide functions in SpaceShip:

```
void SpaceShip::collide(SpaceShip& otherObject)
{
  process a SpaceShip-SpaceShip collision;
}

void SpaceShip::collide(SpaceStation& otherObject)
{
  process a SpaceShip-SpaceStation collision;
}

void SpaceShip::collide(Asteroid& otherObject)
{
  process a SpaceShip-Asteroid collision;
}
```

As you can see, there's no muss, no fuss, no RTTI, no need to throw exceptions for unexpected object types. There can be no unexpected object types — that's the whole point of using virtual functions. In fact, were it not for its fatal flaw, this would be the perfect solution to the double-dispatching problem.

The flaw is one it shares with the RTTI approach we saw earlier: each class must know about its siblings. As new classes are added, the code must be updated. However, the *way* in which the code must be updated is different in this case. True, there are no if-then-elses to modify, but there is something that is often worse: each class definition must be amended to include a new virtual function. If, for example, you decide to add a new class Satellite (inheriting from GameObject) to your game, you'd have to add a new collide function to each of the existing classes in the program.

Modifying existing classes is something you are frequently in no position to do. If, instead of writing the entire video game yourself, you started with an off-the-shelf class library comprising a video game application framework, you might not have write access to the GameObject class or the framework classes derived from it. In that case, adding new member functions, virtual or otherwise, is not an option. Alternatively, you may have *physical* access to the classes requiring modification, but you may not have *practical* access. For example, suppose you *were* hired by Nintendo and were put to work on programs using a library containing GameObject and other useful classes. Surely you wouldn't be the only one using that library, and Nintendo would probably be less than thrilled about recompiling every application using that library each time you decided to add a new type of object to your program. In practice, libraries in wide use are modified only rarely, because the cost of recompiling everything using those libraries is too great.

The long and short of it is if you need to implement double-dispatching in your program, your best recourse is to modify your design to eliminate the need. Failing that, the virtual function approach is safer than the RTTI strategy, but it constrains the extensibility of your system to match that of your ability to edit header files. The RTTI approach, on the other hand, makes no recompilation demands, but, if implemented as shown above, it generally leads to software that is unmaintainable. You pays your money and you takes your chances.

Emulating Virtual Function Tables

There is a way to improve those chances. You may recall from Item 24 that compilers typically implement virtual functions by creating an array of function pointers (the vtbl) and then indexing into that array when a virtual function is called. Using a vtbl eliminates the need for compilers to perform chains of if-then-else-like computations, and it allows compilers to generate the same code at all virtual function call sites: determine the correct vtbl index, then call the function pointed to at that position in the vtbl.

There is no reason you can't do this yourself. If you do, you not only make your RTTI-based code more efficient (indexing into an array and following a function pointer is almost always more efficient than running through a series of if-then-else tests, and it generates less code, too), you also isolate the use of RTTI to a single location: the place where your array of function pointers is initialized. I should mention that the meek may inherit the earth, but the meek of heart may wish to take a few deep breaths before reading what follows.

We begin by making some modifications to the functions in the GameObject hierarchy:

```
class GameObject {
public:
  virtual void collide(GameObject& otherObject) = 0;
  ...
};

class SpaceShip: public GameObject {
public:
  virtual void collide(GameObject& otherObject);
  virtual void hitSpaceShip(SpaceShip& otherObject);
  virtual void hitSpaceStation(SpaceStation& otherObject);
  virtual void hitAsteroid(Asteroid& otherobject);
  ...
};
```

```
void SpaceShip::hitSpaceShip(SpaceShip& otherObject)
{
  process a SpaceShip-SpaceShip collision;
}

void SpaceShip::hitSpaceStation(SpaceStation& otherObject)
{
  process a SpaceShip-SpaceStation collision;
}

void SpaceShip::hitAsteroid(Asteroid& otherObject)
{
  process a SpaceShip-Asteroid collision;
}
```

Like the RTTI-based hierarchy we started out with, the GameObject class contains only one function for processing collisions, the one that performs the first of the two necessary dispatches. Like the virtual-function-based hierarchy we saw later, each kind of interaction is encapsulated in a separate function, though in this case the functions have different names instead of sharing the name collide. There is a reason for this abandonment of overloading, and we shall see it soon. For the time being, note that the design above contains everything we need except an implementation for SpaceShip::collide; that's where the various hit functions will be invoked. As before, once we successfully implement the SpaceShip class, the SpaceStation and Asteroid classes will follow suit.

Inside SpaceShip::collide, we need a way to map the dynamic type of the parameter otherObject to a member function pointer that points to the appropriate collision-handling function. An easy way to do this is to create an associative array that, given a class name, yields the appropriate member function pointer. It's possible to implement collide using such an associative array directly, but it's a bit easier to understand what's going on if we add an intervening function, lookup, that takes a GameObject and returns the appropriate member function pointer. That is, you pass lookup a GameObject, and it returns a pointer to the member function to call when you collide with something of that GameObject's type.

Here's the declaration of lookup:

```
class SpaceShip: public GameObject {
private:
  typedef void (SpaceShip::*HitFunctionPtr)(GameObject&);

  HitFunctionPtr lookup(const GameObject& whatWeHit) const;

  ...
};
```

The syntax of function pointers is never very pretty, and for member function pointers it's worse than usual, so we've typedefed HitFunctionPtr to be shorthand for a pointer to a member function of Space-Ship that takes a GameObject& and returns nothing.

Once we've got lookup, implementation of collide becomes the proverbial piece of cake:

```
void SpaceShip::collide(GameObject& otherObject)
{
  HitFunctionPtr hfp =
    lookup(otherObject);       // find the function to call

  if (hfp) {                   // if a function was found
    (this->*hfp)(otherObject); // call it
  }
  else {
    throw CollisionWithUnknownObject(otherObject);
  }
}
```

Provided we've kept the contents of our associative array in sync with the class hierarchy under GameObject, lookup must always find a valid function pointer for the object we pass it. People are people, however, and mistakes have been known to creep into even the most carefully crafted software systems. That's why we still check to make sure a valid pointer was returned from lookup, and that's why we still throw an exception if the impossible occurs and the lookup fails.

All that remains now is the implementation of lookup. Given an associative array that maps from object types to member function pointers, the lookup itself is easy, but creating, initializing, and destroying the associative array is an interesting problem of its own.

Such an array should be created and initialized before it's used, and it should be destroyed when it's no longer needed. We could use new and delete to create and destroy the array manually, but that would be error-prone: how could we guarantee the array wasn't used before we got around to initializing it? A better solution is to have compilers automate the process, and we can do that by making the associative array a static member of lookup. That way it will be created and initialized the first time lookup is called, and it will be automatically destroyed sometime after main is exited.

Furthermore, we can use the map template from the Standard Template Library (see Item 35) as the associative array, because that's what a map is:

```
class SpaceShip: public GameObject {
private:
  typedef void (SpaceShip::*HitFunctionPtr)(GameObject&);
  typedef map<string, HitFunctionPtr> HitMap;

  ...

};

SpaceShip::HitFunctionPtr
SpaceShip::lookup(const GameObject& whatWeHit) const
{
  static HitMap collisionMap;

  ...

}
```

Here, collisionMap is our associative array. It maps the name of a class (as a string object) to a SpaceShip member function pointer. Because map<string, HitFunctionPtr> is quite a mouthful, we use a typedef to make it easier to swallow. (For fun, try writing the declaration of collisionMap without using the HitMap and HitFunctionPtr typedefs. Most people will want to do this only once.)

Given collisionMap, the implementation of lookup is rather anticlimactic. That's because searching for something is an operation directly supported by the map class, and the one member function we can always (portably) call on the result of a typeid invocation is name (which, predictably, yields the name of the object's dynamic type). To implement lookup, then, we just find the entry in collisionMap corresponding to the dynamic type of lookup's argument.

The code for lookup is straightforward, but if you're not familiar with the Standard Template Library (again, see Item 35), it may not seem that way. Don't worry. The comments in the function explain what's going on.

```
SpaceShip::HitFunctionPtr
SpaceShip::lookup(const GameObject& whatWeHit) const
{
  static HitMap collisionMap;    // we'll see how to
                                 // initialize this below

  // look up the collision-processing function for the type
  // of whatWeHit. The value returned is a pointer-like
  // object called an "iterator" (see Item 35).
  HitMap::iterator mapEntry=
    collisionMap.find(typeid(whatWeHit).name());

  // mapEntry == collisionMap.end() if the lookup failed;
  // this is standard map behavior. Again, see Item 35.
  if (mapEntry == collisionMap.end()) return 0;
```

```
// If we get here, the search succeeded. mapEntry
// points to a complete map entry, which is a
// (string, HitFunctionPtr) pair. We want only the
// second part of the pair, so that's what we return.
return (*mapEntry).second;
}
```

The final statement in the function returns (*mapEntry).second instead of the more conventional mapEntry->second in order to satisfy the vagaries of the STL. For details, see page 96.

Initializing Emulated Virtual Function Tables

Which brings us to the initialization of collisionMap. We'd like to say something like this,

```
// An incorrect implementation
SpaceShip::HitFunctionPtr
SpaceShip::lookup(const GameObject& whatWeHit) const
{
  static HitMap collisionMap;

  collisionMap["SpaceShip"] = &hitSpaceShip;
  collisionMap["SpaceStation"] = &hitSpaceStation;
  collisionMap["Asteroid"] = &hitAsteroid;

  ...

}
```

but this inserts the member function pointers into collisionMap *each time* lookup is called, and that's needlessly inefficient. In addition, this won't compile, but that's a secondary problem we'll address shortly.

What we need now is a way to put the member function pointers into collisionMap only once — when collisionMap is created. That's easy enough to accomplish; we just write a private static member function called initializeCollisionMap to create and initialize our map, then we initialize collisionMap with initializeCollisionMap's return value:

```
class SpaceShip: public GameObject {
private:
  static HitMap initializeCollisionMap();
  ...

};

SpaceShip::HitFunctionPtr
SpaceShip::lookup(const GameObject& whatWeHit) const
{
  static HitMap collisionMap = initializeCollisionMap();
  ...
}
```

But this means we probably have to pay the cost of copying the map object returned from initializeCollisionMap into collisionMap (see Items 19 and 20). We'd prefer not to do that. We wouldn't have to pay if initializeCollisionMap returned a pointer, but then we'd have to worry about making sure the map object the pointer pointed to was destroyed at an appropriate time.

Fortunately, there's a way for us to have it all. We can turn collisionMap into a smart pointer (see Item 28) that automatically deletes what it points to when the pointer itself is destroyed. In fact, the standard C++ library contains a template, auto_ptr, for just such a smart pointer (see Item 9). By making collisionMap a static auto_ptr in lookup, we can have initializeCollisionMap return a pointer to an initialized map object, yet never have to worry about a resource leak; the map to which collisionMap points will be automatically destroyed when collisionMap is. Thus:

```
class SpaceShip: public GameObject {
private:
  static HitMap * initializeCollisionMap();

  ...

};

SpaceShip::HitFunctionPtr
SpaceShip::lookup(const GameObject& whatWeHit) const
{
  static auto_ptr<HitMap>
    collisionMap(initializeCollisionMap());
  ...

}
```

The clearest way to implement initializeCollisionMap would seem to be this,

```
SpaceShip::HitMap * SpaceShip::initializeCollisionMap()
{
  HitMap *phm = new HitMap;

  (*phm)["SpaceShip"] = &hitSpaceShip;
  (*phm)["SpaceStation"] = &hitSpaceStation;
  (*phm)["Asteroid"] = &hitAsteroid;

  return phm;
}
```

but as I noted earlier, this won't compile. That's because a HitMap is declared to hold pointers to member functions that all take the same type of argument, namely `GameObject`. But `hitSpaceShip` takes a `SpaceShip`, `hitSpaceStation` takes a `SpaceStation`, and, `hitAsteroid` takes an `Asteroid`. Even though `SpaceShip`, `SpaceStation`, and `Asteroid` can all be implicitly converted to `GameObject`, there is no such conversion for pointers to functions taking these argument types.

To placate your compilers, you might be tempted to employ `reinterpret_casts` (see Item 2), which are generally the casts of choice when converting between function pointer types:

```
// A bad idea...
SpaceShip::HitMap * SpaceShip::initializeCollisionMap()
{
  HitMap *phm = new HitMap;

  (*phm)["SpaceShip"] =
    reinterpret_cast<HitFunctionPtr>(&hitSpaceShip);

  (*phm)["SpaceStation"] =
    reinterpret_cast<HitFunctionPtr>(&hitSpaceStation);

  (*phm)["Asteroid"] =
    reinterpret_cast<HitFunctionPtr>(&hitAsteroid);

  return phm;
}
```

This will compile, but it's a bad idea. It entails doing something you should never do: lying to your compilers. Telling them that `hitSpaceShip`, `hitSpaceStation`, and `hitAsteroid` are functions expecting a `GameObject` argument is simply not true. `hitSpaceShip` expects a `SpaceShip`, `hitSpaceStation` expects a `SpaceStation`, and `hitAsteroid` expects an `Asteroid`. The casts say otherwise. The casts lie.

More than morality is on the line here. Compilers don't like to be lied to, and they often find a way to exact revenge when they discover they've been deceived. In this case, they're likely to get back at you by generating bad code for functions you call through *phm in cases where `GameObject`'s derived classes employ multiple inheritance or have virtual base classes. In other words, if `SpaceStation`, `SpaceShip`, or `Asteroid` had other base classes (in addition to `GameObject`), you'd probably find that your calls to collision-processing functions in `collide` would behave quite rudely.

Consider again the A-B-C-D inheritance hierarchy and the likely object layout for a D object that is described in Item 24:

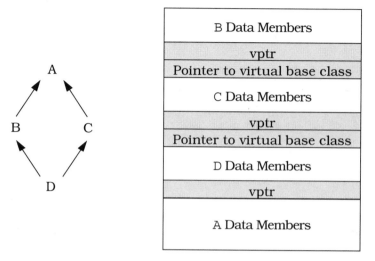

Each of the four class parts in a D object has a different address. This is important, because even though pointers and references behave differently (see Item 1), compilers typically *implement* references by using pointers in the generated code. Thus, pass-by-reference is typically implemented by passing a pointer to an object. When an object with multiple base classes (such as a D object) is passed by reference, it is crucial that compilers pass the *correct* address — the one corresponding to the declared type of the parameter in the function being called.

But what if you've lied to your compilers and told them your function expects a GameObject when it really expects a SpaceShip or a SpaceStation? Then they'll pass the wrong address when you call the function, and the resulting runtime carnage will probably be gruesome. It will also be *very* difficult to determine the cause of the problem. There are good reasons why casting is discouraged. This is one of them.

Okay, so casting is out. Fine. But the type mismatch between the function pointers a HitMap is willing to contain and the pointers to the hitSpaceShip, hitSpaceStation, and hitAsteroid functions remains. There is only one way to resolve the conflict: change the types of the functions so they all take GameObject arguments:

```
class GameObject {                           // this is unchanged
public:
  virtual void collide(GameObject& otherObject) = 0;
  ...
};
```

```
class SpaceShip: public GameObject {
public:
  virtual void collide(GameObject& otherObject);

  // these functions now all take a GameObject parameter
  virtual void hitSpaceShip(GameObject& spaceShip);
  virtual void hitSpaceStation(GameObject& spaceStation);
  virtual void hitAsteroid(GameObject& asteroid);
  ...
};
```

Our solution to the double-dispatching problem that was based on virtual functions overloaded the function name collide. Now we are in a position to understand why we didn't follow suit here — why we decided to use an associative array of member function pointers instead. All the hit functions take the same parameter type, so we must give them different names.

Now we can write initializeCollisionMap the way we always wanted to:

```
SpaceShip::HitMap * SpaceShip::initializeCollisionMap()
{
  HitMap *phm = new HitMap;

  (*phm)["SpaceShip"] = &hitSpaceShip;
  (*phm)["SpaceStation"] = &hitSpaceStation;
  (*phm)["Asteroid"] = &hitAsteroid;

  return phm;
}
```

Regrettably, our hit functions now get a general GameObject parameter instead of the derived class parameters they expect. To bring reality into accord with expectation, we must resort to a dynamic_cast (see Item 2) at the top of each function:

```
void SpaceShip::hitSpaceShip(GameObject& spaceShip)
{
  SpaceShip& otherShip=
    dynamic_cast<SpaceShip&>(spaceShip);

  process a SpaceShip-SpaceShip collision;

}

void SpaceShip::hitSpaceStation(GameObject& spaceStation)
{
  SpaceStation& station=
    dynamic_cast<SpaceStation&>(spaceStation);

  process a SpaceShip-SpaceStation collision;

}
```

```
void SpaceShip::hitAsteroid(GameObject& asteroid)
{
  Asteroid& theAsteroid =
    dynamic_cast<Asteroid&>(asteroid);

  process a SpaceShip-Asteroid collision;

}
```

Each of the dynamic_casts will throw a bad_cast exception if the cast fails. They should never fail, of course, because the hit functions should never be called with incorrect parameter types. Still, we're better off safe than sorry.

Using Non-Member Collision-Processing Functions

We now know how to build a vtbl-like associative array that lets us implement the second half of a double-dispatch, and we know how to encapsulate the details of the associative array inside a lookup function. Because this array contains pointers to *member* functions, however, we still have to modify class definitions if a new type of GameObject is added to the game, and that means everybody has to recompile, even people who don't care about the new type of object. For example, if Satellite were added to our game, we'd have to augment the Space-Ship class with a declaration of a function to handle collisions between satellites and spaceships. All SpaceShip clients would then have to recompile, even if they couldn't care less about the existence of satellites. This is the problem that led us to reject the implementation of double-dispatching based purely on virtual functions, and that solution was a lot less work than the one we've just seen.

The recompilation problem would go away if our associative array contained pointers to non-member functions. Furthermore, switching to non-member collision-processing functions would let us address a design question we have so far ignored, namely, in which class should collisions between objects of different types be handled? With the implementation we just developed, if object 1 and object 2 collide and object 1 happens to be the left-hand argument to processCollision, the collision will be handled inside the class for object 1. If object 2 happens to be the left-hand argument to processCollision, however, the collision will be handled inside the class for object 2. Does this make sense? Wouldn't it be better to design things so that collisions between objects of types A and B are handled by neither A nor B but instead in some neutral location outside both classes?

If we move the collision-processing functions out of our classes, we can give clients header files that contain class definitions without any hit or collide functions. We can then structure our implementation file for processCollision as follows:

```
#include "SpaceShip.h"
#include "SpaceStation.h"
#include "Asteroid.h"

namespace {                        // unnamed namespace — see below
  // primary collision-processing functions
  void shipAsteroid(GameObject& spaceShip,
                    GameObject& asteroid);

  void shipStation(GameObject& spaceShip,
                   GameObject& spaceStation);

  void asteroidStation(GameObject& asteroid,
                       GameObject& spaceStation);
  ...

  // secondary collision-processing functions that just
  // implement symmetry: swap the parameters and call a
  // primary function
  void asteroidShip(GameObject& asteroid,
                    GameObject& spaceShip)
  { shipAsteroid(spaceShip, asteroid); }

  void stationShip(GameObject& spaceStation,
                   GameObject& spaceShip)
  { shipStation(spaceShip, spaceStation); }

  void stationAsteroid(GameObject& spaceStation,
                       GameObject& asteroid)
  { asteroidStation(asteroid, spaceStation); }

  ...

  // see below for a description of these types/functions
  typedef void (*HitFunctionPtr)(GameObject&, GameObject&);
  typedef map< pair<string,string>, HitFunctionPtr > HitMap;

  pair<string,string> makeStringPair(const char *s1,
                                     const char *s2);

  HitMap * initializeCollisionMap();

  HitFunctionPtr lookup(const string& class1,
                        const string& class2);

} // end namespace

void processCollision(GameObject& object1,
                      GameObject& object2)
{
  HitFunctionPtr phf = lookup( typeid(object1).name(),
                               typeid(object2).name() );

  if (phf) phf(object1, object2);
  else throw UnknownCollision(object1, object2);
}
```

Note the use of the unnamed namespace to contain the functions used to implement processCollision. Everything in such an unnamed namespace is private to the current translation unit (essentially the current file) — it's just like the functions were declared static at file scope. With the advent of namespaces, however, statics at file scope have been deprecated, so you should accustom yourself to using un-named namespaces as soon as your compilers support them.

Conceptually, this implementation is the same as the one that used member functions, but there are some minor differences. First, Hit-FunctionPtr is now a typedef for a pointer to a non-member function. Second, the exception class CollisionWithUnknownObject has been renamed UnknownCollision and modified to take two objects instead of one. Finally, lookup must now take two type names and perform both parts of the double-dispatch. This means our collision map must now hold three pieces of information: two types names and a HitFunc-tionPtr.

As fate would have it, the standard map class is defined to hold only two pieces of information. We can finesse that problem by using the standard pair template, which lets us bundle the two type names to-gether as a single object. initializeCollisionMap, along with its makeStringPair helper function, then looks like this:

```
// we use this function to create pair<string,string>
// objects from two char* literals. It's used in
// initializeCollisionMap below. Note how this function
// enables the return value optimization (see Item 20).

namespace {        // unnamed namespace again — see below

    pair<string,string> makeStringPair(const char *s1,
                                       const char *s2)
    { return pair<string,string>(s1, s2); }

} // end namespace

namespace {        // still the unnamed namespace — see below

    HitMap * initializeCollisionMap()
    {
        HitMap *phm = new HitMap;

        (*phm)[makeStringPair("SpaceShip","Asteroid")] =
            &shipAsteroid;

        (*phm)[makeStringPair("SpaceShip", "SpaceStation")] =
            &shipStation;

        ...

        return phm;
    }

} // end namespace
```

lookup must also be modified to work with the pair<string, string> objects that now comprise the first component of the collision map:

```
namespace {        // I explain this below — trust me

  HitFunctionPtr lookup(const string& class1,
                          const string& class2)
  {
    static auto_ptr<HitMap>
      collisionMap(initializeCollisionMap());

    // see below for a description of make_pair
    HitMap::iterator mapEntry=
      collisionMap->find(make_pair(class1, class2));

    if (mapEntry == collisionMap->end()) return 0;

    return (*mapEntry).second;
  }

} // end namespace
```

This is almost exactly what we had before. The only real difference is the use of the make_pair function in this statement:

```
HitMap::iterator mapEntry=
  collisionMap->find(make_pair(class1, class2));
```

make_pair is just a convenience function (template) in the standard library (see Item 35) that saves us the trouble of specifying the types when constructing a pair object. We could just as well have written the statement like this:

```
HitMap::iterator mapEntry=
  collisionMap->find(pair<string,string>(class1, class2));
```

This calls for more typing, however, and specifying the types for the pair is redundant (they're the same as the types of class1 and class2), so the make_pair form is more commonly used.

Because makeStringPair, initializeCollisionMap, and lookup were declared inside an unnamed namespace, each must be implemented within the same namespace. That's why the implementations of the functions above are in the unnamed namespace (for the same translation unit as their declarations): so the linker will correctly associate their definitions (i.e., their implementations) with their earlier declarations.

We have finally achieved our goals. If new subclasses of GameObject are added to our hierarchy, existing classes need not recompile (unless they wish to use the new classes). We have no tangle of RTTI-based switch or if-then-else conditionals to maintain. The addition of new classes to the hierarchy requires only well-defined and localized changes to our system: the addition of one or more map insertions in initializeCollisionMap and the declarations of the new collision-processing functions in the unnamed namespace associated with the implementation of processCollision. It may have been a lot of work to get here, but at least the trip was worthwhile. Yes? Yes?

Maybe.

Inheritance and Emulated Virtual Function Tables

There is one final problem we must confront. (If, at this point, you are wondering if there will *always* be one final problem to confront, you have truly come to appreciate the difficulty of designing an implementation mechanism for virtual functions.) Everything we've done will work fine as long as we never need to allow inheritance-based type conversions when calling collision-processing functions. But suppose we develop a game in which we must sometimes distinguish between commercial space ships and military space ships. We could modify our hierarchy as follows, where we've heeded the guidance of Item 33 and made the concrete classes CommercialShip and MilitaryShip inherit from the newly abstract class SpaceShip:

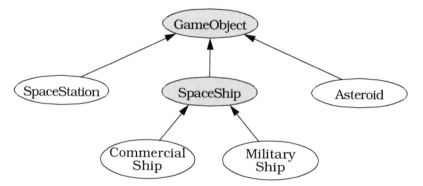

Suppose commercial and military ships behave identically when they collide with something. Then we'd expect to be able to use the same collision-processing functions we had before CommercialShip and MilitaryShip were added. In particular, if a MilitaryShip object and an Asteroid collided, we'd expect

```
void shipAsteroid(GameObject& spaceShip,
                  GameObject& asteroid);
```

to be called. It would not be. Instead, an UnknownCollision exception would be thrown. That's because lookup would be asked to find a function corresponding to the type names "MilitaryShip" and "Asteroid," and no such function would be found in collisionMap. Even though a `MilitaryShip` can be treated like a `SpaceShip`, `lookup` has no way of knowing that.

Furthermore, there is no easy way of telling it. If you need to implement double-dispatching and you need to support inheritance-based parameter conversions such as these, your only practical recourse is to fall back on the double-virtual-function-call mechanism we examined earlier. That implies you'll also have to put up with everybody recompiling when you add to your inheritance hierarchy, but that's just the way life is sometimes.

Initializing Emulated Virtual Function Tables (Reprise)

That's really all there is to say about double-dispatching, but it would be unpleasant to end the discussion on such a downbeat note, and unpleasantness is, well, unpleasant. Instead, let's conclude by outlining an alternative approach to initializing `collisionMap`.

As things stand now, our design is entirely static. Once we've registered a function for processing collisions between two types of objects, that's it; we're stuck with that function forever. What if we'd like to add, remove, or change collision-processing functions as the game proceeds? There's no way to do it.

But there can be. We can turn the concept of a map for storing collision-processing functions into a class that offers member functions allowing us to modify the contents of the map dynamically. For example:

```
class CollisionMap {
public:
  typedef void (*HitFunctionPtr)(GameObject&, GameObject&);

  void addEntry(const string& type1,
                const string& type2,
                HitFunctionPtr collisionFunction,
                bool symmetric = true);       // see below

  void removeEntry(const string& type1,
                   const string& type2);

  HitFunctionPtr lookup(const string& type1,
                        const string& type2);

  // this function returns a reference to the one and only
  // map — see Item 26
  static CollisionMap& theCollisionMap();

private:
  // these functions are private to prevent the creation
  // of multiple maps — see Item 26
  CollisionMap();
  CollisionMap(const CollisionMap&);
};
```

This class lets us add entries to the map, remove them from it, and look up the collision-processing function associated with a particular pair of type names. It also uses the techniques of Item 26 to limit the number of CollisionMap objects to one, because there is only one map in our system. (More complex games with multiple maps are easy to imagine.) Finally, it allows us to simplify the addition of symmetric collisions to the map (i.e., collisions in which the effect of an object of type T1 hitting an object of type T2 are the same as that of an object of type T2 hitting an object of type T1) by automatically adding the implied map entry when addEntry is called with the optional parameter symmetric set to true.

With the CollisionMap class, each client wishing to add an entry to the map does so directly:

```
void shipAsteroid(GameObject& spaceShip,
               GameObject& asteroid);
CollisionMap::theCollisionMap().addEntry("SpaceShip",
                                         "Asteroid",
                                         &shipAsteroid);

void shipStation(GameObject& spaceShip,
               GameObject& spaceStation);
CollisionMap::theCollisionMap().addEntry("SpaceShip",
                                         "SpaceStation",
                                         &shipStation);

void asteroidStation(GameObject& asteroid,
                   GameObject& spaceStation);
CollisionMap::theCollisionMap().addEntry("Asteroid",
                                         "SpaceStation",
                                         &asteroidStation);
...
```

Care must be taken to ensure that these map entries are added to the map before any collisions occur that would call the associated functions. One way to do this would be to have constructors in GameObject subclasses check to make sure the appropriate mappings had been added each time an object was created. Such an approach would exact a small performance penalty at runtime. An alternative would be to create a RegisterCollisionFunction class:

```
class RegisterCollisionFunction {
public:
  RegisterCollisionFunction(
            const string& type1,
            const string& type2,
            CollisionMap::HitFunctionPtr collisionFunction,
            bool symmetric = true)
  {
    CollisionMap::theCollisionMap().addEntry(type1, type2,
                                             collisionFunction,
                                             symmetric);
  }
};
```

Clients could then use global objects of this type to automatically register the functions they need:

```
RegisterCollisionFunction cf1("SpaceShip", "Asteroid",
                                &shipAsteroid);

RegisterCollisionFunction cf2("SpaceShip", "SpaceStation",
                                &shipStation);

RegisterCollisionFunction cf3("Asteroid", "SpaceStation",
                                &asteroidStation);

...

int main(int argc, char * argv[])
{
  ...
}
```

Because these objects are created before main is invoked, the functions their constructors register are also added to the map before main is called. If, later, a new derived class is added

```
class Satellite: public GameObject { ... };
```

and one or more new collision-processing functions are written,

```
void satelliteShip(GameObject& satellite,
                   GameObject& spaceShip);

void satelliteAsteroid(GameObject& satellite,
                       GameObject& asteroid);
```

these new functions can be similarly added to the map without disturbing existing code:

```
RegisterCollisionFunction cf4("Satellite", "SpaceShip",
                                &satelliteShip);

RegisterCollisionFunction cf5("Satellite", "Asteroid",
                                &satelliteAsteroid);
```

This doesn't change the fact that there's no perfect way to implement multiple dispatch, but it does make it easy to provide data for a map-based implementation if we decide such an approach is the best match for our needs.

Miscellany

We thus arrive at the organizational back of the bus, the chapter containing the guidelines no one else would have. We begin with two Items on C++ software development that describe how to design systems that accommodate change. One of the strengths of the object-oriented approach to systems building is its support for change, and these Items describe specific steps you can take to fortify your software against the slings and arrows of a world that refuses to stand still.

We then examine how to combine C and C++ in the same program. This necessarily leads to consideration of extralinguistic issues, but C++ exists in the real world, so sometimes we must confront such things.

Finally, I summarize changes to the C++ language standard since publication of the *de facto* reference. I especially cover the sweeping changes that have been made in the standard library. If you have not been following the standardization process closely, you are probably in for some surprises — many of them quite pleasant.

Item 32: Program in the future tense

Things change.

As software developers, we may not know much, but we do know that things will change. We don't necessarily know what will change, how the changes will be brought about, when the changes will occur, or why they will take place, but we do know this: things will change.

Good software adapts well to change. It accommodates new features, it ports to new platforms, it adjusts to new demands, it handles new inputs. Software this flexible, this robust, and this reliable does not come about by accident. It is designed and implemented by programmers who conform to the constraints of today while keeping in mind the probable needs of tomorrow. This kind of software — software that accepts change gracefully — is written by people who *program in the future tense.*

To program in the future tense is to accept that things will change and to be prepared for it. It is to recognize that new functions will be added to libraries, that new overloadings will occur, and to watch for the potentially ambiguous function calls that might result. It is to acknowledge that new classes will be added to hierarchies, that present-day derived classes may be tomorrow's base classes, and to prepare for that possibility. It is to accept that new applications will be written, that functions will be called in new contexts, and to write those functions so they continue to perform correctly. It is to remember that the programmers charged with software maintenance are typically not the code's original developers, hence to design and implement in a fashion that facilitates comprehension, modification, and enhancement by others.

One way to do this is to express design constraints in C++ instead of (or in addition to) comments or other documentation. For example, if a class is designed to never have derived classes, don't just put a comment in the header file above the class, use C++ to prevent derivation; Item 26 shows you how. If a class requires that all instances be on the heap, don't just tell clients that, enforce the restriction by applying the approach of Item 27. If copying and assignment make no sense for a class, prevent those operations by declaring the copy constructor and the assignment operator private. C++ offers great power, flexibility, and expressiveness. Use these characteristics of the language to enforce the design decisions in your programs.

Given that things will change, write classes that can withstand the rough-and-tumble world of software evolution. Avoid "demand-paged" virtual functions, whereby you make no functions virtual unless somebody comes along and demands that you do it. Instead, determine the *meaning* of a function and whether it makes sense to let it be redefined in derived classes. If it does, declare it virtual, even if nobody redefines it right away. If it doesn't, declare it nonvirtual, and don't change it later just because it would be convenient for someone; make sure the change makes sense in the context of the entire class and the abstraction it represents.

Handle assignment and copy construction in every class, even if "nobody ever does those things." Just because they don't do them now doesn't mean they won't do them in the future. If these functions are difficult to implement, declare them `private`. That way no one will inadvertently call compiler-generated functions that do the wrong thing (as often happens with default assignment operators and copy constructors).

Adhere to the principle of least astonishment: strive to provide classes whose operators and functions have a natural syntax and an intuitive semantics. Preserve consistency with the behavior of the built-in types: when in doubt, do as the `int`s do.

Recognize that anything somebody *can* do, they *will* do. They'll throw exceptions, they'll assign objects to themselves, they'll use objects before giving them values, they'll give objects values and never use them, they'll give them huge values, they'll give them tiny values, they'll give them null values. In general, if it will compile, somebody will do it. As a result, make your classes easy to use correctly and hard to use incorrectly. Accept that clients will make mistakes, and design your classes so you can prevent, detect, or correct such errors (see, for example, Item 33).

Strive for portable code. It's not much harder to write portable programs than to write unportable ones, and only rarely will the difference in performance be significant enough to justify unportable constructs (see Item 16). Even programs designed for custom hardware often end up being ported, because stock hardware generally achieves an equivalent level of performance within a few years. Writing portable code allows you to switch platforms easily, to enlarge your client base, and to brag about supporting open systems. It also makes it easier to recover if you bet wrong in the operating system sweepstakes.

Design your code so that when changes are necessary, the impact is localized. Encapsulate as much as you can; make implementation details private. Where applicable, use unnamed namespaces or file-`static` objects and functions (see Item 31). Try to avoid designs that lead to virtual base classes, because such classes must be initialized by every class derived from them — even those derived indirectly (see Item 4). Avoid RTTI-based designs that make use of `switch`-on-type statements (see Item 31 again). Every time the class hierarchy changes, each such `switch` statement must be updated, and if you forget one, you'll almost certainly receive no warning from your compilers.

These are well known and oft-repeated exhortations, but most programmers are still stuck in the present tense. As are many authors, unfortunately. Consider this advice by a well-regarded C++ expert:

> You need a virtual destructor whenever someone deletes a B* that actually points to a D.

Here B is a base class and D is a derived class. In other words, this author suggests that if your program looks like this, you don't need a virtual destructor in B:

```
    class B { ... };                    // no virtual dtor needed
    class D: public B { ... };

    B *pb = new D;
```

However, the situation changes if you add this statement:

```
    delete pb;                          // NOW you need the virtual
                                        // destructor in B
```

The implication is that a minor change to client code — the addition of
a `delete` statement — can result in the need to change the class definition for B. When that happens, all B's clients must recompile. Following this author's advice, then, the addition of a single statement in one
function can lead to extensive code recompilation and relinking for all
clients of a library. This is anything but effective software design.

On the same topic, a different author writes:

> If a public base class does not have a virtual destructor, no de-
> rived class nor members of a derived class should have a de-
> structor.

In other words, this is okay,

```
    class string {                      // from the standard C++ library
    public:
      ~string();
    };

    class B { ... };                    // no data members with dtors,
                                        // no virtual dtor needed
```

but if a new class is derived from B, things change:

```
    class D: public B {
      string name;                      // NOW ~B needs to be virtual
    };
```

Again, a small change to the way B is used (here, the addition of a derived class that contains a member with a destructor) may necessitate
extensive recompilation and relinking by clients. But small changes in
software should have small impacts on systems. This design fails that
test.

The same author writes:

> If a multiple inheritance hierarchy has any destructors, every
> base class should have a virtual destructor.

In all these quotations, note the present-tense thinking. How do clients
manipulate pointers *now*? What class members have destructors *now*?
What classes in the hierarchy have destructors *now*?

Future-tense thinking is quite different. Instead of asking how a class is used now, it asks how the class is *designed* to be used. Future-tense thinking says, if a class is *designed* to be used as a base class (even if it's not used as one now), it should have a virtual destructor. Such classes behave correctly both now and in the future, and they don't affect other library clients when new classes derive from them. (At least, they have no effect as far as their destructor is concerned. If additional changes to the class are required, other clients may be affected.)

A commercial class library (one that predates the `string` specification in the C++ library standard) contains a string class with no virtual destructor. The vendor's explanation?

> We didn't make the destructor virtual, because we didn't want `String` to have a vtbl. We have no intention of ever having a `String*`, so this is not a problem. We are well aware of the difficulties this could cause.

Is this present-tense or future-tense thinking?

Certainly the vtbl issue is a legitimate technical concern (see Item 24). The implementation of most `String` classes contains only a single `char*` pointer inside each `String` object, so adding a vptr to each `String` would double the size of those objects. It is easy to understand why a vendor would be unwilling to do that, especially for a highly visible, heavily used class like `String`. The performance of such a class might easily fall within the 20% of a program that makes a difference (see Item 16).

Still, the total memory devoted to a string object — the memory for the object itself plus the heap memory needed to hold the string's value — is typically much greater than just the space needed to hold a `char*` pointer. From this perspective, the overhead imposed by a vptr is less significant. Nevertheless, it is a legitimate technical consideration. (Certainly the ANSI/ISO standardization committee seems to think so: the standard `string` class has a nonvirtual destructor.)

Somewhat more troubling is the vendor's remark, "We have no intention of ever having a `String*`, so this is not a problem." That may be true, but their `String` class is part of a library they make available to *thousands* of developers. That's a lot of developers, each with a different level of experience with C++, each doing something unique. Do those developers understand the consequences of there being no virtual destructor in `String`? Are they likely to know that because `String` has no virtual destructor, deriving new classes from `String` is a high-risk venture? Is this vendor confident their clients will understand that in the absence of a virtual destructor, deleting objects through `String*` pointers will not work properly and RTTI operations on pointers and references to Strings may return incorrect information? Is this class easy to use correctly and hard to use incorrectly?

This vendor should provide documentation for its String class that makes clear the class is not designed for derivation, but what if programmers overlook the caveat or flat-out fail to read the documentation?

An alternative would be to use C++ itself to prohibit derivation. Item 26 describes how to do this by limiting object creation to the heap and then using auto_ptr objects to manipulate the heap objects. The interface for String creation would then be both unconventional and inconvenient, requiring this,

```
auto_ptr<String> ps(String::makeString("Future tense C++"));

...                                    // treat ps as a pointer to
                                       // a String object, but don't
                                       // worry about deleting it
```

instead of this,

```
String s("Future tense C++");
```

but perhaps the reduction in the risk of improperly behaving derived classes would be worth the syntactic inconvenience. (For String, this is unlikely to be the case, but for other classes, the trade-off might well be worth it.)

There is a need, of course, for present-tense thinking. The software you're developing has to work with current compilers; you can't afford to wait until the latest language features are implemented. It has to run on the hardware you currently support and it must do so under configurations your clients have available; you can't force your customers to upgrade their systems or modify their operating environment. It has to offer acceptable performance *now*; promises of smaller, faster programs some years down the line don't generally warm the cockles of potential customers' hearts. And the software you're working on must be available "soon," which often means some time in the recent past. These are important constraints. You cannot ignore them.

Future-tense thinking simply adds a few additional considerations:

- Provide complete classes, even if some parts aren't currently used. When new demands are made on your classes, you're less likely to have to go back and modify them.

- Design your interfaces to facilitate common operations and prevent common errors. Make the classes easy to use correctly, hard to use incorrectly. For example, prohibit copying and assignment for classes where those operations make no sense. Prevent partial assignments (see Item 33).

- If there is no great penalty for generalizing your code, generalize it. For example, if you are writing an algorithm for tree traversal, consider generalizing it to handle any kind of directed acyclic graph.

Future tense thinking increases the reusability of the code you write, enhances its maintainability, makes it more robust, and facilitates graceful change in an environment where change is a certainty. It must be balanced against present-tense constraints. Too many programmers focus exclusively on current needs, however, and in doing so they sacrifice the long-term viability of the software they design and implement. Be different. Be a renegade. Program in the future tense.

Item 33: Make non-leaf classes abstract

Suppose you're working on a project whose software deals with animals. Within this software, most animals can be treated pretty much the same, but two kinds of animals — lizards and chickens — require special handling. That being the case, the obvious way to relate the classes for animals, lizards, and chickens is like this:

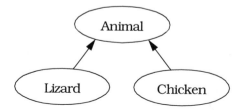

The `Animal` class embodies the features shared by all the creatures you deal with, and the `Lizard` and `Chicken` classes specialize `Animal` in ways appropriate for lizards and chickens, respectively.

Here's a sketch of the definitions for these classes:

```
class Animal {
public:
  Animal& operator=(const Animal& rhs);
  ...

};
```

```
class Lizard: public Animal {
public:
  Lizard& operator=(const Lizard& rhs);
  ...

};

class Chicken: public Animal {
public:
  Chicken& operator=(const Chicken& rhs);
  ...

};
```

Only the assignment operators are shown here, but that's more than enough to keep us busy for a while. Consider this code:

```
Lizard liz1;
Lizard liz2;

Animal *pAnimal1 = &liz1;
Animal *pAnimal2 = &liz2;

...

*pAnimal1 = *pAnimal2;
```

There are two problems here. First, the assignment operator invoked on the last line is that of the Animal class, even though the objects involved are of type Lizard. As a result, only the Animal part of liz1 will be modified. This is a *partial* assignment. After the assignment, liz1's Animal members have the values they got from liz2, but liz1's Lizard members remain unchanged.

The second problem is that real programmers write code like this. It's not uncommon to make assignments to objects through pointers, especially for experienced C programmers who have moved to C++. That being the case, we'd like to make the assignment behave in a more reasonable fashion. As Item 32 points out, our classes should be easy to use correctly and difficult to use incorrectly, and the classes in the hierarchy above are easy to use incorrectly.

One approach to the problem is to make the assignment operators virtual. If Animal::operator= were virtual, the assignment would invoke the Lizard assignment operator, which is certainly the correct one to call. However, look what happens if we declare the assignment operators virtual:

```
class Animal {
public:
  virtual Animal& operator=(const Animal& rhs);
  ...
};
```

```
.ass Lizard: public Animal {
 ıblic:
   virtual Lizard& operator=(const Animal& rhs);
   ...
 };

 class Chicken: public Animal {
 public:
   virtual Chicken& operator=(const Animal& rhs);
   ...
 };
```

Due to relatively recent changes to the language, we can customize the return value of the assignment operators so that each returns a reference to the correct class, but the rules of C++ force us to declare identical *parameter* types for a virtual function in every class in which it is declared. That means the assignment operator for the Lizard and Chicken classes must be prepared to accept *any* kind of Animal object on the right-hand side of an assignment. That, in turn, means we have to confront the fact that code like the following is legal:

```
Lizard liz;
Chicken chick;

Animal *pAnimal1 = &liz;
Animal *pAnimal2 = &chick;

...

*pAnimal1 = *pAnimal2;          // assign a chicken to
                                // a lizard!
```

This is a mixed-type assignment: a Lizard is on the left and a Chicken is on the right. Mixed-type assignments aren't usually a problem in C++, because the language's strong typing generally renders them illegal. By making Animal's assignment operator virtual, however, we opened the door to such mixed-type operations.

This puts us in a difficult position. We'd like to allow same-type assignments through pointers, but we'd like to forbid mixed-type assignments through those same pointers. In other words, we want to allow this,

```
Animal *pAnimal1 = &liz1;
Animal *pAnimal2 = &liz2;

...

*pAnimal1 = *pAnimal2;          // assign a lizard to a lizard
```

but we want to prohibit this:

```
Animal *pAnimal1 = &liz;
Animal *pAnimal2 = &chick;

...

*pAnimal1 = *pAnimal2;          // assign a chicken to a lizard
```

Distinctions such as these can be made only at runtime, because sometimes assigning *pAnimal2 to *pAnimal1 is valid, sometimes it's not. We thus enter the murky world of type-based runtime errors. In particular, we need to signal an error inside operator= if we're faced with a mixed-type assignment, but if the types are the same, we want to perform the assignment in the usual fashion.

We can use a dynamic_cast (see Item 2) to implement this behavior. Here's how to do it for Lizard's assignment operator:

```
Lizard& Lizard::operator=(const Animal& rhs)
{
  // make sure rhs is really a lizard
  const Lizard& rhs_liz = dynamic_cast<const Lizard&>(rhs);

  proceed with a normal assignment of rhs_liz to *this;

}
```

This function assigns rhs to *this only if rhs is really a Lizard. If it's not, the function propagates the bad_cast exception that dynamic_cast throws when the cast fails. (Actually, the type of the exception is std::bad_cast, because the components of the standard library, including the exceptions thrown by the standard components, are in the namespace std. For an overview of the standard library, see Item 35.)

Even without worrying about exceptions, this function seems needlessly complicated and expensive — the dynamic_cast must consult a type_info structure; see Item 24 — in the common case where one Lizard object is assigned to another:

```
Lizard liz1, liz2;

...

liz1 = liz2;                    // no need to perform a
                                // dynamic_cast: this
                                // assignment must be valid
```

We can handle this case without paying for the complexity or cost of a dynamic_cast by adding to Lizard the conventional assignment operator:

```
class Lizard: public Animal {
public:
  virtual Lizard& operator=(const Animal& rhs);

  Lizard& operator=(const Lizard& rhs);          // add this

  ...

};

Lizard liz1, liz2;

...

liz1 = liz2;                    // calls operator= taking
                                // a const Lizard&

Animal *pAnimal1 = &liz1;
Animal *pAnimal2 = &liz2;

...

*pAnimal1 = *pAnimal2;          // calls operator= taking
                                // a const Animal&
```

In fact, given this latter operator=, it's simplicity itself to implement the former one in terms of it:

```
Lizard& Lizard::operator=(const Animal& rhs)
{
  return operator=(dynamic_cast<const Lizard&>(rhs));
}
```

This function attempts to cast rhs to be a Lizard. If the cast succeeds, the normal class assignment operator is called. Otherwise, a bad_cast exception is thrown.

Frankly, all this business of checking types at runtime and using dynamic_casts makes me nervous. For one thing, many compilers still lack support for dynamic_cast, so code that uses it, though theoretically portable, is not really portable in practice. More importantly, it requires that clients of Lizard and Chicken be prepared to catch bad_cast exceptions and do something sensible with them each time they perform an assignment. In my experience, there just aren't that many programmers who are willing to program that way. If they don't, it's not clear we've gained a whole lot over our original situation where we were trying to guard against partial assignments.

Given this rather unsatisfactory state of affairs regarding virtual assignment operators, it makes sense to regroup and try to find a way to prevent clients from making problematic assignments in the first place. If such assignments are rejected during compilation, we don't have to worry about them doing the wrong thing.

The easiest way to prevent such assignments is to make operator= private in Animal. That way, lizards can be assigned to lizards and chickens can be assigned to chickens, but partial and mixed-type assignments are forbidden:

```cpp
class Animal {
private:
  Animal& operator=(const Animal& rhs);        // this is now
  ...                                          // private
};

class Lizard: public Animal {
public:
  Lizard& operator=(const Lizard& rhs);
  ...
};

class Chicken: public Animal {
public:
  Chicken& operator=(const Chicken& rhs);
  ...
};

Lizard liz1, liz2;
...
liz1 = liz2;                          // fine

Chicken chick1, chick2;
...
chick1 = chick2;                      // also fine

Animal *pAnimal1 = &liz1;
Animal *pAnimal2 = &chick1;
...
*pAnimal1 = *pAnimal2;                // error! attempt to call
                                      // private Animal::operator=
```

Unfortunately, Animal is a concrete class, and this approach also makes assignments between Animal objects illegal:

```cpp
Animal animal1, animal2;

...

animal1 = animal2;                    // error! attempt to call
                                      // private Animal::operator=
```

Moreover, it makes it impossible to implement the Lizard and Chicken assignment operators correctly, because assignment operators in derived classes are responsible for calling assignment operators in their base classes:

```
Lizard& Lizard::operator=(const Lizard& rhs)
{
  if (this == &rhs) return *this;

  Animal::operator=(rhs);           // error! attempt to call
                                    // private function. But
                                    // Lizard::operator= must
                                    // call this function to
  ...                               // assign the Animal parts
}                                   // of *this!
```

We can solve this latter problem by declaring Animal::operator= protected, but the conundrum of allowing assignments between Animal objects while preventing partial assignments of Lizard and Chicken objects through Animal pointers remains. What's a poor programmer to do?

The easiest thing is to eliminate the need to allow assignments between Animal objects, and the easiest way to do that is to make Animal an abstract class. As an abstract class, Animal can't be instantiated, so there will be no need to allow assignments between Animals. Of course, this leads to a new problem, because our original design for this system presupposed that Animal objects were necessary. There is an easy way around this difficulty. Instead of making Animal itself abstract, we create a new class — AbstractAnimal, say — consisting of the common features of Animal, Lizard, and Chicken objects, and we make *that* class abstract. Then we have each of our concrete classes inherit from AbstractAnimal. The revised hierarchy looks like this,

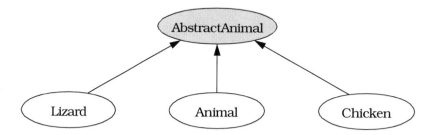

and the class definitions are as follows:

```
class AbstractAnimal {
protected:
  AbstractAnimal& operator=(const AbstractAnimal& rhs);
  virtual ~AbstractAnimal() = 0;              // see below
  ...
};
```

```
class Animal: public AbstractAnimal {
public:
  Animal& operator=(const Animal& rhs);
  ...
};
class Lizard: public AbstractAnimal {
public:
  Lizard& operator=(const Lizard& rhs);
  ...
};
class Chicken: public AbstractAnimal {
public:
  Chicken& operator=(const Chicken& rhs);
  ...
};
```

This design gives you everything you need. Homogeneous assignments are allowed for lizards, chickens, and animals; partial assignments and heterogeneous assignments are prohibited; and derived class assignment operators may call the assignment operator in the base class. Furthermore, none of the code written in terms of the Animal, Lizard, or Chicken classes requires modification, because these classes continue to exist and to behave as they did before Abstract-Animal was introduced. Sure, such code has to be recompiled, but that's a small price to pay for the security of knowing that assignments that compile will behave intuitively and assignments that would behave unintuitively won't compile.

For all this to work, AbstractAnimal must be abstract — it must contain at least one pure virtual function. In most cases, coming up with a suitable function is not a problem, but on rare occasions you may find yourself facing the need to create a class like AbstractAnimal in which none of the member functions would naturally be declared pure virtual. In such cases, the conventional technique is to make the destructor a pure virtual function; that's what's shown above. In order to support polymorphism through pointers correctly, base classes need virtual destructors anyway, so the only cost associated with making such destructors pure virtual is the inconvenience of having to implement them outside their class definitions. (For an example, see page 195.)

(If the notion of implementing a pure virtual function strikes you as odd, you just haven't been getting out enough. Declaring a function pure virtual doesn't mean it has no implementation, it means

- the current class is abstract, and

- any concrete class inheriting from the current class must declare the function as a "normal" virtual function (i.e., without the "=0").

True, most pure virtual functions are never implemented, but pure virtual destructors are a special case. They *must* be implemented, because they are called whenever a derived class destructor is invoked. Furthermore, they often perform useful tasks, such as releasing resources (see Item 9) or logging messages. Implementing pure virtual functions may be uncommon in general, but for pure virtual destructors, it's not just common, it's mandatory.)

You may have noticed that this discussion of assignment through base class pointers is based on the assumption that concrete base classes like Animal contain data members. If there are no data members, you might point out, there is no problem, and it would be safe to have a concrete class inherit from a second, dataless, concrete class.

One of two situations applies to your data-free would-be concrete base class: either it might have data members in the future or it might not. If it might have data members in the future, all you're doing is postponing the problem until the data members are added, in which case you're merely trading short-term convenience for long-term grief (see also Item 32). Alternatively, if the base class should truly never have any data members, that sounds very much like it should be an abstract class in the first place. What use is a concrete base class without data?

Replacement of a concrete base class like Animal with an abstract base class like AbstractAnimal yields benefits far beyond simply making the behavior of operator= easier to understand. It also reduces the chances that you'll try to treat arrays polymorphically, the unpleasant consequences of which are examined in Item 3. The most significant benefit of the technique, however, occurs at the design level, because replacing concrete base classes with abstract base classes forces you to explicitly recognize the existence of useful abstractions. That is, it makes you create new abstract classes for useful concepts, even if you aren't aware of the fact that the useful concepts exist.

If you have two concrete classes C1 and C2 and you'd like C2 to publicly inherit from C1, you should transform that two-class hierarchy into a three-class hierarchy by creating a new abstract class A and having both C1 and C2 publicly inherit from it:

Your initial idea

Your transformed hierarchy

The primary value of this transformation is that it forces you to identify the abstract class A. Clearly, C1 and C2 have something in common; that's why they're related by public inheritance. With this transformation, you must identify what that something is. Furthermore, you must formalize the something as a class in C++, at which point it becomes more than just a vague something, it achieves the status of a formal *abstraction*, one with well-defined member functions and well-defined semantics.

All of which leads to some worrisome thinking. After all, every class represents *some* kind of abstraction, so shouldn't we create two classes for every concept in our hierarchy, one being abstract (to embody the abstract part of the abstraction) and one being concrete (to embody the object-generation part of the abstraction)? No. If you do, you'll end up with a hierarchy with too many classes. Such a hierarchy is difficult to understand, hard to maintain, and expensive to compile. That is not the goal of object-oriented design.

The goal is to identify *useful* abstractions and to force them — and only them — into existence as abstract classes. But how do you identify useful abstractions? Who knows what abstractions might prove useful in the future? Who can predict who's going to want to inherit from what?

Well, I don't know how to predict the future uses of an inheritance hierarchy, but I do know one thing: the need for an abstraction in one context may be coincidental, but the need for an abstraction in more than one context is usually meaningful. Useful abstractions, then, are those that are needed in more than one context. That is, they correspond to classes that are useful in their own right (i.e., it is useful to have objects of that type) and that are also useful for purposes of one or more derived classes.

This is precisely why the transformation from concrete base class to abstract base class is useful: it forces the introduction of a new abstract class only when an existing concrete class is about to be used as a base class, i.e., when the class is about to be (re)used in a new context. Such abstractions are *useful*, because they have, through demonstrated need, shown themselves to be so.

The first time a concept is needed, we can't justify the creation of both an abstract class (for the concept) and a concrete class (for the objects corresponding to that concept), but the second time that concept is needed, we *can* justify the creation of both the abstract and the concrete classes. The transformation I've described simply mechanizes this process, and in so doing it forces designers and programmers to represent explicitly those abstractions that are useful, even if the designers and programmers are not consciously aware of the useful concepts. It also happens to make it a lot easier to bring sanity to the behavior of assignment operators.

Let's consider a brief example. Suppose you're working on an application that deals with moving information between computers on a network by breaking it into packets and transmitting them according to some protocol. All we'll consider here is the class or classes for representing packets. We'll assume such classes make sense for this application.

Suppose you deal with only a single kind of transfer protocol and only a single kind of packet. Perhaps you've heard that other protocols and packet types exist, but you've never supported them, nor do you have any plans to support them in the future. Should you make an abstract class for packets (for the concept that a packet represents) as well as a concrete class for the packets you'll actually be using? If you do, you could hope to add new packet types later without changing the base class for packets. That would save you from having to recompile packet-using applications if you add new packet types. But that design requires two classes, and right now you need only one (for the particular type of packets you use). Is it worth complicating your design now to allow for future extension that may never take place?

There is no unequivocally correct choice to be made here, but experience has shown it is nearly impossible to design good classes for concepts we do not understand well. If you create an abstract class for packets, how likely are you to get it right, especially since your experience is limited to only a single packet type? Remember that you gain the benefit of an abstract class for packets only if you can design that class so that future classes can inherit from it without its being changed in any way. (If it needs to be changed, you have to recompile all packet clients, and you've gained nothing.)

It is unlikely you could design a satisfactory abstract packet class unless you were well versed in many different kinds of packets and in the varied contexts in which they are used. Given your limited experience in this case, my advice would be not to define an abstract class for packets, adding one later only if you find a need to inherit from the concrete packet class.

The transformation I've described here is *a* way to identify the need for abstract classes, not *the* way. There are many other ways to identify good candidates for abstract classes; books on object-oriented analysis are filled with them. It's not the case that the only time you should introduce abstract classes is when you find yourself wanting to have a concrete class inherit from another concrete class. However, the desire to relate two concrete classes by public inheritance is usually indicative of a need for a new abstract class.

As is often the case in such matters, brash reality sometimes intrudes on the peaceful ruminations of theory. Third-party C++ class libraries are proliferating with gusto, and what are you to do if you find yourself wanting to create a concrete class that inherits from a concrete class in a library to which you have only read access?

You can't modify the library to insert a new abstract class, so your choices are both limited and unappealing:

- Derive your concrete class from the existing concrete class, and put up with the assignment-related problems we examined at the beginning of this Item. You'll also have to watch out for the array-related pitfalls described in Item 3.

- Try to find an abstract class higher in the library hierarchy that does most of what you need, then inherit from that class. Of course, there may not be a suitable class, and even if there is, you may have to duplicate a lot of effort that has already been put into the implementation of the concrete class whose functionality you'd like to extend.

- Implement your new class in terms of the library class you'd like to inherit from. For example, you could have an object of the library class as a data member, then reimplement the library class's interface in your new class:

```cpp
class Window {             // this is the library class
public:
  virtual void resize(int newWidth, int newHeight);
  virtual void repaint() const;

  int width() const;
  int height() const;
};

class SpecialWindow {      // this is the class you
public:                    // wanted to have inherit
  ...                      // from Window

  // pass-through implementations of nonvirtual functions
  int width() const { return w.width(); }
  int height() const { return w.height(); }

  // new implementations of "inherited" virtual functions
  virtual void resize(int newWidth, int newHeight);
  virtual void repaint() const;

private:
  Window w;
};
```

This strategy requires that you be prepared to update your class each time the library vendor updates the class on which you're dependent. It also requires that you be willing to forego the ability to redefine virtual functions declared in the library class, because you can't redefine virtual functions unless you inherit them.

- Make do with what you've got. Use the concrete class that's in the library and modify your software so that the class suffices. Write non-member functions to provide the functionality you'd like to add to the class, but can't. The resulting software may not be as clear, as efficient, as maintainable, or as extensible as you'd like, but at least it will get the job done.

None of these choices is particularly attractive, so you have to apply some engineering judgment and choose the poison you find least unappealing. It's not much fun, but life's like that sometimes. To make things easier for yourself (and the rest of us) in the future, complain to the vendors of libraries whose designs you find wanting. With luck (and a lot of comments from clients), those designs will improve as time goes on.

Still, the general rule remains: non-leaf classes should be abstract. You may need to bend the rule when working with outside libraries, but in code over which you have control, adherence to it will yield dividends in the form of increased reliability, robustness, comprehensibility, and extensibility throughout your software.

Item 34: Understand how to combine C++ and C in the same program

In many ways, the things you have to worry about when making a program out of some components in C++ and some in C are the same as those you have to worry about when cobbling together a C program out of object files produced by more than one C compiler. There is no way to combine such files unless the different compilers agree on implementation-dependent features like the size of $ints$ and $doubles$, the mechanism by which parameters are passed from caller to callee, and whether the caller or the callee orchestrates the passing. These pragmatic aspects of mixed-compiler software development are quite properly ignored by language standardization efforts, so the only reliable way to know that object files from compiler A and compiler B can be safely combined in a program is to obtain assurances from the vendors of A and B that their products produce compatible output. This is as true for programs made up of C++ and C as it is for all-C++ or all-C programs, so before you try to mix C++ and C in the same program, make sure your C++ and C compilers generate compatible object files.

Having done that, there are four other things you need to consider: name mangling, initialization of statics, dynamic memory allocation, and data structure compatibility.

Name Mangling

Name mangling, as you may know, is the process through which your C++ compilers give each function in your program a unique name. In C, this process is unnecessary, because you can't overload function names, but nearly all C++ programs have at least a few functions with the same name. (Consider, for example, the iostream library, which declares several versions of `operator<<` and `operator>>`.) Overloading is incompatible with most linkers, because linkers generally take a dim view of multiple functions with the same name. Name mangling is a concession to the realities of linkers; in particular, to the fact that linkers usually insist on all function names being unique.

As long as you stay within the confines of C++, name mangling is not likely to concern you. If you have a function name `drawLine` that a compiler mangles into `xyzzy`, you'll always use the name `drawLine`, and you'll have little reason to care that the underlying object files happen to refer to `xyzzy`.

It's a different story if `drawLine` is in a C library. In that case, your C++ source file probably includes a header file that contains a declaration like this,

```
void drawLine(int x1, int y1, int x2, int y2);
```

and your code contains calls to `drawLine` in the usual fashion. Each such call is translated by your compilers into a call to the mangled name of that function, so when you write this,

```
drawLine(a, b, c, d);     // call to unmangled function name
```

your object files contain a function call that corresponds to this:

```
xyzzy(a, b, c, d);     // call to mangled function mame
```

But if `drawLine` is a C function, the object file (or archive or dynamically linked library, etc.) that contains the compiled version of `draw-Line` contains a function called *drawLine*; no name mangling has taken place. When you try to link the object files comprising your program together, you'll get an error, because the linker is looking for a function called `xyzzy`, and there is no such function.

To solve this problem, you need a way to tell your C++ compilers not to mangle certain function names. You never want to mangle the names of functions written in other languages, whether they be in C, assembler, FORTRAN, Lisp, Forth, or what-have-you. (Yes, what-have-you would include COBOL, but then what would you have?) After all, if you call a C function named drawLine, it's really called drawLine, and your object code should contain a reference to that name, not to some mangled version of that name.

To suppress name mangling, use C++'s extern "C" directive:

```
// declare a function called drawLine; don't mangle
// its name
extern "C"
void drawLine(int x1, int y1, int x2, int y2);
```

Don't be drawn into the trap of assuming that where there's an extern "C", there must be an extern "Pascal" and an extern "FORTRAN" as well. There's not, at least not in the standard. The best way to view extern "C" is not as an assertion that the associated function is written in C, but as a statement that the function should be called as if it *were* written in C. (Technically, extern "C" means the function has C linkage, but what that means is far from clear. One thing it always means, however, is that name mangling is suppressed.)

For example, if you were so unfortunate as to have to write a function in assembler, you could declare it extern "C", too:

```
// this function is in assembler — don't mangle its name
extern "C" void twiddleBits(unsigned char bits);
```

You can even declare C++ functions extern "C". This can be useful if you're writing a library in C++ that you'd like to provide to clients using other programming languages. By suppressing the name mangling of your C++ function names, your clients can use the natural and intuitive names you choose instead of the mangled names your compilers would otherwise generate:

```
// the following C++ function is designed for use outside
// C++ and should not have its name mangled
extern "C" void simulate(int iterations);
```

Often you'll have a slew of functions whose names you don't want mangled, and it would be a pain to precede each with extern "C". Fortunately, you don't have to. extern "C" can also be made to apply to a whole set of functions. Just enclose them all in curly braces:

```
extern "C" {                        // disable name mangling for
                                    // all the following functions

  void drawLine(int x1, int y1, int x2, int y2);
  void twiddleBits(unsigned char bits);
  void simulate(int iterations);
  ...

}
```

This use of extern "C" simplifies the maintenance of header files that must be used with both C++ and C. When compiling for C++, you'll want to include extern "C", but when compiling for C, you won't. By taking advantage of the fact that the preprocessor symbol __cplusplus is defined only for C++ compilations, you can structure your polyglot header files as follows:

```
#ifdef __cplusplus

extern "C" {

#endif

  void drawLine(int x1, int y1, int x2, int y2);
  void twiddleBits(unsigned char bits);
  void simulate(int iterations);
  ...

#ifdef __cplusplus

}

#endif
```

There is, by the way, no such thing as a "standard" name mangling algorithm. Different compilers are free to mangle names in different ways, and different compilers do. This is a good thing. If all compilers mangled names the same way, you might be lulled into thinking they all generated compatible code. The way things are now, if you try to mix object code from incompatible C++ compilers, there's a good chance you'll get an error during linking, because the mangled names won't match up. This implies you'll probably have other compatibility problems, too, and it's better to find out about such incompatibilities sooner than later,

Initialization of Statics

Once you've mastered name mangling, you need to deal with the fact that in C++, lots of code can get executed before and after main. In particular, the constructors of static class objects and objects at global, namespace, and file scope are usually called before the body of main is executed. This process is known as *static initialization*. This is in direct opposition to the way we normally think about C++ and C programs, in which we view main as the entry point to execution of the program. Similarly, objects that are created through static initialization must have their destructors called during *static destruction*; that process typically takes place after main has finished executing.

To resolve the dilemma that main is supposed to be invoked first, yet objects need to be constructed before main is executed, many compilers insert a call to a special compiler-written function at the beginning of main, and it is this special function that takes care of static initialization. Similarly, compilers often insert a call to another special function at the end of main to take care of the destruction of static objects. Code generated for main often looks as if main had been written like this:

```
int main(int argc, char *argv[])
{
  performStaticInitialization();     // generated by the
                                     // implementation

  the statements you put in main go here;

  performStaticDestruction();        // generated by the
                                     // implementation
}
```

Now don't take this too literally. The functions performStaticInitialization and performStaticDestruction usually have much more cryptic names, and they may even be generated inline, in which case you won't see any functions for them in your object files. The important point is this: if a C++ compiler adopts this approach to the initialization and destruction of static objects, such objects will be neither initialized nor destroyed unless main is written in C++. Because this approach to static initialization and destruction is common, you should try to write main in C++ if you write any part of a software system in C++.

Sometimes it would seem to make more sense to write main in C — say if most of a program is in C and C++ is just a support library. Nevertheless, there's a good chance the C++ library contains static objects (if it doesn't now, it probably will in the future — see Item 32), so it's still a good idea to write main in C++ if you possibly can. That doesn't mean you need to rewrite your C code, however. Just rename the main you wrote in C to be realMain, then have the C++ version of main call realMain:

```
extern "C"                            // implement this
int realMain(int argc, char *argv[]); // function in C

int main(int argc, char *argv[])      // write this in C++
{
  return realMain(argc, argv);
}
```

If you do this, it's a good idea to put a comment above main explaining what is going on.

If you cannot write main in C++, you've got a problem, because there is no other portable way to ensure that constructors and destructors for static objects are called. This doesn't mean all is lost, it just means you'll have to work a little harder. Compiler vendors are well acquainted with this problem, so almost all provide some extralinguistic mechanism for initiating the process of static initialization and static destruction. For information on how this works with your compilers, dig into your compilers' documentation or contact their vendors.

Dynamic Memory Allocation

That brings us to dynamic memory allocation. The general rule is simple: the C++ parts of a program use new and delete (see Item 8), and the C parts of a program use malloc (and its variants) and free. As long as memory that came from new is deallocated via delete and memory that came from malloc is deallocated via free, all is well. Calling free on a newed pointer yields undefined behavior, however, as does deleteing a malloced pointer. The only thing to remember, then, is to segregate rigorously your news and deletes from your mallocs and frees.

Sometimes this is easier said than done. Consider the humble (but handy) strdup function, which, though standard in neither C nor C++, is nevertheless widely available:

```
char * strdup(const char *ps);    // return a copy of the
                                  // string pointed to by ps
```

If a memory leak is to be avoided, the memory allocated inside strdup must be deallocated by strdup's caller. But how is the memory to be deallocated? By using delete? By calling free? If the strdup you're calling is from a C library, it's the latter. If it was written for a C++ library, it's probably the former. What you need to do after calling strdup, then, varies not only from system to system, but also from compiler to compiler. To reduce such portability headaches, try to avoid calling functions that are neither in the standard library (see Item 35) nor available in a stable form on most computing platforms.

Data Structure Compatibility

Which brings us at long last to passing data between C++ and C programs. There's no hope of making C functions understand C++ features, so the level of discourse between the two languages must be limited to those concepts that C can express. Thus, it should be clear there's no portable way to pass objects or to pass pointers to member functions to routines written in C. C does understand normal pointers, however, so, provided your C++ and C compilers produce compatible output, functions in the two languages can safely exchange pointers to objects and pointers to non-member or static functions. Naturally, structs and variables of built-in types (e.g., ints, chars, etc.) can also freely cross the C++/C border.

Language lawyers will be quick to point out that the rules governing the layout of a struct in C++ are not the same as in C, but if you are using C++ and C compilers whose output is otherwise compatible, it is safe to assume that a structure definition that compiles in both languages is laid out the same way by both compilers. Such structs can be safely passed back and forth between C++ and C. If you add *nonvirtual* functions to the C++ version of the struct, its memory layout should not change, so objects of a struct (or class) containing only non-virtual functions should be compatible with their C brethren whose structure definition lacks only the member function declarations. Adding *virtual* functions ends the game, because the addition of virtual functions to a class causes objects of that type to use a different memory layout (see Item 24). Having a struct inherit from another struct (or class) usually changes its layout, too, so structs with base structs (or classes) are also poor candidates for exchange with C functions.

From a data structure perspective, it boils down to this: it is safe to pass data structures from C++ to C and from C to C++ provided the definition of those structures compiles in both C++ and C. Adding non-virtual member functions to the C++ version of a struct that's otherwise compatible with C will probably not affect its compatibility, but almost any other change to the struct will.

Summary

If you want to mix C++ and C in the same program, remember the following simple guidelines:

- Make sure the C++ and C compilers produce compatible object files.

- Declare functions to be used by both languages extern "C".

- If at all possible, write main in C++.

- Always use delete with memory from new; always use free with memory from malloc.

- Limit what you pass between the two languages to data structures that compile under C; the C++ version of structs may contain non-virtual member functions.

Item 35: Familiarize yourself with the language standard

Since its publication in 1990, *The Annotated C++ Reference Manual* (see page 285) has been the definitive reference for working programmers needing to know what is in C++ and what is not. In the years since the ARM (as it's fondly known) came out, the ANSI/ISO committee standardizing the language has changed (primarily extended) the language in ways both big and small. As a definitive reference, the ARM no longer suffices.

The post-ARM changes to C++ significantly affect how good programs are written. As a result, it is important for C++ programmers to be familiar with the primary ways in which the C++ specified by the emerging standard differs from that described by the ARM.

This "emerging standard" is the joint ANSI/ISO standard for C++ that's been under development since 1989 and is now in more or less final form. It will probably be at least 1997 before all the *i*s are dotted, all the *t*s are crossed, and all the red tape that makes an official standard official has been dispensed with, but, practically speaking, the current draft standard specifies the programming language C++. This standard is what vendors will consult when implementing compilers, what authors will examine when preparing books, and what programmers will look to for definitive answers to questions about C++.

Among the most important changes to C++ since the ARM are the following:

- **New features have been added**: RTTI, namespaces, `bool`, the `mutable` and `explicit` keywords, the ability to overload operators for enums, and the ability to initialize constant integral static class members within a class definition.

- **Templates have been extended**: member templates are now allowed, there is a standard syntax for forcing template instantiations, non-type arguments are now allowed in function templates, and class templates may themselves be used as template arguments.

- **Exception handling has been refined**: exception specifications are now more rigorously checked during compilation, and the unexpected function may now throw a `bad_exception` object.

- **Memory allocation routines have been modified**: `operator new[]` and `operator delete[]` have been added, the operators `new/new[]` now throw an exception if memory can't be allocated, and there are now alternative versions of the operators `new/new[]` that return 0 when an allocation fails.

- **New casting forms have been added**: static_cast, dynamic_cast, const_cast, and reinterpret_cast.

- **Language rules have been refined**: redefinitions of virtual functions need no longer have a return type that exactly matches that of the function they redefine, and the lifetime of temporary objects has been defined precisely.

Almost all these changes are described in *The Design and Evolution of C++* (see page 285). Current C++ textbooks (those written after 1994) should include them, too. (If you find one that doesn't, reject it.) In addition, *More Effective C++* (that's this book) contains examples of how to use most of these new features. If you're curious about something on this list, try looking it up in the index.

The changes to C++ proper pale in comparison to what's happened to the standard library. Furthermore, the evolution of the standard library has not been as well publicized as that of the language. *The Design and Evolution of C++*, for example, makes almost no mention of the standard library. The few books that do discuss the library are generally out of date, because the library changed quite substantially in 1994.

The capabilities of the standard library can be broken down into the following general categories:

- **Support for the standard C library**. Fear not, C++ still remembers its roots. Some minor tweaks have brought the C++ version of the C library into conformance with C++'s stricter type checking, but for all intents and purposes, everything you know and love (or hate) about the C library continues to be knowable and lovable (or hateable) in C++, too.

- **Support for strings**. As Chair of the working group for the standard C++ library, Mike Vilot was told, "If there isn't a standard string class, there will be blood in the streets!" (Some people get so emotional.) Calm yourself and put away those hatchets and truncheons — the standard C++ library has strings.

- **Support for localization**. Different cultures use different character sets and follow different conventions when displaying dates and times, sorting strings, printing monetary values, etc. Localization support within the standard library facilitates the development of programs that accommodate such cultural differences.

- **Support for I/O**. The iostream library remains part of the C++ standard, but the committee has tinkered with it a bit. Though some classes have been eliminated (notably iostream and fstream) and some have been replaced (e.g., string-based stringstreams replace char*-based strstreams, which are now deprecated), the basic capabilities of the soon-to-be-standard iostream classes mirror those of the implementations that have existed for several years.

- **Support for numeric applications**. Complex numbers, long a mainstay of examples in C++ texts, have finally been enshrined in the standard library. In addition, the library contains special array classes (valarrays) that restrict aliasing. These arrays are eligible for more aggressive optimization than are built-in arrays, especially on multiprocessing architectures. The library also provides a few commonly useful numeric functions, including partial sum and adjacent difference.

- **Support for general-purpose containers and algorithms**. Contained within the standard C++ library is a set of class and function templates collectively known as the Standard Template Library (STL). The STL is the most revolutionary part of the standard C++ library. I summarize its features below.

Before I describe the STL, though, I must dispense with two idiosyncrasies of the standard C++ library you need to know about.

First, almost everything in the library is a *template*. Many times in this book I've referred to the standard string class, but in fact there is no such class. Instead, there is a class template called basic_string that represents sequences of characters, and this template takes as a parameter the type of the characters making up the sequences. This allows for strings to be made up of chars, wide chars, Unicode chars, whatever.

What we normally think of as the string class is really the template instantiation basic_string<char>. Because its use is so common, the standard library provides a typedef:

```
typedef basic_string<char> string;
```

Even this glosses over many details, because the basic_string template takes three arguments; all but the first have default values. To *really* understand the string class, you must face this full, unexpurgated declaration of basic_string:

```
template<class charT,
         class traits = string_char_traits<charT>,
         class Allocator = allocator>
  class basic_string;
```

You don't need to understand this gobbledygook to use the string class, because even though string is a typedef for The Template Instantiation from Hell, it behaves as if it were the unassuming non-template class the typedef makes it appear to be. Just tuck away in the back of your mind the fact that if you ever need to customize the types of characters that go into strings, or if you want to fine-tune the behavior of those characters, or if you want to seize control over the way memory for strings is allocated, the basic_string template allows you to do these things.

The approach taken in the design of the string class — generalize it and make the generalization a template — is repeated throughout the standard C++ library. IOstreams? They're templates; a type parameter defines the type of character making up the streams. Complex numbers? Also templates; a type parameter defines how the components of the numbers should be stored. Valarrays? Templates; a type parameter specifies what's in each array. And of the course the STL consists almost entirely of templates. If you are not comfortable with templates, now would be an excellent time to start making serious headway toward that goal.

The other thing to know about the standard library is that virtually everything it contains is inside the namespace std. To use things in the standard library without explicitly qualifying their names, you'll have to employ a using directive or (preferably) using declarations. Fortunately, this syntactic administrivia is automatically taken care of when you #include the appropriate headers.

The Standard Template Library

The biggest news in the standard C++ library is the STL, the Standard Template Library. (Since almost everything in the C++ library is a template, the name STL is not particularly descriptive. Nevertheless, this is the name of the containers and algorithms portion of the library, so good name or bad, this is what we use.)

The STL is likely to influence the organization of many — perhaps most — C++ libraries, so it's important that you be familiar with its general principles. They are not difficult to understand. The STL is based on three fundamental concepts: containers, iterators, and algorithms. Containers hold collections of objects. Iterators are pointer-like objects that let you walk through STL containers just as you'd use pointers to walk through built-in arrays. Algorithms are functions that work on STL containers and that use iterators to help them do their work.

It is easiest to understand the STL view of the world if we remind ourselves of the C++ (and C) rules for arrays. There is really only one rule we need to know: a pointer to an array can legitimately point to any element of the array *or to one element beyond the end of the array.* If the pointer points to the element beyond the end of the array, it can be compared only to other pointers to the array; the results of dereferencing it are undefined.

We can take advantage of this rule to write a function to find a particular value in an array. For an array of integers, our function might look like this:

```
int * find(int *begin, int *end, int value)
{
  while (begin != end && *begin != value) ++begin;
  return begin;
}
```

This function looks for value in the range between begin and end (excluding end — end points to one beyond the end of the array) and returns a pointer to the first occurrence of value in the array; if none is found, it returns end.

Returning end seems like a funny way to signal a fruitless search. Wouldn't 0 (the null pointer) be better? Certainly null seems more natural, but that doesn't make it "better." The find function must return some distinctive pointer value to indicate the search failed, and for this purpose, the end pointer is as good as the null pointer. In addition, as we'll soon see, the end pointer generalizes to other types of containers better than the null pointer.

Frankly, this is probably not the way you'd write the find function, but it's not unreasonable, and it generalizes astonishingly well. If you followed this simple example, you have mastered most of the ideas on which the STL is founded.

You could use the find function like this:

```
int values[50];

...

int *firstFive = find(values,          // search the range
                      values+50,        // values[0] - values[49]
                      5);               // for the value 5

if (firstFive != values+50) {          // did the search succeed?
    ...                                 // yes
}
else {
    ...                                 // no, the search failed
}
```

You can also use find to search subranges of the array:

```
int *firstFive = find(values,        // search the range
                      values+10,     // values[0] - values[9]
                      5);            // for the value 5

int age = 36;

...

int *firstValue = find(values+10,    // search the range
                       values+20,    // values[10] - values[19]
                       age);         // for the value in age
```

There's nothing inherent in the find function that limits its applicability to arrays of ints, so it should really be a template:

```
template<class T>
T * find(T *begin, T *end, const T& value)
{
  while (begin != end && *begin != value) ++begin;
  return begin;
}
```

In the transformation to a template, notice how we switched from pass-by-value for value to pass-by-reference-to-const. That's because now that we're passing arbitrary types around, we have to worry about the cost of pass-by-value. Each by-value parameter costs us a call to the parameter's constructor and destructor every time the function is invoked. We avoid these costs by using pass-by-reference, which involves no object construction or destruction.

This template is nice, but it can be generalized further. Look at the operations on begin and end. The only ones used are comparison for inequality, dereferencing, prefix increment (see Item 6), and copying (for the function's return value — see Item 19). These are all operations we can overload, so why limit find to using pointers? Why not allow *any* object that supports these operations to be used in addition to pointers? Doing so would free the find function from the built-in meaning of pointer operations. For example, we could define a pointer-like object for a linked list whose prefix increment operator moved us to the next element in the list.

This is the concept behind STL *iterators*. Iterators are pointer-like objects designed for use with STL containers. They are first cousins to the smart pointers of Item 28, but smart pointers tend to be more ambitious in what they do than do STL iterators. From a technical viewpoint, however, they are implemented using the same techniques.

Embracing the notion of iterators as pointer-like objects, we can replace the pointers in find with iterators, thus rewriting find like this:

```
template<class Iterator, class T>
Iterator find(Iterator begin, Iterator end, const T& value)
{
  while (begin != end && *begin != value) ++begin;
  return begin;
}
```

Congratulations! You have just written part of the Standard Template Library. The STL contains dozens of algorithms that work with containers and iterators, and find is one of them.

Containers in STL include bitset, vector, list, deque, queue, priority_queue, stack, set, and map, and you can apply find to *any* of these container types:

```
list<char> charList;              // create STL list object
                                  // for holding chars

...

// find the first occurrence of 'x' in charList
list<char>::iterator it = find(charList.begin(),
                               charList.end(),
                               'x');
```

"Whoa!", I hear you cry, "This doesn't look *anything* like it did in the array examples above!" Ah, but it does; you just have to know what to look for.

To call find for a list object, you need to come up with iterators that point to the first element of the list and to one past the last element of the list. Without some help from the list class, this is a difficult task, because you have no idea how a list is implemented. Fortunately, list (like all STL containers) obliges by providing the member functions begin and end. These member functions return the iterators you need, and it is those iterators that are passed into the first two parameters of find above.

When find is finished, it returns an iterator object that points to the found element (if there is one) or to charList.end() (if there's not). Because you know nothing about how list is implemented, you also know nothing about how iterators into lists are implemented. How, then, are you to know what type of object is returned by find? Again, the list class, like all STL containers, comes to the rescue: it provides a typedef, iterator, that is the type of iterators into lists. Since charList is a list of chars, the type of an iterator into such a list is list<char>::iterator, and that's what's used in the example above. (Each STL container class actually defines two iterator types, iterator and const_iterator. The former acts like a normal pointer, the latter like a pointer-to-const.)

Exactly the same approach can be used with the other STL containers. Furthermore, C++ pointers *are* STL iterators, so the original array examples work with the STL find function, too:

```
int values[50];

...

int *firstFive = find(values, values+50, 5);   // fine, calls
                                                // STL find
```

At its core, STL is very simple. It is just a collection of class and function templates that adhere to a set of conventions. The STL collection classes provide functions like begin and end that return iterator objects of types defined by the classes. The STL algorithm functions move through collections of objects by using iterator objects over STL collections. STL iterators act like pointers. That's really all there is to it. There's no big inheritance hierarchy, no virtual functions, none of that stuff. Just some class and function templates and a set of conventions to which they all subscribe.

Which leads to another revelation: STL is extensible. You can add your own collections, algorithms, and iterators to the STL family. As long as you follow the STL conventions, the standard STL collections will work with your algorithms and your collections will work with the standard STL algorithms. Of course, your templates won't be part of the standard C++ library, but they'll be built on the same principles and will be just as reusable.

There is much more to the C++ library than I've described here. Before you can use the library effectively, you must learn more about it than I've had room to summarize, and before you can write your own STL-compliant templates, you must learn more about the conventions of the STL. The standard C++ library is far richer than the C library, and the time you take to familiarize yourself with it is time well spent. Furthermore, the design principles embodied by the library — those of generality, extensibility, customizability, efficiency, and reusability — are well worth learning in their own right. By studying the standard C++ library, you not only increase your knowledge of the ready-made components available for use in your software, you learn how to apply the features of C++ more effectively, and you gain insight into how to design better libraries of your own.

Recommended Reading

So your appetite for information on C++ remains unsated. Fear not, there's more — much more. In the sections that follow, I put forth my recommendations for further reading on C++. It goes without saying that such recommendations are both subjective and selective, but in view of the litigious age in which we live, it's probably a good idea to say it anyway.

Books

There are hundreds — possibly thousands — of books on C++, and new contenders join the fray with increasing frequency. I haven't seen all these books, much less read them, but my experience has been that while some books are very good, some of them, well, some of them aren't.

What follows is the list of books I find myself consulting when I have questions about software development in C++. Other good books are available, I'm sure, but these are the ones I use, the ones I can truly *recommend*.

A good place to begin is with the books that describe the language itself. Until the ANSI/ISO standard is finalized and becomes generally available, most programmers make do with these, and unless you are crucially dependent on the nuances of the official standards documents, I suggest you do, too.

> *The Annotated C++ Reference Manual*, Margaret A. Ellis and Bjarne Stroustrup, Addison-Wesley, 1990, ISBN 0-201-51459-1.

> *The Design and Evolution of C++*, Bjarne Stroustrup, Addison-Wesley, 1994, ISBN 0-201-54330-3.

These books contain not just a description of what's in the language, they also explain the rationale behind the design decisions — something you won't find in the official standard documents. *The Anno-*

tated C++ Reference Manual is now incomplete (several language features have been added since it was published — see Item 35) and is in some cases out of date, but it is still the best reference for the core parts of the language, including templates and exceptions. *The Design and Evolution of C++* covers most of what's missing in *The Annotated C++ Reference Manual*; the only thing it lacks is a discussion of the Standard Template Library (again, see Item 35). These books are not tutorials, they're references, but you can't truly understand C++ unless you understand the material in these books.

For a more general reference on the language and how to apply it, there is no better place to look than the book by the man responsible for C++ in the first place:

> *The C++ Programming Language (Second Edition)*, Bjarne Stroustrup, Addison-Wesley, 1991, ISBN 0-201-53992-6.

Stroustrup has been intimately involved in the language's design, implementation, application, and standardization since its inception, and he probably knows more about it than anybody else does. His descriptions of language features make for dense reading, but that's primarily because they contain so much information. The chapters on approaches to library design are a nice complement to the more feature-oriented material that precedes it.

If you're ready to move beyond the language itself and are interested in how to apply it effectively, you might consider my other book on the subject:

> *Effective C++: 50 Specific Ways to Improve Your Programs and Designs*, Scott Meyers, Addison-Wesley, 1992, ISBN 0-201-56364-9.

That book is organized similarly to this one, but it covers different (arguably more fundamental) material.

A book pitched at roughly the same level as my *Effective C++* books, but covering different topics, is

> *C++ Strategies and Tactics*, Robert Murray, Addison-Wesley, 1993, ISBN 0-201-56382-7.

Murray's book is especially strong on the fundamentals of template design, a topic to which he devotes two chapters. He also includes a chapter on the important topic of migrating from C development to C++ development. Much of my discussion on reference counting (see Item 29) is based on the ideas in *C++ Strategies and Tactics*.

If you're the kind of person who likes to learn proper programming technique by reading *code*, the book for you is

C++ Programming Style, Tom Cargill, Addison-Wesley, 1992, ISBN 0-201-56365-7.

Each chapter in this book starts with some C++ software that has been published as an example of how to do something correctly. Cargill then proceeds to dissect — nay, *vivisect* — each program, identifying likely trouble spots, poor design choices, brittle implementation decisions, and things that are just plain wrong. He then iteratively rewrites each example to eliminate the weaknesses, and by the time he's done, he's produced code that is more robust, more maintainable, more efficient, and more portable, and it still fulfills the original problem specification. Anybody programming in C++ would do well to heed the lessons of this book, but it is especially important for those involved in code inspections.

(One topic Cargill does not discuss in *C++ Programming Style* is exceptions. He turns his critical eye to this language feature in the following article, however, which demonstrates why writing exception-safe code is more difficult than most programmers realize:

"Exception Handling: A False Sense of Security," *C++ Report*, Volume 6, Number 9, November-December 1994, pages 21-24.

If you are contemplating the use of exceptions, read this article before you proceed. If you don't have access to back issues of the *C++ Report*, you can find the article at the Addison-Wesley Internet site. The World Wide Web URL is `http://www.aw.com/cp/mec++.html`. If you prefer anonymous FTP, you can get the article from `ftp.aw.com` in the directory `cp/mec++`.)

Once you've mastered the basics of C++ and are ready to start pushing the envelope, you must familiarize yourself with

Advanced C++: Programming Styles and Idioms, James Coplien, Addison-Wesley, 1992, ISBN 0-201-54855-0.

I generally refer to this as "the LSD book," because it's purple and it will expand your mind. Coplien covers some straightforward material, but his focus is really on showing you how to do things in C++ you're not supposed to be able to do. You want to construct objects on top of one another? He shows you how. You want to bypass strong typing? He gives you a way. You want to add data and functions to classes as your programs are running? He explains how to do it. Most of the time, you'll want to steer clear of the techniques he describes, but sometimes they provide just the solution you need for a tricky problem you're facing. Furthermore, it's illuminating just to see what kinds of things can be done with C++. This book may frighten you, it may dazzle you, but when you've read it, you'll never look at C++ the same way again.

If you have anything to do with the design and implementation of C++ libraries, you would be foolhardy to overlook

> *Designing and Coding Reusable C++*, Martin D. Carroll and Margaret A. Ellis, Addison-Wesley, 1995, ISBN 0-201-51284-X.

Carroll and Ellis discuss many practical aspects of library design and implementation that are simply ignored by everybody else. Good libraries are small, fast, extensible, easily upgraded, graceful during template instantiation, powerful, and robust. It is not possible to optimize for each of these attributes, so one must make trade-offs that improve some aspects of a library at the expense of others. *Designing and Coding Reusable C++* examines these trade-offs and offers down-to-earth advice on how to go about making them.

Regardless of whether you write software for scientific and engineering applications, you owe yourself a look at

> *Scientific and Engineering C++*, John J. Barton and Lee R. Nackman, Addison-Wesley, 1994, ISBN 0-201-53393-6.

The first part of the book explains C++ for FORTRAN programmers (now *there's* an unenviable task), but the latter parts cover techniques that are relevant in virtually any domain. The extensive material on templates is close to revolutionary; it's probably the most advanced that's currently available, and I suspect that when you've seen the miracles these authors perform with templates, you'll never again think of them as little more than souped-up macros.

Finally, the emerging discipline of *patterns* in object-oriented software development (see page 123) is described in

> *Design Patterns: Elements of Reusable Object-Oriented Software*, Erich Gamma, Richard Helm, Ralph Johnson, and John Vlissides, Addison-Wesley, 1995, ISBN 0-201-63361-2.

This book provides an overview of the ideas behind patterns, but its primary contribution is a catalogue of 23 fundamental patterns that are useful in many application areas. A stroll through these pages will almost surely reveal a pattern you've had to invent yourself at one time or another, and when you find one, you're almost certain to discover that the design in the book is superior to the ad-hoc approach you came up with. The names of the patterns here have already become part of an emerging vocabulary for object-oriented design; failure to know these names may soon be hazardous to your ability to communicate with your colleagues. A particular strength of the book is its emphasis on designing and implementing software so that future evolution is gracefully accommodated (see Items 32 and 33).

Magazines

For hard-core C++ programmers, there's really only one game in town:

> *C++ Report*, SIGS Publications, New York, NY.

The magazine has made a conscious decision to move away from its "C++ only" roots, but the increased coverage of domain- and system-specific programming issues is worthwhile in its own right, and the material on C++, if occasionally a bit off the deep end, continues to be the best available.†

If you're more comfortable with C than with C++, or if you find the *C++ Report*'s material too extreme to be useful, you may find the articles in this magazine more to your taste:

> *C/C++ Users Journal*, Miller Freeman, Inc., Lawrence, KS.

As the name suggests, this covers both C and C++. The articles on C++ tend to assume a weaker background than those in the *C++ Report*. In addition, the editorial staff keeps a tighter rein on its authors than does the *Report*, so the material in the magazine tends to be relatively mainstream. This helps filter out ideas on the lunatic fringe, but it also limits your exposure to techniques that are truly cutting-edge.

Usenet Newsgroups

Three Usenet newsgroups are devoted to C++. The general-purpose anything-goes newsgroup is comp.lang.c++. The postings there run the gamut from detailed explanations of advanced programming techniques to rants and raves by those who love or hate C++ to undergraduates the world over asking for help with the homework assignments they neglected until too late. Volume in the newsgroup is extremely high. Unless you have hours of free time on your hands, you'll want to employ a filter to help separate the wheat from the chaff. Get a good filter — there's a lot of chaff.

In November 1995, a moderated version of comp.lang.c++ was created. Named comp.lang.c++.moderated, this newsgroup is also designed for general discussion of C++ and related issues, but the moderators aim to weed out implementation-specific questions and

---

† I am a columnist for the *C++ Report*, so it is fair to assume I am less than unbiased in making this assessment.

comments, questions covered in the extensive on-line FAQ ("Frequently Asked Questions" list), flame wars, and other matters of little interest to most C++ practitioners.

A more narrowly focused newsgroup is `comp.std.c++`, which is devoted to a discussion of the C++ standard itself. Language lawyers abound in this group, but it's a good place to turn if your picky questions about C++ go unanswered in the references otherwise available to you. The newsgroup is moderated, so the signal-to-noise ratio is quite good; you won't see any pleas for homework assistance here.

An `auto_ptr` Implementation

Items 9, 10, 26, 31 and 32 attest to the remarkable utility of the `auto_ptr` template. Unfortunately, few compilers currently provide an implementation. Items 9 and 28 sketch how you might write one yourself, but it's nice to have more than a sketch when embarking on real-world projects.

Below are two presentations of a complete implementation for `auto_ptr`. The first presentation documents the class interface and implements all the member functions outside the class definition. The second implements each member function within the class definition. Stylistically, the second presentation is inferior to the first, because it fails to separate the class interface from its implementation. However, `auto_ptr` is a simple class, and the second presentation brings that out much more clearly than does the first.

Here is `auto_ptr` with its interface documented:

```
template<class T>
class auto_ptr {
public:
  explicit auto_ptr(T *p = 0);    // see Item 5 for a
                                  // description of "explicit"

  template<class U>               // copy constructor member
  auto_ptr(auto_ptr<U>& rhs);     // template (see Item 28):
                                  // initialize a new auto_ptr
                                  // with any compatible
                                  // auto_ptr

  ~auto_ptr();

  template<class U>
  auto_ptr<T>& operator=(auto_ptr<U>& rhs);
                                  // assignment operator
                                  // member template (see
                                  // Item 28): assign from any
                                  // compatible auto_ptr
```

```
  T& operator*() const;          // see Item 28
  T* operator->() const;         // see Item 28

  T* get() const;                // return value of current
                                 // dumb pointer

  T* release();                  // relinquish ownership of
                                 // current dumb pointer and
                                 // return its value

  void reset(T *p = 0);          // delete owned pointer;
                                 // assume ownership of p
private:
  T *pointee;
};

template<class T>
inline auto_ptr<T>::auto_ptr(T *p)
: pointee(p)
{}

template<class T>
  template<class U>
  inline auto_ptr<T>::auto_ptr(auto_ptr<U>& rhs)
  : pointee(rhs.release())
  {}

template<class T>
inline auto_ptr<T>::~auto_ptr()
{ delete pointee; }

template<class T>
  template<class U>
  inline auto_ptr<T>& auto_ptr<T>::operator=(auto_ptr<U>& rhs)
  {
    if (this != &rhs) reset(rhs.release());
    return *this;
  }

template<class T>
inline T& auto_ptr<T>::operator*() const
{ return *pointee; }

template<class T>
inline T* auto_ptr<T>::operator->() const
{ return pointee; }

template<class T>
inline T* auto_ptr<T>::get() const
{ return pointee; }
```

```
template<class T>
inline T* auto_ptr<T>::release()
{
  T *oldPointee = pointee;
  pointee = 0;
  return oldPointee;
}

template<class T>
inline void auto_ptr<T>::reset(T *p)
{
  delete pointee;
  pointee = p;
}
```

Here is auto_ptr with all the functions defined in the class definition. As you can see, there's no brain surgery going on here:

```
template<class T>
class auto_ptr {
public:
  explicit auto_ptr(T *p = 0): pointee(p) {}

  template<class U>
  auto_ptr(auto_ptr<U>& rhs): pointee(rhs.release()) {}

  ~auto_ptr() { delete pointee; }

  template<class U>
  auto_ptr<T>& operator=(auto_ptr<U>& rhs)
  {
    if (this != &rhs) reset(rhs.release());
    return *this;
  }

  T& operator*() const { return *pointee; }

  T* operator->() const { return pointee; }

  T* get() const { return pointee; }

  T* release()
  {
    T *oldPointee = pointee;
    pointee = 0;
    return oldPointee;
  }

  void reset(T *p = 0) { delete pointee; pointee = p; }
private:
  T *pointee;
};
```

If your compilers don't yet support `explicit`, you may safely `#define` it out of existence:

```
#define explicit
```

This won't make `auto_ptr` any less functional, but it will render it slightly less safe. For details, see Item 5.

If your compilers lack support for member templates, you can use the non-template `auto_ptr` copy constructor and assignment operator described in Item 28. This will make your `auto_ptrs` less convenient to use, but there is, alas, no way to approximate the behavior of member templates. If member templates (or other language features, for that matter) are important to you, let your compiler vendors know. The more customers ask for new language features, the sooner vendors will implement them.

General Index

This index is for everything in this book except the classes, functions, and templates I use as examples. If you're looking for a reference to a particular class, function, or template I use as an example, please turn to the index beginning on page 313. For everything else, this is the place to be. In particular, classes, functions, and templates in the standard C++ library (e.g., string, auto_ptr, list, vector, etc.) are indexed here.

For the most part, operators are listed under *operator*. For example, operator<< is listed under operator<<, not under <<, etc. However, operators whose names are words or are word-like (e.g., new, delete, sizeof, const_cast, etc.) are listed under the appropriate words (e.g., new, delete, sizeof, const_cast, etc.).

Example uses of new and lesser-known language features are indexed under *example uses*.

Before A

#define 294
?:, vs. if/then 56
__cplusplus 273
">>", vs. "> >" 29
80-20 rule 79, 82–85, 106
90-10 rule xi, 82

A

abort
  and assert 167
  and object destruction 72
  relationship to terminate 72
abstract classes
  and inheritance 258–270
  and vtbls 115

  drawing 5
  identifying 267, 268
  transforming from concrete 266–269
abstract mixin base classes 154
abstractions
  identifying 267, 268
  useful 267
access-declarations 144
adding data and functions to classes at runtime 287
Addison-Wesley Internet site 8, 287
address comparisons to determine object locations 150–152
address-of operator —
  see *operator&*

W

Y

Index of Example Classes, Functions, and Templates

**Functions and Function
Templates**